ADOLESCENCE IN INDIA

Adolescence in India: An Interdisciplinary Perspective highlights the need and importance of studying adolescence in the domain of education. Using an interdisciplinary approach, it discusses adolescence from the perspective of sociology, psychology, education and health studies.

Against the backdrop of economic development and globalization, the book looks at adolescence in the changing social milieu. It offers an understanding of adolescence by exploring the sociocultural influences on adolescents and their interactions in various spaces such as the school, among peers, family and the media. The book reflects on classroom group processes and instructional practices for better psychosocial growth of adolescents as well as discusses the need for a greater emphasis on making resources available for adolescents to realize and strengthen their skills and agency. The book outlines various life-skills policies and programmes in India and uses vignettes, anecdotes, emerging classroom discussions, case studies, activities plus self-assessment tools and questionnaires to facilitate a deeper understanding of the concept.

The book will be of interest to students, teachers, and educators in teaching programmes, including educational psychology, adolescent psychology and human development. It will also be useful for policymakers, NGOs, and public and private sector bodies who work in the field of adolescent psychology.

Gomathi Jatin is associate professor at the Centre of Excellence in Teacher Education (formerly, CEIAR), TISS, Mumbai, where she teaches and researches within the broader area of psychology. She is a teacher educator, and her research areas and publications comprise the domains of adolescent psychology, psychology of learners, life skills and well-being.

Sybil Thomas is a faculty member at the Department of Education, University of Mumbai. She has been in the field of teacher education for over two decades with a short stint of administrative experience as a principal of a College of Education. Her doctoral study was in the area of studying attitudes of adolescence towards educated and working women. She teaches courses related to the philosophical and sociological basis of education and e-learning. Her area of research centres around transformative pedagogies for developing agency, advocacy and social responsibilities.

Principles-based Adaptive Teaching

Series Editors: Mythili Ramchand, *Tata Institute of Social Science, Mumbai* and Nishevita Jayendran, *Tata Institute of Social Sciences, Mumbai*

This series bring together critical discussions of educational practices and pedagogies in India. The teaching profession has undergone rapid changes and advancements in recent years. The books in this series will identify the changes which are affecting teaching-learning practices in schools and the range of knowledge development required for educators to develop and adopt innovative pedagogical practices to adapt to uncertain futures. The books in the series include worksheets, vignettes, emerging classroom discussions, case studies along with other additional resources for teachers and students. The series caters to a range of teacher education programmes and are envisioned as resources, primarily for teacher educators and student-teachers and others engaged in the education sector. It focuses on topics such as Adolescence in India, Pedagogy of Language (English), Pedagogy of Mathematics and Pedagogy of Science, the nature and purpose of education, philosophy of education, knowledge and curriculum, learners and learning, educational policies and practices,, teachers and teaching, inclusive education, pedagogies of language, social sciences and assessments and evaluation, within the themes of education.

Language Education: Teaching English in India
Nishevita Jayendran, Anusha Ramanathan and Surbhi Nagpal

Adolescence in India
An Interdisciplinary Perspective
Gomathi Jatin and Sybil Thomas

For more information about this series, please visit: www.routledge.com/Principles-based-Adaptive-Teaching/book-series/PAT

ADOLESCENCE IN INDIA

An Interdisciplinary Perspective

Gomathi Jatin and Sybil Thomas

LONDON AND NEW YORK

Cover image: Ramesh Khade

First published 2022
by Routledge
2 Park Square, Milton Park, Abingdon, Oxon OX14 4RN

and by Routledge
605 Third Avenue, New York, NY 10158

Routledge is an imprint of the Taylor & Francis Group, an informa business

© 2022 Gomathi Jatin and Sybil Thomas

The right of Gomathi Jatin and Sybil Thomas to be identified as authors of this work has been asserted in accordance with sections 77 and 78 of the Copyright, Designs and Patents Act 1988.

All rights reserved. No part of this book may be reprinted or reproduced or utilised in any form or by any electronic, mechanical, or other means, now known or hereafter invented, including photocopying and recording, or in any information storage or retrieval system, without permission in writing from the publishers.

Trademark notice: Product or corporate names may be trademarks or registered trademarks, and are used only for identification and explanation without intent to infringe.

British Library Cataloguing-in-Publication Data
A catalogue record for this book is available from the British Library

Library of Congress Cataloging-in-Publication Data
A catalog record has been requested for this book

ISBN: 978-0-367-48571-9 (hbk)
ISBN: 978-0-367-51548-5 (pbk)
ISBN: 978-1-003-05435-1 (ebk)

DOI: 10.4324/9781003054351

Typeset in Bembo
by Apex CoVantage, LLC

CONTENTS

List of figures vi
Series editors' note ix
Foreword xii
Acknowledgments xiv

1 Conceptualizing adolescence for the educational space   1

2 Developmental patterns and processes   37

3 Social contexts in adolescence   94

4 Adolescence and well-being   171

5 The adolescent in the classroom   209

Index   250

FIGURES

1.1	Etymological Definition of Adolescence	3
1.2	Life Span as Stages of Life	3
1.3	Phase 1 – Characterized by Cartesian Splits	4
1.4	The Specific Character of Scientific Study of Adolescence	5
1.5	Phase 2 – Ideal Natural Ontogenetic Laboratory	6
1.6	Reasons for the Special Salience of the Study of Adolescent Development	7
1.7	Four Defining Features of the Second Phase of Science of Adolescent Development	8
1.8	Phase 3 – Moving Forward	9
1.9	Adolescence – Distinct or Transient?	14
2.1	Salient Features of Identity	40
2.2	Socialization Through Education: Contributor to Individual Development	42
2.3	Culture as a Determinant of Identity	42
2.4	Culture and Its Influences in Experiences of Reality	43
2.5	Need for Deliberate Socialization	44
2.6	Identity: A Lifelong Development	47
2.7	Assimilation and Accommodation in Cognitive Development	59
2.8	Theory of Cognitive Development as Proposed by Piaget	60
2.9	Stages of Cognitive Development as Proposed by Piaget	60
2.10	Illustration of Personal Fable in Adolescent Egocentrism	69
2.11	Stages of Moral Development as Proposed by Kohlberg	76
2.12	Themes Identified with Vygotsky's Ideas of Sociocultural learning	81
2.13	Zone of Proximal Development and Scaffolding	82
3.1	Social Contexts in Adolescence	95
3.2	Adolescent Daydreaming	97

3.3	Adolescent Dialogue Indicating the Fortuitous Character of an Adolescent's Life	97
3.4	Four Core Features of Human Agency	98
3.5	Bronfenbrenner's Ecological Theory of Development	102
3.6	Channelling, Selection, Adjustment and Reflection as Mechanisms of Adolescents' Socialization	104
3.7	Socio-ecological and Sociocultural Framework of Socialization Processes	108
3.8	Contextual-developmental Perspective of Socialization Processes	109
3.9	Self as Actor, Agent and Author and Its Features	111
3.10	Family Factors Impacting Adolescents' Identity (Social Contexts in Adolescence)	112
3.11a	Parent-Adolescent Interaction (Mother Understands Her Adolescent Child)	121
3.11b	Parent-Adolescent Interaction (Adolescent Values Friends' Company than Family Gathering	122
3.11c	Parent-Adolescent Interaction (Father is Irritated with His Adolescent Child's Behaviour of Isolating from Family)	122
3.12	Key Constituents in Adolescent Identity Formation	128
3.13a	Parents' Influence on Adolescents	131
3.13b	Adolescents' Influence on Parents	131
3.14	Bidirectional and Transactional Nature of Social Processes and Interactions	144
3.15	Assumptions with Respect to Interpersonal Processes of Adolescent Identity in Relation to Peer and Peer Groups	145
3.16a	Adolescent Vulnerable to Peer Influence	148
3.16b	Adolescent Influenced by Positive Peer Pressure	149
3.17	Adolescent's Feeling of Being Recognized and Acknowledged on Social Media, Boosting Her Self-worth	161
4.1	Eudemonic and Hedonic Perspectives of Well-Being	176
4.2	Participatory Framework of Well-Being	178
4.3	PERMA Model of Flourishing	180
4.4	The Realm of Potentialities and Environmental Resources for Adolescent Well-Being	182
4.5	Soutter et al.'s (2010) Framework for Well-being	202
4.6	Adolescents' Well-being Using Soutter et al.'s (2010) Framework for Well-being	203
5.1	Classroom Ecology	210
5.2	Classroom Dynamics: Teacher and Learner Agency	212
5.3	The Relationally Organized Nature of Classroom Contexts	213
5.4a	Studies Highlighting 'Social Group' as the Variable Related to Adolescents and the Factors Resulting in Adolescent Problems	218

5.4b	Studies Highlighting 'Health and Behaviour' as the Variable Related to Adolescents and the Factors Resulting in Adolescent Problems	219
5.4c	Studies Highlighting 'Gender Role and Differences' as the Variable Related to Adolescents and the Factors Resulting in Adolescent Problems	219
5.4d	Studies Highlighting 'Adjustment' as the Variable Related to Adolescents and the Factors Resulting in Adolescent Problems	220
5.4e	Studies Highlighting 'Academics and Classroom' as the Variable Related to Adolescents and the Factors Resulting in Adolescent Problems	220
5.4f	Studies Highlighting 'Technology' as the Variable Related to Adolescents and the Factors Resulting in Adolescent Problems	221
5.5	Factors Affecting Adolescents and Need for Life Skills to Combat Adolescent Problems	221
5.6	P21 Framework for 21st-Century Learning	236

SERIES EDITORS' NOTE

The last two decades have seen developments of national importance in school education in India. With the Right of Children to Free and Compulsory Education (RtE Act 2009) and the National Curriculum Framework (NCF, 2005), changes have been afoot to enable access to quality education for children at scale. Responding to the concurrent need for teacher education to support the vision of a robust education system, the National Curriculum Framework for Teacher Education (NCFTE, 2009) recommended substantive changes in curriculum and practice of teacher education in the country. Subsequently, the high-powered committee on teacher education set up by the Hon. Supreme Court of India (Justice Verma Committee, 2012) endorsed these curricular reforms and called for an overhaul of the sector. Notably, similar shifts have been observed across the world, as teacher education programmes discuss pathways for professional development to enable teachers to work as transformative professionals in the 21st century. UNESCO's Sustainable Development Goals (SDG) call for transformative pedagogies, with a shift towards active, self-directed participatory and collaborative learning, problem orientation, inter- and trans-disciplinarity and linking formal and informal learning (UNESCO 2017, 7). Acknowledging the need for gearing up the Indian education system to meet SDGs, particularly SDG 4 to ensure inclusive and equitable quality education and promote lifelong learning opportunities for all, the recent National Education Policy (2020) has proposed re-envisioning teacher education in multidisciplinary institutions that can prepare teachers to meet the needs of learners in the 21st century.

With rapid advancements in science and technology, and the pervasiveness of ICT and media in our lives, the education sector stands witness to radical changes that are affecting teaching-learning practices in schools. Arguably, the onset of the Fourth Industrial Revolution requires preparing learners for a range of competences including effective communication, intercultural sensitivity, analytical and critical thinking, problem-solving skills and creativity, which extend beyond content knowledge. In this context, educators are required to gain adaptive expertise to prepare themselves and their students for uncertain futures.

A dearth of good curricular resources has been consistently identified as a key lacuna by the first national commission on education in independent India in preparing teachers as professional educators. In the light of the present education policy calling for substantial changes to teacher education, there is an urgent need for quality teaching-learning materials that can trigger critical inquiry, invoke a sense of adventure and provoke the curiosity of both student-teachers and teacher-educators to embark on the complex task of learning to teach.

To this end, the Centre of Excellence in Teacher Education (formerly the Centre for Education, Innovation and Action Research, or CEIAR) at the Tata Institute of Social Sciences, Mumbai, has developed a series of textbooks under the theme "Principles-based Adaptive Teaching" that make inroads into the content and pedagogical domains of study relevant to teaching-learning practice. The titles for these books have been identified based on a consideration of the NCFTE 2009; emerging understandings from comparative studies of teacher education curriculum in the international context; and demands from the field to address the needs of preparing teachers for the 21st century. Drawing from current research in education, the textbooks adopt an innovative, practice-based approach to transact the selected topics. The themes covered in the series include adolescent learners in India, titles in subject pedagogies (English, Mathematics, Science and Social Science), knowledge and learning, ICT and new media in education, and state, education and policy.

Each book covers key concepts, constructs, theories, conceptual and empirical frameworks, and contemporary discourses around the topic. The content and discussions are meant to broaden and deepen readers' understanding of the topic. Cases, narratives and vignettes are used for contextual illustration of ideas. It is desirable that educators bring supplementary illustrations to problematize local issues. The references, range of activities and discussion triggers provided in each volume are meant to enable readers to explore issues further. The books are meant to be used as one among many 'resources' rather than as 'a textbook'.

Additionally, with the purchase of the books in this series, readers can avail supplementary resources hosted on the TISSx platform, which can be accessed at this URL: *www.tissx.tiss.edu/*. Each book comes with a QR code on its cover that serves as a coupon to access the resources on this platform. Readers may follow these simple steps to reach the pages.

1 Click on *https://www.tissx.tiss.edu/* taking care that the text is entered correctly. You can also scan the QR code on the cover of this book to access the website.
2 Register on the platform with a valid email ID by clicking on the 'Register' button on the top of the page. Fill in the details requested.

3   A verification link will be sent to your registered email address as soon as you register. Click on the link to activate your account.
4   You can now login to the TISSx platform, and visit the e-resource page of the specific book/s you have purchased, through the link provided. Enrol into the relevant course by entering the coupon code provided (PBAT0_) in the respective books.

It is hoped that this book series will help readers gain nuanced perspectives on the topics, along with relevant skills and dispositions to integrate into their teaching repertoire.

Dr Mythili Ramchand
Dr Nishevita Jayendran
Centre of Excellence in Teacher Education (formerly, CEIAR)
Tata Institute of Social Sciences, Mumbai

Note: The coupon code for the course related to the book *Adolescence in India: An Interdisciplinary Perspective* **is PBAT03.**

FOREWORD

The discipline of education and professional development of teachers in India and the broader South Asian region has been undergoing radical redefinition over the last thirty years, with significant advancements in its conceptual base, approaches to theory and practice, and the formation of practice of teachers. Policy documents such as the National Curriculum Framework (2005) and the National Curriculum Framework for Teacher Education (2009) in India lay out for us the scope and depth of ideas that are of contemporary disciplinary interest. Resources that enable students of education to engage with these ideas relevant to the developing world contexts are, however, very few. This has been a key problem in widespread dissemination and for the ideas taking root in disciplinary discourses and practices in the university and colleges of teacher education. While planning the scope of work of the Centre of Excellence in Teacher Education at the Tata Institute of Social Sciences, seeded by the Tata Trusts, therefore, we included the development of resources as one of the major activities that will be needed in order to revitalize the sector. Dr Mythili Ramchand and Dr Nishevita Jayendran, as series editors, have laid out the scope and vision of such resources built around a series of textbooks to be developed in English and major modern Indian languages. Recognizing the importance of such an initiative, several colleagues from universities in India have joined this effort as collaborators.

Textbooks are essential to support the formation and advancement of disciplines. Important scientific ideas became integrated into disciplinary thinking through textbooks written by scientists themselves. In the colonized world, textbooks came to represent 'colonizers' knowledge' and the cornerstone of the examination system, defining 'official knowledge' and strongly framing academic discourse from the world outside. Many of us trained in education, therefore, retain a suspicion of textbooks that may come to dominate the intellectual mental scape of students, and have sought out 'original writings' to include in our course reading compendia.

Important as the reading of original texts is, particularly in the social sciences, they do not address what good textbooks can do and need to do for their students: performing a disciplinary landscaping function that is contextually relevant, drawing on contemporary research and practice, putting ideas to use as tools for thinking, scaffolding engagement and stimulating inquiry. In developing the textbooks in this series, authors have drawn on their experiences of teaching, research, reading and field engagement. We hope that faculty of education, students of education and teachers will all find the resources useful.

Padma M. Sarangapani
Chairperson, Centre of Excellence in Teacher Education
(formerly, CEIAR)

ACKNOWLEDGMENTS

"It's a gratifying moment as we sit down to pen these thanks, calmness in the mind in a chaotic world around." For a passionate and wholehearted work, "We are submerged in gratitude. We'll need a minute."

Writing this book on 'Adolescence' has been an intellectual exercise of immense joy and profound learning derived from teaching and research across programs at the Centre of Excellence in Teacher Education (formerly, CEIAR), Tata Institute of Social Sciences (TISS), Mumbai, and at the Department of Education, University of Mumbai. It is a dream come true accomplished through discourses on the area of adolescence with colleagues at the Centre and beyond, who have helped us learn and practice both the art and science of writing.

First and foremost, we would like to thank the Almighty, who gave us the power to believe in our passion and pursue our dreams. We are extremely grateful to Prof. Padma Sarangapani, Chairperson of CETE, for being the driving force and for being open and flexible to every action that we undertook through the course of exploring resources and domains in the area of adolescence.

We would like to acknowledge our colleagues and friends for their undaunted support towards the completion of this book. We can't thank our series editors, Dr Mythili Ramchand and Dr Nishevita Jayendran, enough for being our unrelenting source of inspiration to overcome challenges and move forward towards achieving our goals.

Special thanks to Ms Farrah Kerawalla for her support and contribution to the writing of the book. We are thankful to Dr Gauri Hardikar for her contribution towards a box article in our book. Satej Shende and Ramesh Khade have been invaluable in supporting us through the creation of media content for this book and the TISSx platform for our online resources.

We are indebted to the team at Routledge, Lubna Irfan, Shloka Chauhan and Shoma Chaudhary, for their tolerance and thoughtful consideration during these unprecedented, challenging times of the pandemic and for helping us meet our deadlines in completing this book.

And last but not the least, this journey would not have been possible without the dedicated support of our families who constantly supported us in all our peaks and valleys through the completion of this book.

1
CONCEPTUALIZING ADOLESCENCE FOR THE EDUCATIONAL SPACE

CHAPTER 1: Conceptualizing Adolescence in the Educational Space

Overview

After reading this chapter, you will be able to achieve the following objectives

- Gain an overview to the evolving multi disciplinary concept of dolescence

- Able to reflect on the individual context relations, developmental systems, plasticity and diversity dimensions of the concept of adolescent development

- Envision a working definition of adolescence consistent with its conceptualization understood at the level of interactions between biological, behavioral and social domains from historical and transitional perspectives

- Understand the sharp contrast in the lives of adolescents in general and a collectivist society like India

- Widen the awareness of the cultural context of adolescent development, specific to India, given the growing attention of the phenomenon of globalization having reached the field of adolescent research

What do you understand by this word 'Adolescence'?

?

When you think of the word "Adolescent" what comes to mind?

DOI: 10.4324/9781003054351-1

2 Adolescence for the educational space

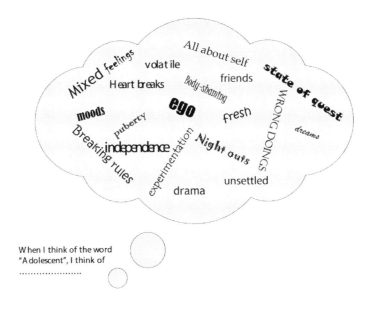

Understanding the study of adolescence development: an introduction

The World Health Organization (WHO) and UNICEF define adolescents as persons between ages 10 and 19 (Population Council & UNICEF, 2013). Adolescence is mostly referred to by societies as the period of time from the onset of puberty until an individual achieves social and economic independence. However, with the delayed onset of puberty, timing of role transitions, including completion of education, marriage and parenthood, the span of years that define adolescence has been proposed to a new extended adolescence beyond 19 years, thus yielding a fluid and kaleidoscopic age definition.

Discourses in the area of adolescence and adolescence education seem to be largely pervaded by universal definitions on adolescence and their characteristics. This gives an impression and a global acceptance of adolescent characteristics, tending to look at adolescence sharing similar characteristic features, going through roughly the same kind of changes and encountering identical challenges based on the widely accepted Western concept of 'the teenager'.

However, the term 'adolescent' is a *dynamic and evolving construct embedded in the psychological, social, temporal and cultural lenses* resulting in inconsistencies in the criteria of constructing the concept of adolescent stage and its substages. To understand this assertion, we need to take a peep into the short history and a long past of understanding adolescents and their development.

Adolescence for the educational space **3**

A brief history of the study of adolescent development

FIGURE 1.1 Etymological Definition of Adolescence

The first use of the term 'adolescence' appeared in the 15th century. The term adolescence was referred as a derivative of the Latin term *adolescere, which means to grow up or to grow to maturity* (Lerner & Steinberg, 2004).

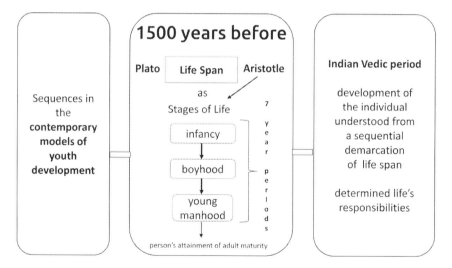

FIGURE 1.2 Life Span as Stages of Life

More than 1,500 years before this explicit use of the term, both Plato and Aristotle proposed a sequential demarcation of the life span, and Aristotle in particular proposed stages of life that are not too dissimilar from sequences that might be included in contemporary models of youth development. Aristotle proposed three successive stages that preceded the person's attainment of full, adult maturity. Seven-year periods (infancy, boyhood and young manhood) were the three stages prior to adulthood. About 2,000 years have lapsed between the philosophical discussions of adolescence and the emergence of a scientific approach to the understanding of adolescence.

4 Adolescence for the educational space

The history of the scientific study of adolescence has two overlapping phases, and we have entered into the third phase of understanding adolescence.

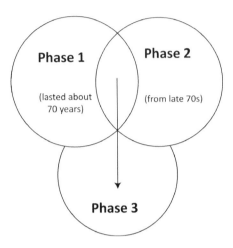

The First phase, lasted for about 70 years, was characterized by cartesian splits that created false dichotomies that in turn limited the intellectual development of the field (Lerner & Steinberg, 2004).

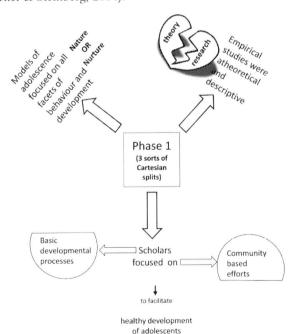

FIGURE 1.3 Phase 1 – Characterized by Cartesian Splits

Lerner and Steinberg (2004) in their book claim that the first of these polarization, "grand" models of adolescence dealt with all aspects of behavior and development.), but these theories were limited because they largely dealt with either nature (e.g. genetic or maturational; or all nurture. We then had the splits between the scholars whose work was focused on basic development processes and practitioners whose focus was on community-based efforts to facilitate the healthy development of adolescents.

These debates, which were characterized by Cartesian splits, restricted the understanding of adolescence. The Cartesian splits were of different types – nature-nurture, empirical-based but lacking theoretical foundations, and basic developmental processes versus community-based development of adolescents. Many parallel discourses criticized the Cartesian dualistic notion of the approach to the understanding of development in general and adolescence in particular. L.S.Vygotski (1896–1934) proposed to analyze the complexity of development as a totality. The notion of complexity of development facilitates the understanding of development of adolescence comprising subjective experiences, as complex, contradictory, dynamic and unique, but at the same time, historical, cultural and universal.

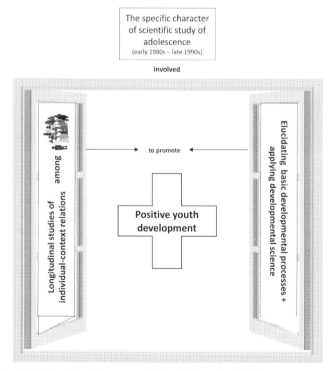

FIGURE 1.4 The Specific Character of Scientific Study of Adolescence

6 Adolescence for the educational space

This polarization phase and the grand theories of adolescence that dominated the field during its first phase of scientific development have elicited made several contributions to the scientific study of adolescents between the late 1980s and 1990s. This scientific study **primarily contributed** to the further approach of using *longitudinal studies that looked into relationships between individual-context relationships between diverse groups of adolescents and elucidating several basic developmental processes and applying developmental science to promote positive youth development* (Lerner & Steinberg, 2004). Therefore, we see that the first phase of adolescent development not only contributed to the establishment of adolescents as a concept of scientific enquiry, it also contributed to the scientific approaches to adolescent development. Thus, we can safely say that the first phase provided an ontogenetic window to the understanding of person–context processes involved in coping and adaptation of adolescents. First phase the *second phase* had begun with a prediction about the research on adolescence (Lerner & Steinberg, 2004).

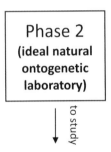

FIGURE 1.5   Phase 2 – Ideal Natural Ontogenetic Laboratory

The second phase of scientific study was from the late 1970s through this writing. The adolescent period came to be regarded as an ideal natural ontogenetic laboratory for studying key theoretical and methodological issues in development science (Lerner & Steinberg, 2004).

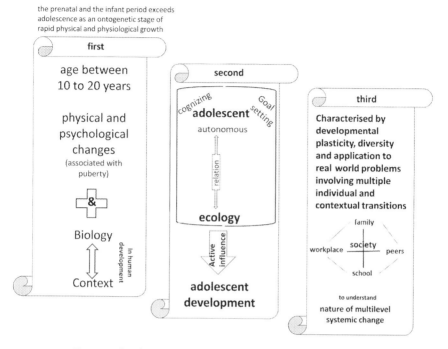

FIGURE 1.6 Reasons for the Special Salience of the Study of Adolescent Development

There are several reasons for the special salience of the study of adolescent development to the understanding of broad life-span development. First, although the prenatal and the infant period exceeds adolescence as an ontogenetic stage of rapid physical and physiological growth, the years from approximately 10 years to 20 years not only include considerable physical and physiological changes associated with puberty but also mark a time when the interdependency of biology and context in human development is apparent. Second, as compared to infants, the cognizing, goal setting and relatively autonomous adolescent can, through reciprocal relations with his or her ecology, serve as an active influence on his or her development. Third, the multiple individual and contextual transitions into, throughout and out of this period, involving the major institutions of society (family, peers, schools and workplace), engage scholars interested in broader as well as individual levels of organization and also provide a rich opportunity for understanding the nature of change at multilevels.

8 Adolescence for the educational space

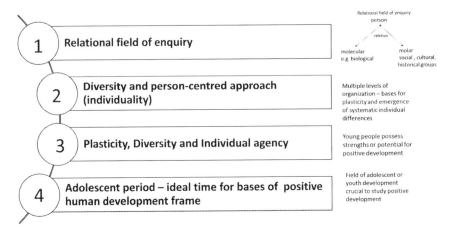

FIGURE 1.7 Four Defining Features of the Second Phase of Science of Adolescent Development

Four defining features of the second phase of science of adolescent development are worth noting. First, the empirical study of adolescence emerged as a relational field of inquiry. It became an area of scholarship in which implicitly and sometimes explicitly, the key unit of analysis in understanding the development was the person. This person, the unit of analysis, is now understood in relation with both more molecular (e.g. biological) and more molar (social groups cultural and historical) levels of organization. In such a relational frame, no one level of organization was seen as a prime mover of development.

Second, the coming together of the multiple levels of organization involved in the development system provides the bases for plasticity and significant emergence of individual difference. This concept of individual differences now begins to indicate that every individual has its individuality, which serves as a key bases of a person's ability to act as an agent of one's own development. This has contributed to the awareness of the need for a person-centred approach to research in human development. Third, although there is a focus on the problems of this development period, the focus on plasticity, diversity of development of people and individual agency has also surfaced as important themes in adolescence literature.

The strength and the capacity of an adolescent to influence his/her development for better or worse have been the important premise of this phase, where problems of the adolescent phase is just one of an array of the strands in the literature. This idea of personal agency playing a role in the adolescent's development has provided a basis for the positive human development framework, which forms the *fourth* defining feature of this phase.

The study of adolescence is now characterized by efforts made to understand how relational processes provide for a basis of diverse trajectories across adolescents and how these ecological variables can be altered in order to bring about a positive development in youth. These ecological variables were termed as *ecological assets* (Lerner & Steinberg, 2004)

Advent of the third phase of scientific study of adolescence;

- there exists a system of relations between individuals and contexts that is the core of the study of human development.

- a belief that theories that explain the relationship between the interacting systems are more important than theories whose groundings are exclusively nature or nurture

Moving forward

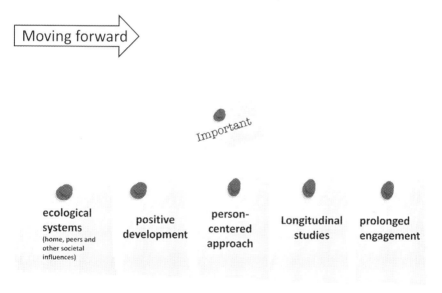

FIGURE 1.8 Phase 3 – Moving Forward

The other broader issues that have and must engage developmental scientists is that the study of adolescence pertained to the understanding of the bases, parameters and limits of plasticity of human development. This also legitimized an optimistic view that interventions in ecological systems such as home, peers and other societal influences have the potential to alter the course of life for improved life outcomes. This gave rise to the concept of positive development that can be promoted among adolescents. It also attested the belief that for understanding human behaviour, using the person-centred approach is necessary. It also brought about changes in the methodologies used for study of human development at large. Longitudinal studies and prolonged engagement using techniques such as interviews, observations and various triangulation techniques developed.

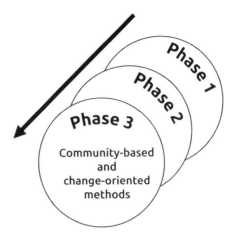

The emergence of the third phase leads us to an idea of adolescence representing at any point in history the generational cohort that needs to be ready to assume the quality of leadership of self, family, community and society with an aim of maintaining and improving human life. It presents the need for the generation of basic and applied knowledge to enable adolescents to become fully engaged citizens capable of, and committed to, making contributions to society and self. The initiation of this phase shows how the study of adolescent development can inform and be informed by the concerns of all stakeholders including communities, practitioners and policymakers.

Tracing the concept of adolescence: G. Stanley's comprehensive theory

After going through the previously noted phases, we can draw parallelism with the kind of efforts located in G. Stanley Hall's work on adolescence, which resulted in a comprehensive theory of adolescence in modern times.

Before we take a look at the time when the formal concept of adolescence found its expression and at the immediate following movement for systematic 'child study' (inspired and guided by G. Stanley Hall) that came into existence, we will attempt to discuss the roots and the growth of the concept of adolescence to the point in the early 20th century when it had become well established in the public consciousness.

To begin with, we need to familiarize ourselves with the common ideas about childhood and "youth" during the period 1800–1875 as derived from a rapidly developing literature of child-rearing advice and from books and pamphlets directed to young people bearing especially on their moral problems. This will enable us to understand the relationship between the idea of adolescence and the social phenomena to which it was a response.

Adolescence in general was considered an American discovery and hence the need to look at sources from American history. Prior to 1825, hardly any books on child-rearing were found in America, and those that were available were primarily from England. These books did not reflect any needs or problems in people's lives. Post 1825, child-rearing books began to appear in an American context. These books largely looked at childhood as a distinct period from adolescence in terms of maturity. The 'native' literature disclosed deep anxieties about the quality of American family life. The authors of these books used words like 'disorder', 'disobedience' and so on, emphasizing the need for authority of parents early in a child's life and throughout the years of growth. The growth of a 'child-centred' attitude was observed and criticized by many authors. Children were pampered and given utmost attention, resulting in children becoming self-centred and selfish. Another major outcome of this was that children started resorting to support outside the family and among peer groups. This gave rise to the separation of youth and age. A sense of 'youth' as a critical transition period in the life emerged, and they were characterized by words such as 'pliant', 'plastic' and 'formative'. These characterizations gave way to the vulnerability of youth with experiences of high emotional turbulence and roaring of passions, though there was no direct reference made to the physiological changes that occur at puberty. The dangers confronted by youth was assumed to come from the larger society, thus giving a social dimension to the problems. Towards the end of the 19th century, these dangers were identified with urban life, pointing to cities as the source of negative influences on adolescents' growth towards adulthood as a result of its chaotic social and economic life, its varied population, highly energetic commercial environment and its hypnotizing entertainments.

The formal concept of adolescence started gaining its impression at this time, and Stanley Hall's work gained a new movement for systematic 'child study'. It aimed to deepen the understanding of human development through reflections of ordinary citizens about the behaviour of their children. Hall's work on "The Moral and Religious Training of Children" gave rise to the idea of 'storm and stress'. Associations were made between adolescents' crisis and a wide range of personal and social phenomenon with religious conversion and with the rising rate of juvenile delinquency.

Hall's thinking had been profoundly influenced by Darwinism, and the psychology he proposed was explicitly bound to an evolutionary, or 'genetic', model. According to him, adolescence represented the various stages of development in a specific order. He believed that adolescence is a bundle of a variety of contradictions and "antithetic impulses" such as hyperactivity and lassitude, happiness and depression, egotism and self-abasement, selfishness and altruism, gregariousness and shyness, sensitivity and cruelty, radicalism and conservatism. This is what led to the idea of adolescence as a period of 'storm and stress'. This notion of adolescence became widespread among people, who started looking at adolescence as problematic. Scholars criticized Hall's idea of viewing growth in terms of set 'stages'. Critics also accused Hall of exaggerating the 'storm and stress' phenomena and depicting adolescence as problematic. Yet today, growth of adolescence is regarded in terms of set 'stages', and adolescence as a whole is viewed as problematic, retaining the strength of the "special cult of adolescence" as proposed by Stanley Hall. Further, the work of Margaret Mead on Samoan children indicated adolescent 'storm and stress' as a function of certain cultural determinants.

Hall's idea of adolescence was shaped by the integration of certain aspects of popular beliefs about youth and the new ideas of evolution, reflecting a reasonable degree of continuity with the concept of adolescence as described prior to his conceptualization of the term. Yet there had been questions raised about the concept of adolescence.

The discontinuity in the conceptualization of the term 'adolescence' can be explained through the long-term transformation of the United States from an agricultural into an urban and industrial society which has had immense influence on family structures. The traditional agrarian family structures were characterized by high degree of internal unity, where children and adults shared the same tasks, the same entertainments, the same friends and the same expectations. This resulted in a continuum between generations where the child was considered a miniature model of his/her parent.

As people started migrating to cities, urban children did not perform the same tasks as adults as it was not needed; at the same time poor children were also likely to be doing different work than that of their parents. This resulted in separating children from their families and bringing them in contact with other adults and peers leading to a discontinuity of age groups. Children were now seen as a separate entity from adults, and their behaviour was observed to be a bit deviating from that of adults. This gave rise to the concept of child-rearing whereby the adults developed tolerance for such deviant behaviour. Most of the cultures reflected sharp discontinuities of this kind, and hence a system of age-grading defining the steps in transition from childhood to adulthood, emerged. This situation gave rise to the 'youth culture' as suggested by Kenneth Keniston and it was institutionalized as adolescence. Though the 19th century was not characterized by the same items found in modern culture such as 'teen magazines', 'rock and roll' or specific dressing styles, the fact of wanting to be and with one's own kind was very prominent then with their specific characteristics.

Another point of discontinuity was a consequence of separation between parents and children within individual families that led to intrafamily conflicts where the adolescent is left to form his or her own identity. The ample number of choices and alternatives with respect to careers and lifestyles for the adolescent also gave rise to a unique temporary identity of being part of the youth culture.

The disparity between generations increased. Adolescents became the first generation learners who had the opportunity to go to school, leading to the formation of a youth culture.

The growth of the concept of adolescent was a response to innumerable facts observed in the American society. The culmination of all the efforts of conceptualizing adolescence is reflected in G. Stanley's work proving the first comprehensive theory of adolescence in modern history.

Adolescence: concept, construct and stage

Anthropologist Margaret Mead was probably the first to question the universality of the experience of adolescence in the 1950s. Universal definitions of adolescence were quite restricted and confined to describing adolescence as a 'period of transition', in which "although no longer considered a child, the young person is not yet considered an adult" (Dehne & Riedner, 2001). Literature on adolescent health, usually dominated by international organizations including the United Nations, WHO and the Commonwealth Youth Programme, have considered variedly the period of adolescence to be between the ages of 15–19, 15–24, 10–19 or 10–24 and likewise. The terms 'young people', 'youth' and 'young adult' are often used to constitute these age groups. There are biological, legal, sociohistorical, demographic and behavioural markers which render adolescence (and youth) a dynamic concept. This concept appears to be well established in a few countries and settings, whereas it appears to be just emerging in few other settings.

The concept of adolescence as a stage in the life course has undergone several important changes since the term 'adolescence' was first popularized in the early 1900s. Since then the concept has emerged as a cultural construct and evolved in the study of social sciences as a result of the effects of cultural, economic, and political influences and the role of institutions in shaping adolescence.

In many developing countries, the condition of adolescence has been slowly emerging. Children are looked upon as adults by making them undergo certain initiation rites of passage such as circumcision or arranged marriage; many other such rites vary from culture to culture or among societies. It is perceived that, in India, especially in rural areas, arranged marriage for girls is a common feature which is believed to be achieved post-puberty (Dehne & Riedner, 2001). Instead of attaining schooling and interacting with peers, which is considered a characteristic feature of this age, childbearing at an early age of 16 is quite common in rural girls of India. The concept of adolescence is a waning concept as these girls shift instantly from childhood to motherhood. This concept of adolescence from a biological perspective thus develops into a cultural and social construct determined to a great extent by cultural and social markers.

Issues closely associated with the adolescent life stage such as initiation ceremonies, sexual practices, courtship and marital customs, and intergenerational relations were the focus of anthropological inquiry. This inquiry generally approached adolescence from the perspective of adulthood by undermining the interactions between adolescents and the influence of culture and placing more emphasis on the transition to adulthood. Biological and psychological stages of development of adolescence were the prime concern. The emphasis on adolescence as a universal stage in the biological and psychological development of the individual usefully highlights selfhood as a process rather than a state. Lately, the field of inquiry into adolescence has transcended beyond the range of anthropological inquiry as there have been shifts in disciplines and cultures worldwide. Recent developments in the anthropology of adolescence deals with not just the notion of culture, but also focuses on the practices through which culture is produced. Cultural and social transformations, although a possible result of cultural practices within, can also be viewed in the face of cultural pressures from without; this emphasizes that cultural shifts are drastically revising the meaning of adolescents in many societies.

The impact of modernity and economic restructuring ('development') on adolescents in earlier societies is thought to give rise to psychological stress of a kind in which they are likely to undergo 'identity crises' as they resolve psychic conflicts with their adult roles as proposed by Erikson (Hoose, N.A.). But changing times may bring in rapid changes in society both with respect to cultural practices and social influences and expectations. New educational structures in changing societies also give rise to different kinds of psychological distress in adolescents as a result of competition, social mobility and changing family structures among many other factors. These crises in adolescence can be located in specific social and economic processes. The adolescents are also vulnerable to the extreme shifts of modernization which further questions the relationships between adolescents and adults. On one hand, we can see the intergenerational conflict whereby internal conflicts are experienced by adolescents in the process of cultural change; on the other hand, there are conflicts created by the incongruence between the promises of modernity and the expectations of traditional mindsets of adults.

Adolescence thus characterizes a historically based, socially specific period of transition from childhood to adulthood, as well as a distinct physiological, sexual and psychological life stage. While adolescents worldwide experience similar physical changes during this period, the varied interpretations by individuals in societies give rise to different social and legal meanings of adolescence as a concept or construct or even stages.

Exploring the nature of adolescence

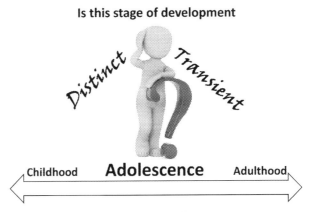

FIGURE 1.9 Adolescence – Distinct or Transient?

Adolescence for the educational space   **15**

To explore the nature of adolescence, a survey was conducted among a group of students studying in higher education institutions. Questions regarding 'Understanding of the concept of adolescence' were administerd to the respondents. The questions posed to them were:

- *What kind of adolescent were you?*
- *What kind of adolescent were your parents?*
- *What kind of adolescents do you see today?*

Responses of three of the respondents have been provided here to get an insight into the nature of adolescence.
Learning Task: Read the responses of the three cases carefully and try to identify the nature of the concept within a period and across different periods in time.

Case 1

Not that I am too old but honestly, I do not remember myself too much as an adolescent. And I have a reason for this. Whichever stage of life I have been, I have been in it to my fullest. So have no regrets or much of remembrance as I strive to make my upcoming stages of life more and more beautiful.

16 Adolescence for the educational space

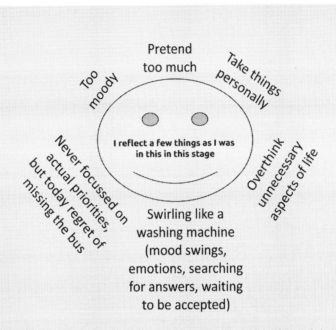

As I reflect today, my parents probably understood what adolescence is and gave me the ideal desired space that every teenager needed. This gave me the sense of independence of my life as an adolescent. I am fortunate I got that which made me surpass this phase smoothly compared to my other friends.

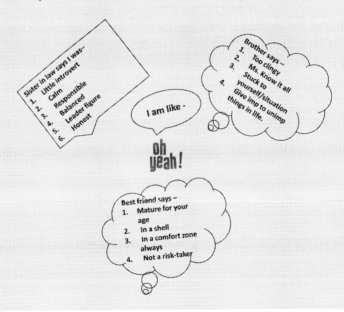

It's in my adolescence that my spiritual inclination grew. The value system and morality were strong since teen age. As an adolescent, I would watch saintly serials and grasp the values needed to live an ethical, moral and a pious life. I will confess that at the age of 13–16 I was going further from my parents. I regret that immensely today. But new day, new things kept happening and like horses I just looked forward and ran. I never stopped to understand what actually the crux of adolescence was and why emotions fluctuated so much.

Case 2

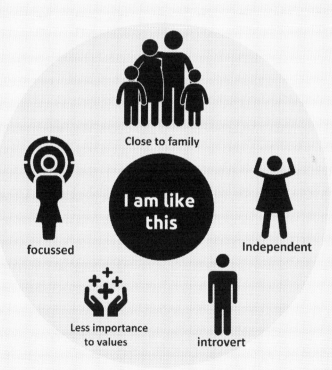

Case 3

> I basically was close to my mother, listened to her at all phases, never had any desire for independence but still some instances like having night out. As adolescent I was too sentimental and moody I didn't possess the courage to confront people or state my view point. I would take things personally, short tempered. I had a jumbled concept of what to do, constant in conflicts, I was more of introvert, indecisive, various thoughts going on in mind altogether. All in all a period wrapped up with emotional turmoils, experiments, lots of immaturity, broken friendships, yet all those made me who I am now. Parents, friends saw me as innocent, honest, immature, not at all a risk taker, responsible and a cry baby.

Case 1

My parents have shared of their lives as adolescent[s] when they intended to narrate and compare their lives with ours. I feel their lives was calmer and more peaceful compared to my adolescence. Though they had siblings and ups and down and, in their comparison, I have no siblings but a joint family environment, I still feel they are more sedentary. They speak of the best times they encountered as teens, the games

Adolescence for the educational space **19**

they played, the friends they had, the dominance of a few siblings and how other siblings reacted to that. However, I couldn't see the complexity of the adolescence period in their talks. I feel their adolescence was peaceful compared to mine. They had hardships in their times as adolescence which I never had and so it can be that they had to take up responsibilities soon and may have turned towards adulthood much earlier than they were [expecting].

Case 2

As far as the adolescent period of my parents is concerned, they found it to be very interesting. It was the same like a normal adolescent where they were engaged more with their friends, and they usually had fun with more of indoor and outdoor games rather than the current scenario where adolescents are mainly engaged and glued to computers and cell phones. The love between the siblings among them was also very much valued and equal importance was given to both friends and family.

They learnt to take responsibilities right from very early age and continued their education alongside their job and other responsibilities. But now they made sure that I don't face those hardships and can live a better life and be successful with strong values and respect.

Case 3

My parents had shared bits and pieces of their adolescence while comparing mine. I believe their adolescence was quite peaceful and full of clarity. Their youth was however full of strains and hardships, yet joy for them was very simple as like having evening tea under the banyan tree. Saving money since months by not eating tiffin to buy books! Going barefeet to do little bit grocery, shopping, flying kites, playing cards, hiding from my grandparents- are some of the incidents they did.

20 Adolescence for the educational space

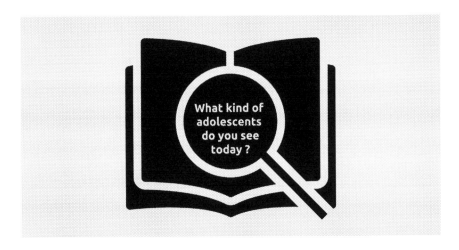

Case 1

Honestly, I find a huge difference in today's adolescents and their behaviour and experiences compared to mine. However, we need to accept that as the time passes, the generation transition also takes place. I will not say they are bad or good. They are just perfect for their time. But this perfect may not be the same for people of my generation or older.

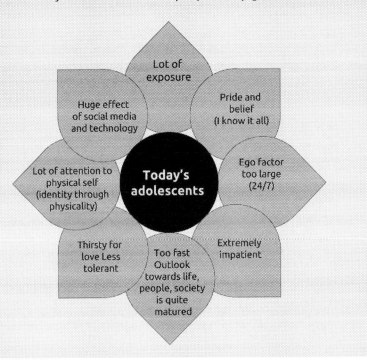

Case 2

Adolescents of today

- Experiment with new skills since they are exploring their reasoning abilities.
- Sometimes they tend to find faults in adult's position and reasoning.
- Adolescents in today's age are more competent in nature.
- There might be certain risk-taking behaviours identified with some adolescents.
- These days adolescents are more creative and energetic.
- Most of the part of their lives are discussed on social media rather than in real context.
- Adolescents nowadays are more career-oriented.

Case 3

Yes, definitely with time there had been huge changes from me being adolescent to today's adolescents. Today's adolescents are open to exposure to a lot of extent; which led them to be full of themself, more self-conscious, egoistic and thinking 'I know it all'. In terms of attitude, behaviour they are full of pride, a bit of over-smart, have an implicit tendency of outshine others. For them 'beauty', body shamming is a grave issue. With so many social networking sites, porn sites, they have one-two many options to get engaged to, and lack a critical thinking to discard bad and accept good. They are very intolerant with respect to constructive criticism as well. The adjective I would use for them will be Volatile. The age I am talking about can be roughly 14 - 18 years.

The responses to the survey are very limited to a confined context reflecting a homogeneous group of individuals having experienced a unique yet distinct adolescent period. Thus, we can see how adolescence is a distinct, yet transient, period of development between childhood and adulthood characterized by increased experimentation and risk-taking, a tendency to discount long-term consequences, and

> heightened sensitivity to peers and other social influences, (National Research Council, 2013). A key function of adolescence is developing an integrated sense of self, including individuation, separation from parents and personal identity. In the process of establishing self and identity, it is seen that risk-taking behaviour, experimentation and engaging in activities that bring in novelty are unique to this stage of development (National Research Council, 2013).
>
> As individuals, as a community and a society, we look at the historical evolution of the concept of adolescence, and eventually our understanding of the concept is also evolving considering the shading of these phases into one another, thus providing new horizons for conceptualization of the idea of adolescence.

Cultural structuring of adolescence

The nature of adolescence as discovered through the survey responses portray adolescence as a distinct, yet transient, period of development. Worldwide, there are diverse cultures that distinguish differently between adolescents and adults. India by itself is a land of diverse culture, wherein most of the cultures assign a certain period of preparation for adulthood parallel to the period of adolescence as known universally. It is also observed that within the broader uniformities in the characterization of adolescence, the structure and content of the adolescent period varies remarkably from culture to culture in ways that reflect broader social and institutional patterns (Crockett, 1997). Adolescence, a very significant phase in the course of life span development, serves as a conceptual continuity between childhood and adulthood. Socially and culturally, this translates into wide variations in what may be described as the stage of adolescence in the Indian context.

Adolescence can be viewed as a social construct – a stage of life between childhood and adulthood – and as a biological construct associated with the onset of reproductive maturation (i.e. puberty). But every society assigns a varied period of adolescence based on critical markers aligned with the cultural practices and arrangements of that society. The adolescent experiences are shaped within cultures by assigning social significance to certain developmental signs such as menarche, puberty, physical development or acquired skills. And these signs become the social markers to which the adolescents' privileges or responsibilities are attached and eventually become psychologically meaningful as well. The culturally developed markers attain social significance and determine the organization of adolescents' activities and expectations in the respective society, thus defining the normative course of adolescent development in that society.

These developmental markers also seem to be associated to the social and economic organization of society. Biological markers of maturation are celebrated in a few societies where puberty is linked to marriage, which has important political and economic functions (Crockett, 1997). For example, marriage is used politically to strengthen interfamilial ties; the marriage market is used to increase a daughter's value in labour-intensive agrarian economies. Puberty is thus celebrated as a political or economic asset.

On one hand there are some societies with less differentiated economies in which adolescents become equipped with adult skills and tasks by the time they attain puberty and are ready to function like adults; on the other hand there are industrialized societies in which the focus is on achieved rather than ascribed social status, and school completion is emphasized for adulthood. Social and technical competence in adolescents is reached much later after the attainment of puberty. Puberty is more of a private affair than being a public celebration. If we look at the former type of society, marriage can be considered the end of adolescence and beginning of adulthood, but if we look at the latter type of society, the completion of formal schooling followed by full-time employment, being away from parent's homes and becoming financially independent can be considered as the beginning of adulthood. As we observe, different cultures mark the social transition from childhood to adolescence at different ages. The choice of developmental markers and the timing of these markers are embedded in cultural arrangements (Crockett, 1997).

Developmental markers in the Indian context

If we look at the Indian context with regard to marriages and puberty in adolescents, fertility is highly valued within marriages. Adolescent girls are married off at a very early age in the fear of getting pregnant prior to marriage, which is strongly condemned by Indian society. A positive relationship is observed between early marriage and the socio-economic development of different regions in India. The poorer states consistently show a lower age of marriage than the developed states. Girls of this age hailing from lower social classes are likely to be less educated and hence marry early and have children at a very young age. Age of marriage and fertility behaviour also correlate highly with the level of education. Girls from the middle class and above have shown a steady increase in the age of marriage with metropolitan cities showing an average above 25 years (Indian Express, April 2012). Women have become more ambitious and career-oriented with changing times, and they either delay marriage for the sake of career or even choose to remain unmarried or not have children after marriage. These age differences of marriage also determines the varied period of adolescence as a result of the economic conditions of society. Regional variations in the country also affect the temporal boundaries of adolescence. One cannot think of a Tamil Brahmin, or the Bengali Kayastha, or the Goan Christian to be uneducated, whereas, the number of literate children especially girls from the tribal belts of Bihar and Rajasthan are very few. Kerala has almost every child completing elementary education and moving to secondary education, while Bihar has hardly one out of two children in the relevant age group in school (Sarawathi & Oke, 2013). This kind of divide caused by gender, class, caste, urban-rural residence and regional variations in India is responsible for different developmental markers and the timing of these markers, rooted in the social and cultural practices (Sarawathi & Oke, 2013).

Intersection of multiple perspectives to the concept of puberty

Puberty viewed as an integrated biological and social construction has aroused curiosity among researchers, scholars, adolescents and stakeholders. Cultures have celebrated puberty to varying degrees. The biological changes of puberty are universal, but the timing and social significance of these changes to adolescents themselves, societies and scientific inquiry vary across historical time and cultures. Puberty is considered to be a complex biosocial period beginning with reproductive-function awakening and culminating in sexual maturity. A downward trend in the age of puberty has been observed and attributed to changing environmental conditions and circumstances. These changes in response to shifting environmental demands reflect puberty as more of a secular environmental trend than being an evolutionary process. Yet one cannot totally discard the role of genes which may be a function of environmental demands and thus bring in varied timing of puberty in contemporary generations.

In addition to the evolutionary and physical developmental properties of puberty, the social component of puberty historically was seen as a transition contributing to the adolescents' storm and stress as conceived by Stanley Hall. Adolescence was viewed as universal and biological in origin till contemporary researches rejected this idea. Contemporary studies attempted to present a more balanced view of adolescence as a period of development characterized by biological, cognitive, emotional and social reorganization with the aim of adapting to cultural expectations of becoming an adult. It also asserts that problems specific to the period of adolescence are not universal. Adolescents by taking on multiple roles are both influenced by and influence the social environment.

A multitude of changes with respect to the molecular-biological, molar-psychological and social changes characterize puberty and provoke scientific interests that comprise the biomedical, behavioural and social sciences. There is a need for interdisciplinary perspectives to characterize adolescent development (Susman & Rogol, 2004). Later researches on pubertal development included genetic and neuroendocrine mechanisms that initiate puberty; influences from the molecular to the social contextual; the significance of timing of puberty; and the dynamic interactive processes among physical growth changes, emotions, problem behaviour, cognition and risky sexual activity. Puberty is thus considered as a biopsychosocial transition that initiates psychological changes and that simultaneously initiates changes in the social contexts in which adolescents are situated. This approach refers to the dynamic integration of psychological, biological and contextual levels of functioning and the interactions between them. Eventually behaviourism, contextualism and learning theory superseded theories of development and evolution. Empirical studies assessing the relationships between physical growth and pubertal hormone levels and psychological development studied issues of family interaction, adjustment, aggressive behaviour, emotions and sexuality (Susman & Rogol, 2004).

A life span perspective played a formative role in the genesis of contextualism, a concept that integrates biological and psychological levels with the contextual levels of analysis. Developmental plasticity at puberty was constrained as a result of both genetics and nutritional aspects. The degree of plasticity in pubertal processes is influenced by genes, neuroendocrine systems, experiential history and the multiple contexts of development, though plasticity is relative because all developmental modifications are neither desirable nor possible, and the normative age of onset of puberty is narrow. Reactions to the biological changes of puberty vary systematically with the social context in which they occur (Susman & Rogol, 2004). Family, peers, community and neighbourhood individually and collectively function differently for adolescents at different times. Family structure and other related experiences are influencers for timing of puberty. Conflict in families did predict earlier menarche, and girls in broken families attained early puberty than girls in secure and ideal families. The peer network also plays an important role in moderating the timing of puberty. Pubertal timing effects vary depending on whether girls are in co-ed schools or same-sex schools (Susman & Rogol, 2004). Studies conducted in developing and economic transition countries have found girls from lower socio-economic status to reach menarche at a later age as compared with girls from higher socio-economic status. These associations can be related to different risk factors like malnutrition or excessive physical activity prevalent in societies of low socio-economic status (James et al., 2010). Thus, it can be seen that processes of development can only be understood by considering the multiple systems that function at multiple levels of development. One needs to take into consideration interdisciplinary models combining the biological, psychological and contextual levels of functioning, bringing together the expertise of diverse disciplines.

Adolescence: a critical bridge between childhood and adulthood

Adolescence lies between childhood and early adulthood. Based on the premise of an understanding of the stage that has gone by, i.e. childhood, and a preparation for a stage called adulthood, attempting to understand these stages necessitates a deeper examination of the concept through psychological, biological and sociological lenses.

There is transformation generally observed as children turn from a warm cuddly behaviour to an emotionally distant and independent individual. These developmental changes do not occur all of a sudden or in a uniform manner. There is an observable change in terms of the kind of activities and interests gradually shifting from watching cartoons and animated movies to preferring reality shows and sitcoms especially focused on teenage issues or the shift in types of relationships pulling away from parents and inclined more towards peers and others.

Adolescent brains are not simply 'advanced' child brains or 'immature' adult brains, but have evolved to meet the needs of this stage of life. The temporal discrepancy in the specialization of and connections between brain regions makes adolescence unique. Evidence of changes in brain structure and function during adolescence strongly suggests that these cognitive tendencies of adolescents are associated with biological immaturity of the brain and with an imbalance among developing brain systems. This biological perspective proposes an imbalance model. This implies dual systems: one involved in cognitive and behavioural control and one involved in socio-emotional processes. Accordingly, adolescents lack mature capacity for self-regulation because the brain system that influences pleasure-seeking and emotional reactivity develops more rapidly than the brain system that supports self-control (National Research Council, 2013).

The increased cognitive abilities gained throughout adolescence also provide the capacity for other aspects of psychosocial development, such as developing identity and capacity for self-direction. The capacity for self-direction enables the adolescent to think rationally, question the legitimacy and justification of everyday experiences and the social institutions around them. Navigating the social systems in which the adolescents are situated requires independent decision-making skills to support the transition to adulthood and make the period of adolescence contribute to others.

Researches have shown that adolescents differ from children and adults in the following three ways. First, adolescents have less capacity for self-regulation in emotionally charged contexts, relative to adults. Second, adolescents have a heightened sensitivity to proximal external influences, such as peer pressure and immediate incentives, relative to children and adults. Third, adolescents show less ability than adults to make judgments and decisions that require future orientation. The combination of these three cognitive patterns accounts for the tendency of adolescents to prefer and engage in risky behaviours that have a high probability of immediate reward but may have harmful consequences (National Research Council, 2013).

Psychological insights tell us that three conditions are critically important to healthy psychological development in adolescence: (1) the presence of a parent or parent figure who is involved with the adolescent and concerned about his or her successful development, (2) inclusion in a peer group that values and models prosocial behaviour and academic success, and (3) activities that contribute to autonomous decision-making and critical thinking. Social institutions such as education provided through schools, extracurricular activities and work settings can provide opportunities for adolescents to learn to think for themselves, develop self-reliance and self-efficacy and improve reasoning skills (National Research Council, 2013).

This perspective of understanding adolescence also throws light on the significance of attachment theories built on childhood relationships and attachments that foster strong relationships in adolescents. The primary function of the attachment system during infancy is to maximize the safety and protection of the developing infant (McElhaney et al., 2009). Infants in need of security and protection display behaviours that promote proximity to caregivers. As they mature, there is an apparent shift towards emotional support. Gradually, as the child enters the so-called adolescent stage, the attachment system tends more towards 'felt security' rather than physical safety, irrespective of the presence or absence of the attachment figure (McElhaney et al., 2009). To some extent, the emphasis on physical protection and proximity to caregivers decreases with increased maturity due to their capability to interact with their environment on their own. However, in the fostering of these strong relationships with the caregiver, it is quite compelling to note that a combination of autonomy and relatedness is most correlated with optimal outcomes in the parent-child relationship. Allen and Land, emphasized the importance of exploratory system in adolescence relative to infants (McElhaney et al., 2009). The increased autonomous exploration coexisting with parents' basic minimal support facilitates adolescents to turn their attention towards other aspects of development, social and emotional. Relationship building with peers, romantic partners and managing their own emotional states and behaviour thus becomes a characteristic feature of this age.

An adolescent's identity is an emerging reflection of his or her values, beliefs and aspirations, and it can be constructed and reconstructed over time and experience. Multiple factors including family, culture, peers and media shape identity development, but adolescents themselves are also active agents in the process. Ultimately, how adolescents' multifaceted identities are manifested – neurobiologically, behaviourally or otherwise – and what role identity plays in their overall well-being greatly depends on their experiences in particular social contexts.

Thus, looking at adolescence from a sociological lens informs us that at this stage, social systems such as schools, colleges, peers and strong family ties can make a difference for better worse in the lives of adolescents. These social systems and the development of the brain is related to the strong interplay between environmental factors and the brain of the adolescent. It is here that social institutions such as education have a significant role to play.

Although adolescence has been often thought of as a time of turmoil and risk for young people, it is also viewed as a developmental period rich with opportunity for youth to learn and grow. Adolescence thus forms a critical bridge between childhood and adulthood and is a window of opportunity for positive, life-shaping development (National Academies of Sciences, Engineering, and Medicine, 2019).

Characteristics of adolescence (physical, emotional, social)

Physical characteristics

Changing times and new challenges have made it necessary for all those who deal with adolescents to be aware of the normative characteristics of adolescents and what represents early or late physical development so as to be able to prepare the adolescent for the multitude of changes that take place during this time of life.

Physical characteristics are primarily characterized by the change in body size and mass as a result of the increase in the number and size of cells. Entering puberty signals the physical changes of adolescence: a growth spurt and sexual maturation. The process of sexual maturation actually occurs over a period of several years.

The sequence of physical changes is largely predictable, though it is argued that there is great variability in the age of onset of puberty and the pace at which changes occur. Many factors affect the onset of puberty. The growth spurt, which involves rapid skeletal growth, usually begins at about ages 10 to 12 in girls and 12 to 14 in boys and is complete at around age 17 to 19 in girls and 20 in boys. For most adolescents, sexual maturation involves achieving fertility and the physical changes that support fertility. For girls, these changes involve breast budding, which may begin around age 10 or earlier, and menstruation, which typically begins at age 12 or 13.9. For boys, the onset of puberty involves enlargement of the testes at around age 11 or 12 (APA, 2002). The development of secondary sexual characteristics, such as pubic, axillary and facial hair development, breaking of the voice and spermatic formation for boys and pubic and axillary hair development and menarche for girls, occurs later in puberty (Ozdemir et al., 2016). These changes during puberty cause children of the same age to look physically different.

Increase in height as a result of the anabolic effect of gonadal hormones is observed with the symptoms of puberty. Testosterone having a stronger anabolic effect compared to the estrogen group of hormones explains the taller adult height in males compared to females. Increase in height is observed to gradually slow down towards the end of adolescence and completely stops at 16–18 in girls and 18–20 in boys. According to a study by WHO, an average height difference of 12–13 centimetres between adult males and females is due to later sexual development in adolescent boys as compared to girls. This results in boys reaching peak height velocity later than girls. The increase in height during the growth spurt is higher in boys (Ozdemir et al., 2016). The weight gain is largely in the form of fat storage in girls and in the form of growth in muscle and skeleton mass in boys. Rapid progress in bone age is also observed, followed by the joining of pineal bodies.

Physical changes are visible to all and highlight the range and pace of change. This sometimes leads to adolescents feeling more or less mature than others. Physical appearance at this age is usually a very crucial factor for the adolescents and associated with their image and identity in front of society. This takes us ahead to understand the social characteristics of adolescents.

Social characteristics

The physical changes occurring at this stage play great importance to the physical appearance and body image of the adolescent. Both boys and girls are concerned about their image and appearance in order to fit into the groups with whom they identify with and at the same time maintain their own unique style and identity. Developing a sense of identity and establishing a role and purpose reflect the social characteristics of adolescents. This is the time when they rely on family, peers and significant others' support in expressing concerns about their looks, facial features, overweight issues and getting a reassurance from adults, that, "you are looking good", "it's okay to be how you are". They are constantly struggling with their self and the environment around, the society in which they are a part of. More importance is attached to friendships rather than family at this stage.

Peer groups serve important functions throughout adolescence, thus providing a reference point for developing a sense of identity. Peer groups also serve to strengthen the sources of popularity, status, prestige and acceptance during adolescence. At the same time, some adolescents secretly try to find ways to identify with their parents. Adolescents who are accepted by their peers and have mutual friendships have been found to have better self-images and to perform better in school. On the other hand, social isolation among peer-rejected teens has been linked to a variety of negative behaviours, such as delinquency. The nature of involvement with peer groups also differs with increasing age. Younger adolescents typically have at least one primary peer group with whom they identify whose members are usually similar in many respects, including sex (APA, 2002).

Involvement with the peer group in this age appears to be strong, and conformity and concerns about acceptance are at their extremes. Middle adolescence, about the age between 14 and 16, sees peer groups to be more gender-mixed. Less conformity and more tolerance of individual differences in appearance, beliefs and feelings are typical of this group. Late adolescence beyond age of 16 often seems to be replaced by more intimate dyadic relationships, such as one-on-one friendships and romances that have grown in importance as the adolescent has matured (APA, 2002). Social skills are very important in maintaining these relationships. Lack of social skills necessitates the intervention of adults to guide them appropriately in enhancing these skills.

Transition from elementary school to middle or junior high school and then to senior high school in school contexts also pose challenges to the academic performance and well-being of adolescents. Teacher-student relationships, the school's environment and friends at school determine the emotional and psychological well-being of adolescents.

The all-pervasive influence of media and the internet affects the lives of adolescents. On one hand, the influences can be negative by representing aggressiveness, violence, unhealthy sexuality and many more ideas; on the other hand, they can be potentially useful by providing valuable information on handling the previously mentioned issues and health concerns. Social development and emotional development are closely intertwined as young people search for a sense of self and personal identity.

Emotional characteristics

Adolescent development is often characterized by rapidly fluctuating emotions. These emotions may provide varying experiences, thus characterizing a few of them as emotionally balanced; a few others as not.

Adolescence is the first time, however, when individuals have the cognitive capacity to consciously sort through who they are and what makes them unique. Identity exists in adolescence with family ties, friends, relationships, career choices, position in society, goals, worldview and lifestyle. Identity includes two concepts: self-concept, the set of beliefs one has about oneself; and self-esteem, which involves evaluating how one feels about one's self-concept (APA, 2002). The physical changes that occur in adolescence strongly influences their self-esteem, either positively or negatively. Assurance from family, peers or significant others act as judgments for the adolescents, and some of them may consider these groups in establishing their own identity.

In attaining a sense of identity, adolescents are more explorative in nature. This leads them to experiment and take risks in approaching the tasks they encounter. Adolescents who lack experimentation or risk-taking may appear stable, but in reality, these adolescents may be facing more difficulty, not being able to achieve a realistic sense of identity, compared to the risk-taking adolescents.

Emotional development occurs uniquely for each adolescent, with different patterns emerging for different groups of adolescents. Boys and girls can differ in the challenges they face in their emotional development. Gender differences also reflects the way in which boys and girls are socialized in society, which in turn results in differences in ways of forming identity. For example, girls may need more help in learning assertive skills, whereas boys may need help to understand the need to feel and express emotions or be encouraged to have more cooperative rather than competitive relationships with other males.

Scan the QR code to view this video

The Mysterious Workings of the Adolescent Brain

Why do teenagers seem so much more impulsive, so much less self-aware than grown-ups? Cognitive neuroscientist Sarah-Jayne Blakemore compares the prefrontal cortex in adolescents to that of adults, to show us how typically "teenage" behavior is caused by the growing and developing brain.

Adolescence for the educational space

> **Activity:**
>
> List down a few distinguishing characteristics of adolescents. Arrange these characteristic features according to age group, gender, type of characteristics. Construct a pictorial representation of these characteristics indicating the relationship between the various characteristic features that you have listed down.
>
> Observe the pictorial representation carefully and
>
> **Reflect on the following:**
>
> 1. Can the physical, emotional, social characteristics of adolescence be considered in isolation?
>
> If yes,
> - Justify your viewpoint.
>
> If no,
> - Why do you think so?
> - How are these characteristics dependent on each other?
>
> 2. How do cultural contexts influence these characteristics?

There is no 'one correct' construction of the concept of adolescence. Adolescence should be understood as a dynamic concept on a variable continuum dependent on context, culture and various other

Adolescence in the Indian context

Adolescents constitute 16% of the global population, with an absolute number of 1.2 billion. India is home to 253 million adolescents, accounting for 20.9% of the country's population (Ramadass et al., 2017).

In a country like India with a strong diverse cultural and social background, one essentially needs to look at and understand the distinct phases of adolescent development and the striking features of adolescence within its context in comparison with the worldwide understanding of adolescent stages and substages.

There are three factors that need to be taken into consideration while understanding adolescence in India.

1. The role of culture and collectivism in India strongly shapes the growth and developmental aspects of adolescents;
2. Within the Indian context itself, the duration of this stage, occurrences in this phase and the transitional period from childhood through adolescence to

adulthood, differ within the country due to the wide cultural differences that mark Indian cultur;

3   This phase of adolescence and the transitional period from childhood through adolescence to adulthood, differ not only within the country due to the wide cultural differences that mark Indian culture but within the culture too, and historically there are reasons attributed to differential socio-economic conditions, gender-related challenges, caste and class based differences, parental educational attainment, family income, varied experiences as a result of the shrinking world due to technological advances, social networking and so on.

Let us discuss the concept of adolescence as an interaction of the various influences of development such as nutrition, gender differences, socio-economic conditions, and cultural beliefs, advent of technology, western influence, caste, religion and so on. All these stated factors account for the challenges and opportunities that confront the understanding of adolescence as a transient period in India.

The collectivist traits of Indian society often sees the adolescent spending time with the family and residing with parents as opposed to the autonomous and highly independent adolescent of the west. These collectivist traits works as an opportunity for positive influence during this stage, and for many adolescence this could also be their most challenging relationship.

For many generations in Indian society, the acceptance of the idea of adolescence has shown mixed responses. On one hand there has been a resistance to accept this as a separate stage; on the other hand, there is a growing acceptance. With a strong influence of the Western culture on the present generation, a gradual adoption of the concept of 'teen' has strongly taken root. The Indian view of the concept again differs within the society. There have been times that witnessed early marriages of girls immediately at the onset of puberty, but over the past decade, the age of tying the nuptial knot has increased; consequently, child-bearing age has also extended, as a result of better education and healthier lifestyles compared to previous generations for the adolescent for a certain section of the Indian population.

To understand the variations in adolescence within the same culture it is imperative to look at the already mentioned factors like nutrition, gender differences, socio-economic conditions, and cultural beliefs, advent of technology, western influence, caste and religion that may influence the transient nature of adolescence as a result of variations observed within a culture itself.

Though India has made remarkable progress in improving access to education and equal opportunities to all, there appears a wide gender gap in society for various reasons. Unequal gender norms and power imbalances are yet a very significant part of the patriarchal and gender-stratified India. Here again, the varying extent of inequality can be discerned in urban and rural India. Variations are seen within rural and urban areas too. Low enrolment in schools due to poverty is a prime reason for poor education of the adolescent. Especially in rural sections of society, this age group is expected to earn a livelihood for the family, perform the household chores or take care of their siblings when their parents went out to work. This results in an early transition into adulthood both for males and females. Males are initiated into employment and females into marriage and child-bearing. Perception of parents about difficulty in finding a suitable match for educated girls is another reason for poor education of adolescent girls. Region-wise differences are apparent in perceiving gender parity. The northern states of India – Bihar, Rajasthan, Uttar Pradesh and Madhya Pradesh – exhibit gender differences in the educational enrolment, whereas the southern states – Kerala and Tamil Nadu – show better female enrolment rates. Religion and caste differences are also a concern in accessing education.

Data from a survey undertaken by the Social and Rural Research Institute (SRI) and Indian Market Research Bureau (IMRB) in 2009 compared the percentages of children that were out of school and found: more rural (5%) than urban (3%); more girls (6%) than boys (5%) aged 11–13 years; and a significant proportion of Muslims (8%), Scheduled Tribe (ST) and Scheduled Caste (SC) (6%) and Other Backward Caste (OBC) (3%) (Population Council & UNICEF, 2013). Religion and caste disparities in access to education exist particularly for the marginalized, including Muslim, SC, ST and OBC populations. Available evidence indicates very low or absolutely no enrolment of girls from the Muslim community as a result of inhibiting cultural factors, thus making them vulnerable. This is also observed of the boys from the Scheduled castes and scheduled Tribes who either dropped out of school at the elementary level or at the secondary level.

Gripped with issues such as poverty, Indian adolescents are faced with the related problems of malnutrition, illiteracy, poor health and livelihood. Good nutrition is associated with an earlier onset of menarche. Thus, urban girls have an earlier age of menarche than their counterparts in rural sections, and girls in families with higher socio-economic status tend to reach menarche sooner than girls of low socio-economic status because these adolescents typically have access to better-quality food. Indian children in the upper social class typically have a more distinct stage of adolescence than children in the lower social class (Chen & Farruggia, 2002).

Despite a number of national level programmes and policies by the government of India, the country is facing the burden of malnutrition on one hand and overnutrition and obesity on the other. Adolescent girls especially from underprivileged communities are undernourished, and further, their health is compromised by early marriages and child-bearing. Sociocultural barriers deprive these girls from making their own decisions regarding improvement of their health or their children's. Studies have exhibited similar gender biases in urban areas too.

During adolescence, nutrient requirements are utmost essential than at any other stage of life; malnutrition at this stage leads to the stunted growth and development of adolescents. Results from studies have highlighted that an urban slum adolescent girl is subjected to more physical and mental challenges compared to a rural adolescent girl (Prashant & Shaw, 2009). Overweight and obesity are problems arising out of the dietary changes and lifestyle patterns in contemporary society. Gender differences are observed indicating that more boys than girls are overweight and obese.

Another difference is observed with respect to societies and the influencing culture. Girls of affluent societies are observed to be more obese than their counterparts in impoverished societies. The habits of eating junk food and eating out of home frequently are strongly encultured in urban cities or families with high socioeconomic conditions. These habits result in obesity and becoming overweight. Post-pubertal girls, influenced by celebrities and models, become conscious of their image and take harsh steps to control their weight. Irregular dietary habits impact the adolescents' development. Hormonal changes, nutrition, poverty, illiteracy, cultural beliefs, socio-economic background, caste, class and religious differences, media and technology exposure – all these factors influence the development of adolescents with respect to their physical, emotional and social characteristics.

As we can see from the previous discussion, even as we head towards embracing the globalized concept of adolescence, the existing diverse conditions within Indian society attributed to beliefs and cultures, socio-economic conditions, gender disparity and media influence leads to a 'push and pull' of the understanding of adolescence as a construct.

Need for adolescence education

The adolescent phase of a school-going child is primarily spent in schools. However, we cannot be ignorant of the fact that, in a country like India, there are many adolescents who may be out of formal schooling due to various reasons that have been noted earlier in this chapter.

Nevertheless, educational institutions have a very important role to play in the life of a child. Particularly, secondary school years lay the foundation of adolescents' lives through a significant portion of the adolescents' activities while navigating through different contexts. Moving into adulthood and leading a positive life may be highly dependent on either an adverse or a wholesome life as an adolescent. Adolescent development has health implications throughout life.

Educational institutions shoulder an important responsibility. The magnitude of this responsibility needs to be recognized. The importance of ecological systems and person-centred approaches have been recognized as having great potential for the positive development of adolescents. Thus, it is critical that, educators, parents, significant others and the community, realize the value of the adolescent phase and be equipped with the necessary knowledge to understand the processes that take place during adolescence in order to engage adolescents in worthwhile activities for their well-being. This demands a departure from the predisposed notions gained from long-standing discourses about adolescence towards an understanding based upon a more generative consideration of the concept for the benefit of adolescents and those who are associated with them.

The education system will need to be responsive to the changes and developments happening around them and capitalize on adolescent development particularly relevant to the field of education. Adolescence education thus is an investment in terms of promoting adolescents' future lives and consequently wider societal gains in support of the 2030 Agenda for Sustainable Development.

Activity:

In light of the understanding of the period of adolescence, look at the words associated with the term given at the beginning of the chapter and those which have emerged from the responses of these cases. Add or subtract the terms that best suits the concept of adolescence.

List down these terms in the following box under Key terms for your reference.

Key terms: adolescence, dynamic, distinct yet transient, plasticity, diversity, positive development, longitudinal studies, individual agency, age of opportunity, ecological systems, evolving concept, biological concept, brain development, adolescent education

---

Bibliography

Adolescence. (2020). *In Encyclopaedia Britannica.* Retrieved from www.britannica.com/science/adolescence

American Psychological Association. (2002). *Developing adolescents.* Retrieved from www.apa.org/pi/families/resources/develop.pdf

Chaudhary, N., & Sharma, N. (2012). (Adolescence in) India. In J. J. Arnett (Ed.), *Adolescent psychology around the world* (pp. 103–118). New York, NY: Psychology Press.

Chen, C. S., & Farruggia, S. (2002). Culture and adolescent development. *Online Readings in Psychology and Culture, 6*(1). doi:10.9707/2307-0919.1113

Children and Adolescents–Unique Audiences. Retrieved from www.sagepub.com/sites/default/files/upm-assets/54292_book_item_54292.pdf

Crockett, L. J. (1997). Cultural, historical, and subcultural contexts of adolescence: Implications for health and development. In J. Schulenberg, J. L. Maggs, & K. Hurrelmann (Eds.), *Health risks and developmental transitions during adolescence* (pp. 23–53). Cambridge: Cambridge University Press.

Curtis, A. C. (2015). Defining adolescence. *Journal of Adolescent and Family Health, 7*(2), Article 2. Retrieved from https://scholar.utc.edu/jafh/vol7/iss2/2

Dahl, R. E. (2004). Adolescent brain development: A period of vulnerabilities and opportunities. Keynote address. *Annals of the New York Academy of Sciences, 1021*(1), 1–22. doi:10.1196/annals.1308.001

Dehne, K., & Riedner, G. (2001). Adolescence—A dynamic concept. *Reproductive Health Matters, 9*(17), 11–15. doi:10.1016/S0968-8080(01)90003-5

Ember, C. R., Pitek, E., & Ringen, E. J. (2017). Adolescence. In C. R. Ember (Ed.), *Explaining human culture. Human relations area files.* Retrieved from http://hraf.yale.edu/ehc/summaries/adolescence

Hoose. (n.d.). *Identity development theory.* Retrieved from https://courses.lumenlearning.com/adolescent/chapter/identity-development-theory/

James-Todd, T., Tehranifar, P., Rich-Edwards, J., Titievsky, L., & Terry, M. B. (2010). The impact of socioeconomic status across early life on age at menarche among a racially diverse population of girls. *Annals of Epidemiology, 20*(11), 836–842. doi:10.1016/j.annepidem.2010.08.006

Johnson, S. B., Blum, R. W., & Giedd, J. N. (2009). Adolescent maturity and the brain: The promise and pitfalls of neuroscience research in adolescent health policy. *Journal of Adolescent Health, 45*(3), 216–221. doi:10.1016/j.jadohealth.2009.05.016

Lerner, R. M., & Steinberg, L. (2004). The scientific study of adolescent development: Past, present, and future. In R. M. Lerner & L. Steinberg (Eds.), *Handbook of adolescent psychology* (pp. 1–12). Hoboken, NJ: John Wiley & Sons.

McElhaney, K. B., Allen, J. P., Stephenson, J. C., & Hare, A. L. (2009). Attachment and autonomy during adolescence. In R. M. Lerner & L. Steinberg (Eds.), *Handbook of adolescent psychology: Individual bases of adolescent development* (pp. 358–403). Hoboken, NJ: John Wiley & Sons. doi:10.1002/9780470479193.adlpsy001012

National Academies of Sciences, Engineering, and Medicine. (2019). *The promise of adolescence: Realizing opportunity for all youth.* Washington, DC: The National Academies Press. doi:10.17226/25388

National Research Council. (1999). *Adolescent development and the biology of puberty: Summary of a workshop on new research.* Washington, DC: The National Academies Press. doi:10.17226/9634

National Research Council. (2013). *Reforming juvenile justice: A developmental approach.* Washington, DC: The National Academies Press. doi:10.17226/14685

Ozdemir, A., Utkualp, N., & Palloş, A. (2016). Physical and psychosocial effects of the changes in adolescence period. *International Journal of Caring Sciences, 9*(2), 717–723.

Population Council & UNICEF. (2013). *Adolescents in India: A desk review of existing evidence and behaviours, programmes and policies.* New Delhi, India: Author.

Prashant, K., & Shaw, C. (2009). Nutritional status of adolescent girls from an urban slum area in South India. *The Indian Journal of Pediatrics*, (76), 501–504. doi:10.1007/s12098-009-0077-2

Ramadass, S., Gupta, S. K., & Nongkynrih, B. (2017). Adolescent health in urban India. *Journal of Family Medicine and Primary Care, 6,* 468–476.

Saraswathi, T. S., & Oke, M. (2013). Ecology of adolescence in India: Implications for policy and practice. *Psychological Studies, 58*(4), 353–364.

Susman, E. J., & Rogol, A. (2004). Puberty and psychological development. In R. M. Lerner & L. Steinberg (Eds.), *Handbook of adolescent psychology* (2nd ed., pp. 15–44). Hoboken, NJ: John Wiley & Sons.

2
DEVELOPMENTAL PATTERNS AND PROCESSES

CHAPTER 2: Developmental Patterns and Processes

Overview

After reading this chapter, you will be able to achieve the following objectives

- Understand the dynamics of identity formation by engaging with the various discourses on identity
- Able to recognize the importance of identity formation in the adolescence stage by examining the aspects of change and stability, in the light of various influences like gender, culture and media in the Indian context
- Acquire a more general overview of the enormous magnitude and complexity of adolescent development through the critical exploration of Erikson's theory of psychosocial development, Piaget's theory of cognitive development, Vygotsky's Socio Cultural Theory of Cognitive Development and Kohlberg's theory of moral development
- Critically analyze the changing concept of self, integrating cognitive, socio-emotional, and neuroimaging perspectives on self-development
- Expand the comprehension of identity as a set of inter-related beliefs defined as self-concept, self-esteem, and self-efficacy in adolescents' development

---

Identity development in adolescents

What is identity?

From the Latin root *idem*, meaning 'the same', the term 'identity' implies both similarity and difference. On the one hand, identity is something unique to each of us that we assume is more or less consistent (and hence the same) over time. Yet on the other hand, identity also implies a relationship with a broader collective or social group of some kind (Buckingham, 2008).

There is a growing interest in the concept of identity, though most discourses on this concept suggests that it is very difficult to explain because of the complexity of its meaning. However, the basic meaning of identity refers to where one (a person or a group) belongs; what is expressed as 'self-image' or/and 'common-image'; what integrates them inside self or a group existence; and what differentiates them with the 'others'.

DOI: 10.4324/9781003054351-2

38 Developmental patterns and processes

Social identities have a historic context. The concept has been evolving from time to time. We see that the traditional understanding of identity evolves from generation to generation; in modern societies identity is conceived as "a matter of rational action and being dynamic". Giddens thinks that one may speak of identity as "a symbolic construction", which helps people to find their own place in time and preserve continuity (Golubović, 2011).

Looking at this concept from a sociological perspective, the concept of identity has been used in different terms: (a) as a 'primordial identity' being conceived as a naturally given and unchangeable entity – belonging to a particular caste or ethnic group; and (b) as a sociocultural, political or ideologically constructed collective sense of communal or personal identity. The two terms can be differentiated also in the fact that culturally conditioned identity recognizes the existence of individual/unique identity and collective/communal identity, while the primordial identity has only its collective expression according to which all individuals have to submit.

As mentioned earlier this concept is complex and diverse; hence defining or identifying the features too is a challenging task. An attempt to consider different ways in which different academicians have attempted to define identity is given below. These definitions range from suggestive glosses to some fairly complicated and opaque formulations. Some examples, culled mainly but not exclusively from the areas of political science, from international relations are given below:

1. Identity is "people's concepts of who they are, of what sort of people they are, and how they relate to others" (Hogg and Abrams 1988, 2).

2. "Identity is used in this book to describe the way individuals and groups define themselves and are defined by others on the basis of race, ethnicity, religion, language, and culture" (Deng 1995, 1).

3. Identity "refers to the ways in which individuals and collectivities are distinguished in their social relations with other individuals and collectivities" (Jenkins 1996, 4).

4. "National identity describes that condition in which a mass of people have made the same identification with national symbols – have internalised the symbols of the nation ..." (Bloom 1990, 52).

5. Identities are "relatively stable, role-specific understandings and expectations about self" (Wendt 1992, 397).

Source: Fearon, J.D (1999)

Activity: Reinforce your learning

If you recollect, in the previous chapter, we had examined the nature of adolescence through the different cases across three time periods.
Scrutinize the responses of the cases carefully and identify those dimensions of identity which you feel is unique to adolescence due to its consistency over time and those which you feel is a result of a broader collective goal or influence of society.
List the dimensions in a tabular form and reflect on the factors that would have influenced the development of that particular dimension of identity

Features of identity

Zagorka Golubović (2011) gave several features with regard to identity. For our discussion and understanding of identity we will look at the following features of identity.

1   identity is not a neutral category, nor is it an inborn (congenital) trait;
2   there are conditions and mechanisms that lead to the constitution of identity;
3   identity is constituted through phases, and there is a difference between phase I (identification)and phase II (individuation);

A careful examination into the various discourses on identity informs us that individuals do not possess identity upon birth, although they often adopt 'identity image' created by their parents and significant others which does not express their individual dispositions. The process begins the moment the individual is born in the world and begins with the interaction of the individuals with the world. The journey begins with the identification of the individual to the group to which they belong – it may be in most cases the family – then being part of the same age group of individuals, being part of the same culture, which could include even religious groups, and the belongingness then just extends.

It takes a long way and time for a person to grow and become capable of transcending the collective form of identity that is created by their parents and significant other. This is very evident that when we ask an individual to introduce or write about themselves, they usually begin and end with I am the son/daughter/mother/father of, belong to XYZ family and from ABC region. The introduction ends with this collective form of identity that the individual has constructed for themselves. The next phase of realization of who they are as unique individuals is a long and arduous process. Individuals have to move in their understanding of selves from belonging to a social group to a self-identification stage. It is here at this stage of self-identification do individuals recognize themselves as unique members of the society.

To reach this stage individuals have to overcome many obstacles (e.g. the traditionally established habits, parents' authorities), and also to surmount their lack of self-knowledge and find out who they really are. In a traditional society, self-identification is not easy a task to achieve. Golubović (2011) recalls Erich Fromm's quote that says: "Many individuals die before they have been born"; that is to say, they have not become aware of who they are as persons, but lived with the identity prescribed to them – either by parents, social groups, or authorities.

In the process of constitution of identity/ies of a person, the first step is to adopt a group identity. This adoption satisfies the individuals need for belonging somewhere as a member of a community (of a family, or a larger community, to the given society/state, to a generation, etc.). A person recognizes her/himself through the concept of 'we' as a primary form of an understanding where one belongs. Therefore, the person then adheres to the norms and believes and trusts its members, and developing a sense of security which helps them cope with the world. So collective identity not only helps in adaption and sense of security but it also influences the individuals' mentality system, providing an interpretation of culture through the definition of self.

For Mucchielli it is important to have in mind two forms of identification: "identification with the other" and "identification in the other", which makes a passage from collective identification to individual identity possible – from empirical ego to the Self as a conscious subject ("Je" and "soi" 19), which has developed the sentiment for differences and autonomy (Golubović, 2011).

For this transition to happen, discourses show that there is a need to have an atmosphere which is conducive, an atmosphere of freedom where an individual can express oneself and have adequate opportunities to know oneself. Hence, in many ways social institutions and ideologies also play a role in helping individuals to develop their identities. It is only natural to have a clash between individual self-identification and inherited collective identification. When cultural patterns change and produce conflicting norms and values, it creates a confusion in individuals' thinking on which pattern to accept in an attempt to define their personal identity. The more the universal values and moral principles become relativized, the more acute are conflicts created for individuals. Thus, giving rise to manipulations from different external factors (political, ideological or the influence of authoritarian mechanisms).

Summarizing the three features discussed:

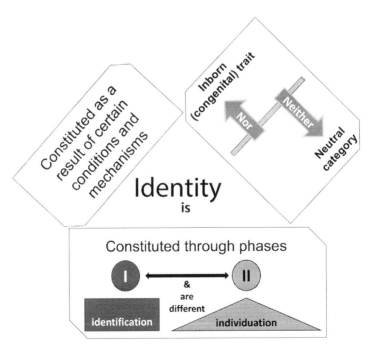

FIGURE 2.1 Salient Features of Identity

What does the process of formation and development of identity entail?

According to Zagorka Golubović (2011), the formation of development of identity is linked to the process of personality development which may be attained only during the process of a reflexive internalization of cultural achievements, and self-estimation of social norms, meanings and claims that have been imposed by historical traditions. This brings to the forefront that on the one side it calls for breaking off with a collective traditional determination, and 'separation' from a 'we' concept to whom one has to be subjected at one hand; and on the other hand, tracing a way to 'selfhood'. This recognized selfhood is expressed as the recognisable 'self', whose difference from the collective image or mass identity represents his/her unique personal character. It is when an individual person emerges as a unique figure, one may speak of individual identity which is emancipating and contributes to the process of ego's development.

It is here that the following concepts play its role. Self-concept or self-representation, that keeps pace with the development of the I, as underscored, of the self's inherent reflexivity; Self-efficacy, referred to the agent-self's beliefs about successful execution of a goal-directed behaviour; and Self-esteem, that refers to evaluation of the progress with respect to those goals – about how the Me is doing (McAdams & Cox, 2010).

As quoted from a Serbian translation, in Aristotelian terminology the process of moving from the collective identity stage to the personal identity stage can be explained by the appearance of phronesis. That is, practical wisdom in terms of a "plan for living" in an ethical-cultural sense starts evolving. When one starts developing and living by one's own plan of living guided by one's own ethical cultural sense, personal character begins to evolve. These relatively permanent dispositions become the personality of an individual and therefore contributes to the individual self-identity of an individual. Development of personal identity (in terms of self-identification) in a democratic society has to pass from the "collective ethos" to one's own self-image and self-esteem in order to become a free citizen Golubović, (2011).

What happens when a person fails to go through the necessary evolutionary passage – from collective ethos to self-understanding of one's own needs and goals? – We reach a point where we have individuals and societies who are conformists and non-critical, so eventually, non-progressive. Which path of development an individuals' growth will take depends in the first place, on the type of socialization and education, which are, however, dependent on the character of social order (be it authoritarian or democratic) and cultural norms as well as the system of values of a particular society Golubović (2011).

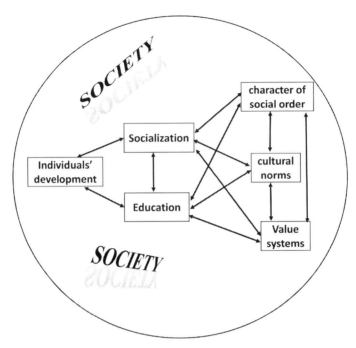

FIGURE 2.2 Socialization Through Education: Contributor to Individual Development

Summarizing, one may say that culture is important to provides patterns of 'ways of life' (for both collective and individual existence); as well as ways/types of thinking and believing. Nevertheless, especially in urban situations, where culture is pluralistic, identity itself may have plural forms not only in different cultures, but within the individual's and collective's expressions and also in the context of their experiences of the given ways of life.

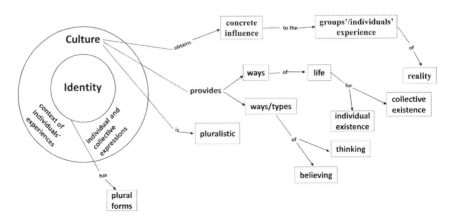

FIGURE 2.3 Culture as a Determinant of Identity

Developmental patterns and processes 43

Using the notion of Dominique Moïsi who explains that, different cultures form different life orientations which in turn lead to different emotions in individuals. He says that culture has much more concrete influence on the group's/individual's experience of reality:

(a) "culture of hope" promotes confidence based on the conviction that tomorrow will be better than today (implying an optimistic view, and thus a positive identity);
(b) "culture of fear" represents the absence of confidence, being apprehensive about the present, expecting the future to become more dangerous (provoking a suspicious view and unstable or confused identity);
(c) "culture of humiliation" represents injured confidence of those who have lost hope in the future, "the feeling that you are no longer in control of your life . . .", producing hopelessness.

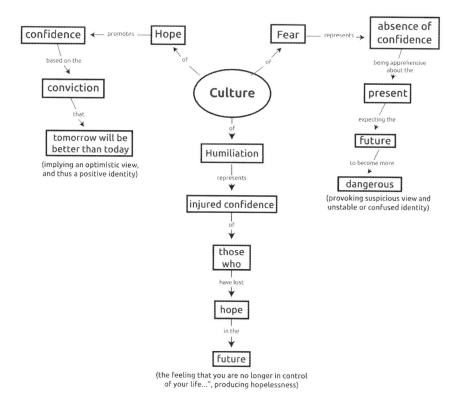

FIGURE 2.4 Culture and Its Influences in Experiences of Reality

Thus, we see that identity has a two-way relationship mediating through emotions with the kind of culture that the individual is a part of. Identity itself may have plural forms not only in different cultures, but within the individual's and collective's expressions.

44 Developmental patterns and processes

So, the following two reasons reiterate the need for deliberate socialisation through social institutions like education. 1. Considering identity as a socioculturally conditioned phenomenon, it evolves through a conscious process and 2. There is a difference between traditional and modern understanding of the type of belonging:

a   group identity may be experienced within a close group with the exclusion of 'others', of those who are different (either ethnically, by social status or other group characteristics); or
b   a liberal comprehension of identity which is open to the differences and tolerates 'otherness', in terms of a close interconnection between 'self' and 'others' (as alter-ego of the former).

It is the kind of socialization that will determine which kind of identity we subscribe to.

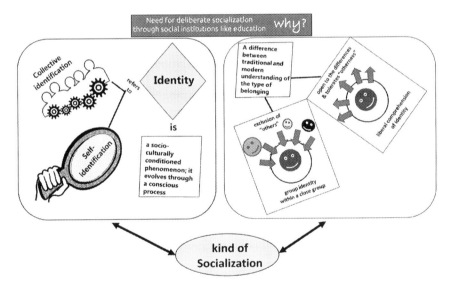

FIGURE 2.5   Need for Deliberate Socialization

Identity and adolescence

This brings out the importance of looking at identity at the stage of its formation, i.e. the adolescents' stage. It is at this stage as we have seen in the previous chapter that those in adolescence begin to define themselves, and there is also a tendency to drift farther away from the parental group and create a unique identity for self. Adolescents usually try to establish their sense of self, depending on others opinions and reactions, and on basis of what they feel is considered acceptable by the contexts in which they reside. They start taking autonomous decisions for themselves according to what they feel about their self from their past and the present as they move further from the stage of childhood (McLean & Pasupathi, 2012).

To take it a step further, very often, people are forced to relook at self-identification and collective identification only when a clash between individual self-identification and inherited collective identification appears, in particular, when cultural patterns change and produce conflicting norms and values. The stage of adolescence forms a fertile ground for these kinds of questioning and confrontation of conflicting norms and values.

Identity theories

To reiterate we saw that there are three important features that we have discussed with respect to the concept of 'Identity'. We recall that identity formation is a complex process and related to several factors in society. Literature suggests a lot of disagreement on definitions of identity. We also saw that individuals have to face many obstacles. It is a socioculturally impregnated expression of both individual/personal and collective way of existence and recognition. This means that it is always a matter of choice, to develop an understanding and explanation of oneself and collective existence.

Since the origin of identity theories, different theorists have looked at various aspects of identity by extending the bases of identities, right from role identity terms, then broadening the understanding of multiple identities, further looking at the role of emotions in identity theory and moving on to find its application in a variety of areas including crime and law, education, gender and many others. The idea of strict identity, which lies at the heart of identity theories, is that something that we call by different names, or encounter in different ways, is despite initial appearances, actually not different, but identical, in the sense of being one and the same thing (Myin & Zahnoun, 2018). Despite theoretical overlap between identity theorists, research has taken different paths delving into innumerable discourses on identity. Today, there are several studies and theories on adolescent identity development to scrutinize. However, the contemporary period, that has undergone transformation and evolved with the times, entails a reappraisal of the identity discourse in order to embrace different perspectives of identity, especially, from the socialization of individuals under consideration for a better understanding of adolescence

We will now advance to get an insight into the different identity theories from the perspectives of psychosocial development, cognitive development, sociocultural development and moral development.

Early theories of identity referred to the term in reference to personality or individuality in an informal manner and gradually; with the emergence of other disciplines, the reference of the term was expanded to a broader social context. The

I/me distinction was theorized, with 'me' representing the identity that influences others responses and 'I' representing the inner self (Hammack, 2015). Erikson was among the first theorists who introduced and elaborated important concepts related to identity in adolescence (Abbassi, 2016). His conceptualization of the terms drew from the work of Sigmund Freud, who initially observed that the self was multitiered, divided among the conscious, preconscious and unconscious, and later introduced a structural model of the mind divided into the id, the ego and the superego.

Would you like to know more about the 'self' according to psychoanalytic theory?

You can read Alex Watson's (2014) article by accessing the QR code given below.

Who Am I? The Self/Subject According to Psychoanalytic Theory

Alex Watson, in this essay argues about Freud's concepts of 'the self' and 'the subject' and elaborates on the topographical and the structural model proposed by Freud.

Scan the QR code to read the article

Erikson's theory of psychosocial development

Erikson alone used a variety of identity-related terms such as identification, identity formation, identity development, identity consolidation, identity foreclosure and identity resolution (Sokol, 2009). According to him, a sense of identity is never fully achieved at one stage of an individual's life; it is "constantly lost and regained" and a lifelong development (Abbassi, 2016).

Developmental patterns and processes 47

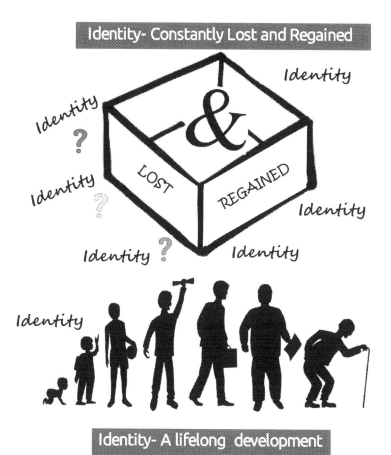

FIGURE 2.6   Identity: A Lifelong Development

He proposed that every individual faces unique kinds of challenges at different periods of his/her life span. This he referred to as the psychological crisis. The successful development of the individual depends on whether s/he is able to cope with such situations of crises and resolve them in a positive manner. Aligned with these crises occurring at different periods in life, Erikson proposed eight consecutive stages ranging from birth to death in his psychosocial theory.

Before we introduce the eight stages of psychosocial development, let us have a brief peek into the most curious aspect of Erikson's biography.

Erik Erikson was not his real name. As a child, he was never secure in his relationship with his mother. He never knew who his father was, so he never knew his heritage. Do you think these factors of his life would have influenced his development?

To know more about Erik Erikson, read his brief Biography at
www.oercommons.org/authoring/22859-personality-theory/7/view

48 Developmental patterns and processes

TABLE 2.1 Erikson's Eight Stages of Psychosocial Development

Stage	Conflict	Age	Characteristic feature of the stage	Virtue attained at the successful completion of this stage
1 Infancy	Trust vs Mistrust	Birth to 1 year/1.5 years	Uncertain about the world in which they live, and looks towards their primary caregiver for stability and consistency of care.	**Hope**
2 Early childhood	Autonomy vs Shame and Doubt	1.5 to 3 years	Focused on developing a sense of personal control over physical skills and a sense of independence.	**Will**
3 Pre-school	Initiative vs Guilt	3 to 6 years	Children assert themselves more frequently and develop a sense of initiative and feel secure in their ability to lead others and make decisions	**Purpose**
4	Industry vs Inferiority	6 to 12 years	Learning to read and write, to do sums, to do things on their own. The child feels the need to win approval by demonstrating specific competencies that are valued by society and begins to develop a sense of pride in their accomplishments.	**Competence**
5 Adolescence	Identity vs Role Confusion	12 to 18 years	Adolescents search for a sense of self and personal identity, through an intense exploration of personal values, beliefs and goals.	**Fidelity**
6 Young Adulthood	Intimacy vs Isolation	19 to 40 years	Major conflict centres on forming intimate, loving relationships with other people.	**Love**
7 Middle Adulthood	Generativity vs Stagnation	40 to 65 years	Experience a need to create or nurture things that will outlast them,	**Care**
8 Maturity	Integrity vs Despair	65 to death	Contemplate our accomplishments and can develop integrity if we see ourselves as leading a successful life.	**Wisdom**

Adolescence and the stage of identity and role confusion

As we can see from Table 2.1, after completion of the four stages of life, the stage of identity vs role confusion is apparent in ages between 12 and 18, referred to as adolescence. Though formation of identity is considered to begin at birth, it is at the age of adolescence that occurrence of identity formation is commonly contemplated.

Erikson described identity as a complicated process which involves forming an opinion of self, depending on what others think about you and also evaluating others opinions about you. This can result in development of either a healthy or a negative identity for individuals (Kelland, M.D.).

> Negative identity has been considered as a serious rejection of one's place in life. Do you feel that there can be times, when negative identity can be used as a potential for some kind of positive change in life? Justify your response with the help of a case in point.

Erikson posited the strong influence of interactions of biological characteristics, psychological aspects and the social and cultural contexts on identity of individuals, emphasizing the significance of social context (Abbassi, 2016).

Look Back and Reflect

> As you recall the various influences and factors that account for the understanding of adolescence in Indian context, you will see both an extended period of adolescence and a period of lost adolescence as well.
> How will you explain the sequential stages of Erikson's psychosocial theory, which talks about entering into a stage only after completion of the previous stage?
> Reflect on the following questions-
> - Are these stages rigidly defined or can there be overlap of these stages?
> - Is it possible for adolescents to skip any of these stages?
> - Will these adolescents be able to tackle the crisis they encounter?
> - Will these adolescents be successful in forming an identity for themselves?
> - Does development of these adolescents get stunted for life time?
> - What attributes to such differential experiences in formation of identity?

Adolescents' identity formation based on psychosocial approach

Erikson's conceptualization of identity formation was more rigid, focusing on the psychosocial crisis during late adolescence, while later, Marcia simplified the concept as a flexible construct without any fixed beginning or end. Marcia also drew attention to the theory's incapability to explain individual differences in degrees of identity formation (Graf, 2003).

Marcia refers to identity formation as starting with a synthesis of childhood skills, beliefs, and identifications and culminating into a coherent, unique whole that provides continuity with the past and direction for the future (Sokol, 2009). The age of adolescence is characterized by onset of puberty leading to acquisition of cognitive skills and many other abilities. Besides, their increased autonomous exploration results in adolescents inclining towards friends, peers and others around them for support. This is also the age when they set aspirations for their future. At the threshold of new adult-like responsibilities, they are trying to search for answers about their identity, their place in the world, their career choices and aspirations, their ability to achieve their goals and many more questions that they are flooded with. This period is typically marked by confusion and experimentation for adolescents in search of identity in their journey of life.

Erikson suggested that many adolescents experience a psychological moratorium, a period where they may take some time off from the ongoing responsibilities and explore other options and possibilities. They ideally come out of this successfully resolving the identity crises, though a very few of them may withdraw into isolation not being able to resolve the crises (Lally & Valentine, 2019).

Erikson was of the opinion that identity formation is successful if individuals are able to strike a balance between their own personal attributes and the possibilities of expressions encountered in their environment; however, if the individual fails to manage this task, role confusion occurs (Sokol, 2009). Erikson put forward two primary modes of identity processing, namely, *identity synthesis*, in which a person creates a stable and consistent sense of self over time and across situations; and *identity confusion*, which manifests signs of inconsistency in representing self and making any decisions in situations (Hansen et al., 2019). Role confusion raises doubts in the individual about one's personality, one's own view of self and others' views about them, thus leading to confusion. Erikson believed that identity is very essential to give direction to the individual and a reason for the individual to be and develop further. However, a few of them do not succeed in resolving the developmental tasks that leads to role confusion (Sokol, 2009).

James Marcia's four identity statuses of psychological identity development

In the 1960s James Marcia expanded on Erikson's work with his identity status model, focusing particularly on the notion of adolescence as a period of "identity crisis" (Buckingham, 2008). He identified four identity statuses through possible combinations of the two components namely, commitment and exploration, that influence identity formation. Here one needs to be mindful that this commitment and exploration is a cyclic act, which needs to be continuously exercised.

Exploration, as the word suggests, refers to the adolescents' nature of questioning and trying out various alternatives for fulfilling roles and responsibilities, while commitment refers to the adolescents' nature of considering choices and decisions and adhering to these for potential achievement of one's goals. The four 'identity statuses', represent different positions of adolescents in this process. The figure below represents these positions in terms of presence and absence of the two components as posited by Marcia. The criteria used for determining the status is the extent of presence or absence of exploration or commitment. At any point of time, you can never say that the exploration and commitment are totally absent or present.

	Exploration	Commitment
Identity Diffusion	X	X
Identity Foreclosure	X	✓
Identity Moratorium	✓	X
Identity Achievement	✓	✓

Identity statuses

Identity diffusion is considered the least mature of all and adolescents in this status are likely to lack self-esteem, self-direction or any agency to achieve in life. Identity achievement is considered as a lengthy process and adolescents in this status are believed to be balanced thinkers and mature in maintaining relationships with others. Adolescents in the identity moratorium status are found to be curious and anxious risk takers and persist in the period of crisis, whereas adolescents in the identity foreclosure status are found to have made their decisions by avoiding the crisis by either conforming to their parents' or others choices or by identifying themselves with their parents or any other role model and thus possess a sense of self-satisfaction (Hansen et al., 2019).

> **Activity: Identity Statuses**
>
> Now that you have learnt about the different identity statuses, let's take a step further in testing your understanding.
> Five different cases given below demonstrate five identity statuses as proposed by the theories that you have studied. For each case, suggest the most appropriate identity status according to you and explain the reasons for your responses.
> *identity achievement, identity foreclosure, identity diffusion, negative identity, and identity moratorium*

Identity Statuses ?

Shehnaz's parents were both in the teaching profession. She was always told, that she too would be a teacher, since school days. She admired her parents. He grew up in a patriarchal Muslim family, where she learned to conform to parents' decisions and not question them. Thus, her belief system was forced upon her by her parents and she feared not to disappoint them in any way. She always excelled in her academics and could have chosen any field to pursue. She was a very confident girl, however, her faith system was not her own.

Akash has just finished his 10th grade. He loves cooking. He helps his mother in cooking and makes variety of dishes for his family. He wanted to spend his summer holidays doing something worthwhile. He looked for some options that he could take up in those holidays. Fortunately, he got to work as a cook in a good restaurant. He enjoyed the job very much and decided to join a culinary school to pursue his career as a chef. He requested to the owner of the restaurant, if he could continue to work there part time while he studied in the culinary school.

Richa's father is an alcoholic who terrified her when she was a child. Her mother was quite conservative in money matters and social values. She had high aspirations for Richa and expected excellence in her academic performance. But Richa always used to day dream a lot as if she has been locked up or being beaten up. She resisted seeing herself as an adult. She was afraid of what she would turn out to be. She got into company of friends who displayed undesirable behaviours and substance abuse. She started stealing money from home to hang out with these friends. She dismissed her plan of going to school or studying further.

Sana is studying in the 9th grade. She looks at her peers play some sport, listen to contemporary music, enjoy bowling in a game parlour and realizes that she never did any of these or enjoyed these activities. She rarely interacts with anyone at home and just stares into her phone all day. She suddenly leaves her house for shopping and comes back home excited with some new thing in the market. She dislikes her parents asking her questions. She is not very interested in academics and studies enough to write her examinations.

Joseph is in the eighth grade. He is doing average in his academics. He takes on various projects in school and participates in different quiz competitions. He keeps thinking a lot and would rather spend his time alone than with friends. He leaves incomplete, a few of the projects and also is not able to focus on his studies. He has suddenly taken interest to religious studies and visits libraries. He spends time in the library reading books related to philosophy and religion.

Identity status?

1. Sana

A. Identity achievement	
B. Identity foreclosure	
C. Identity diffusion	
D. Negative identity	
E. Identity moratorium	

2. Richa

A. Identity achievement	
B. Identity foreclosure	
C. Identity diffusion	
D. Negative identity	
E. Identity moratorium	

3. Joseph

A. Identity achievement	
B. Identity foreclosure	
C. Identity diffusion	
D. Negative identity	
E. Identity moratorium	

4. Akash

A. Identity achievement	
B. Identity foreclosure	
C. Identity diffusion	
D. Negative identity	
E. Identity moratorium	

5. Shehnaz

A. Identity achievement	
B. Identity foreclosure	
C. Identity diffusion	
D. Negative identity	
E. Identity moratorium	

Psychosocial moratorium: "Time out of Life"

Adolescence as a distinctive stage with a beginning and an end or human development as a matter of gradual progression is yet debated. Yet, this approach appears quite normative in terms of our understanding, that, an individual who has attained stable identity will turn out to be a healthy and mature person; on the other hand, an individual who is not able to attain identity and is in continuous state of confusion may end up in behaving in an undesirable and socially unacceptable manner. Adolescence is hereby seen as a state of transition, a matter of "becoming" rather than "being" (Buckingham, 2008). Notwithstanding the criticisms of this theory, Erikson's notion of psychosocial moratorium, a period of delay granted to somebody who is not ready to meet an obligation, empowers the adolescents by providing opportunities for significant exploration of the roles and potential identities (Stroud, 2011).

Vignette: Story of a boy's adolescent days narrated by his friend

He is a mystery. He did not fare too well in academics at school, but he would always be creating something innovative and new with his weird ideas. His room at his house was a messy laboratory full of unique and mysterious things around. He never was able to decide what he wants to do in life. He never spoke of a single discipline that he aimed to pursue, whenever he was asked about his goal in life. He always appeared confused, but never regretted this even then. After high school, he just went out of sight of this usual world. Later, we came to know that he took a break from further studies and ventured into the world to explore his interests. His quest for knowledge was so deep. He did a lot of photography, wrote blogs, explored nature to study birds, and pursued a lot more things than he could have thought of. His parents were very supportive of his decisions all through his journey of exploration.

Review and Reflect:

- What does this narrative suggest about the identity of the adolescent under consideration?
- Can you identify the presence or absence of psychosocial moratorium in the journey of this adolescent? How will you explain the process of identity formation in this particular case?
- Think of any instance of an adolescent which would have been very different from this narrative and how would you explain the process of identity formation in that case?

Gender and cultural differences in adolescents' identity formation

The most significant phase of a gender identity acquisition is adolescence. According to Archer and Waterman, inherent gender differences in individuality are apparent due to the differential upbringing of males and females by the society (Graf, 2003).

It is generally observed that adolescent girls depend on their families more than their male counterparts even after they experience separation from their parents. According to Sartor and Youniss, adolescent boys report lower levels of parental support compared to adolescent girls. This results in greater identity achievement in boys compared to girls in the adolescent years. Erikson has also discussed the female's quest for identity in terms of physical appearance, marriage and motherhood (Graf, 2003).

Gender-based differences in formation of identity is also determined largely by the kinds of opportunities and the autonomy provided to adolescents by the social environment, especially families. Close parent-adolescent relationships and encouragement of autonomy by parents can promote increased identity exploration in both boys and girls. Having said that, culture plays a very important role in differential opportunities for boys and girls in their formation of identity. Girls of this age are usually more initiated towards stereotypic roles that are conventional and accepted by the society and are restricted to relationships with friends and intimate partners and not beyond. This makes it very difficult for women to achieve identity as Matteson conveys, which is due to lack of support and encouragement from society and limits the extent of extended exploration for adolescent girls, which further restricts their identity formation. On the other hand, Mensch et al. communicate that males enjoy the privileges reserved for them and gain autonomy, mobility, opportunity and power which females are generally deprived of (Sandhu et al., 2012).

As it is known, unequal gender norms and power imbalances are yet a very significant part of the patriarchal and gender-stratified India. The varying extent of inequality can be discerned in urban and rural India too. Female individuation has been unacceptable in a traditionally collectivistic Indian culture and has been a neglected practice in child-rearing.

Girls from families of lower socio-economic status, especially from rural areas, are deprived of education and are expected to earn a livelihood for the family, perform the household chores or take care of their siblings when their parents went out to work, compared to boys who may attain education or may be initiated into employment. This leaves hardly any scope for exploration and results in varied forms of identity in girls and boys.

Empirical findings suggest that family context plays a significant role in the adolescents' ability to develop a stable identity. The need for secure relationships and opportunities for self-expression and exploration to develop positive identity has been emphasized. Indian girls tend to take decisions based on their family's expectations without exploring opportunities for themselves and miss out on the virtues associated with healthy resolution of identity crisis (Sandhu et al., 2012).

Parental attitudes of control and overprotection also hinders identity exploration, especially in girls, as generally observed in the Indian context. Ironically, one seeks to understand from literature that youth in the Indian context might benefit from parental control and overprotection for the achievement of identity. According to Pettengil and Rohner, parental control may be perceived as security by children in cultures where it is a prescribed norm (Sandhu, 2012).

Generally, Eastern societies demand compliance with cultural norms and values, in contrast to Western cultures that foster greater individualism in adolescents. Indian culture is more or less aligned with the former. Nonetheless, socio-economic status acts as a mediating factor in fostering individualism in Indian adolescents. Affluent societies are more likely to be individualistic in nature as compared to lower class families. Adolescents from upper class families tend to be more self-reliant and independent as opposed to those from lower class families who would be more compliant towards parental values. This accounts for the differences in identity formation in adolescents as a result of cultural differences arising out of the socio-economic status. Yet one needs to be careful and cautious in evaluating these determinants of adolescent identity, as studies have indicated an experience of increased pressure and confusion in adolescents of Western societies in the process of identity formation (Graf, 2003)

The notion of Indian adolescents being less autonomous than their Western counterparts due to the collectivist nature of Indian society is quite disputable.

Adolescent autonomy is referred to an interplay of both individuation and connectedness and individual's development of a sense of self is based on their relations with others. Close parent-adolescent relationships along with individuation of individuals enable autonomous development in adolescents that further facilitates positive identity formation in adolescents (McElhaney et al., 2009). Cross-cultural findings on identity formation displayed greater autonomy in adolescents from India than their American peers (Graf, 2003).

It has been proposed by Friedman, that globalization in a country like India engenders a basic identity challenge – one that exists at both the societal and the personal level (Rao et al., 2013). Urbanization and globalization brought with it changes in the traditional culture prevailing in India, exposing adolescents to new ways of life and new preferences. These changes had great implications on the identity formation of adolescents.

A study by Rao et al. (2013), of Indian, urban, middle-class 12 to 15-year-olds revealed that adolescents remained strongly identified with traditional Indian collectivist beliefs, values and practices but also identified and participated in individualistic, "minority-world" beliefs, values and practices as well. Male privilege was reflected in the gender differences observed in the study. Adolescents in the study communicated a greater sense of satisfaction and happiness and comparatively lesser stress within a traditional Indian identity, indicating that non-traditional and changing ways caused identity confusion. Findings revealed that adolescents, both males and female, who adopted a blend of traditional- and minority-world identity elements developed bicultural identity and reported highest levels of well-being.

Social media and adolescents' identity

It is often suggested that media has potentially profound effects on the social identity formation of young people. Excessive access to social and digital media has influenced the adolescents' lifestyle patterns associated with the way of dressing, fashion trends, eating habits, physical activity, weight control strategies, identity development, online identity, self-presentation, ambitious career goals and many other aspects of their life and growth. This has also impacted greatly in the formation of identity for both males and females.

For instance, posting a selfie on Facebook, Twitter or Instagram for teens is to claim an identity for oneself in the virtual world. Likes and followers of posts determine the identity for the adolescent who posts on networking sites. At times, to be accepted or belong to a group, teens use a variety of tools offered by different networking sites to manipulate their identity as acceptable to others. This can have both positive and negative influences on an adolescent's development.

Usually, adolescents' excessive use of media and social networking platforms have been associated with its negative effects such as lack of personal interactions with parents, addiction to the gadgets, sleep disruptions, cyberbullying, low level of academic performance and so on. However, theories have contended that use of social networking sites is generally beneficial for the enhancement of adolescents' social connections.

It is inferred from theories that the use of social networking sites provides opportunities for self-disclosure and, in some circumstances, demands self-disclosure, which plays a role in adolescents' identity development. Adolescents' identification of their own self and viewing of themselves in comparison to others based on others' views are factors found to be impact their individual identity. Media and other platforms provide opportunities for this group of children to come together with like-minded individuals which otherwise may be achievable in a face-to-face interaction. This allows them to develop a strong sense of self-identity and augment feelings of belongingness and bonding. With this contention, one needs to invest appropriately in harnessing the potential of media and social networking platforms to promote positive identity development in adolescents (Shapiro & Margolin, 2014).

Looking at identity from the cognitive lens we see that identity formation takes place through the reorganization of schemas and through the process of accommodation and assimilation. Any attempt to know how individuals in general and adolescents in particular develop their identity and use it as a frame of reference for interacting with their environment makes it imperative to understand the concept of cognition and how development happens through the cognitive approach.

Introduction to cognition

The biological perspective asserts puberty as the stage of physical maturation in adolescents. Puberty also initiates a period of major changes and growth in brain structure and function which impacts adolescents' thinking, usually referred to as cognition. Cognition includes processes involved with the acquisition, modification and manipulation of knowledge in particular contexts, covering topics such as memory, attention, problem-solving, metacognition and so on (Hansen et al., 2019).

It has been asserted that, assert that, though rapid cognitive changes occur during childhood, the brain continues to develop throughout adolescence, and even into the 20s. The prefrontal cortex of adolescents' brain as responsible for reasoning, planning and problem-solving as they mature and grow. It has also been observed by Blakemore that adolescents' actions appear quite impulsive rather than being thoughtful due to the slow development of their prefrontal cortex as compared to the development of the emotional parts of the brain and the hormonal changes associated with puberty (Stangor & Walinga, 2014).

The 'I know it all' belief of adolescents gives rise to new feelings of egocentrism as a consequence of their cognitive abilities attained at this stage. They appear to be constantly thinking about their image and believe that others are also watching them and thinking about them. Thinking undergoes an important qualitative change as children enter adolescence. The major aim of cognitive development during adolescence according to Piaget is the achievement of formal operational thinking, which is considered to be a state of equilibrium for this age.

Before we move to the formal operation stage that is considered parallel with the period of adolescence, we will try to understand the various stages of intellectual development suggested by Piaget.

> **Stop and Think**
>
> Have you ever played peek a boo with kids? You would have definitely observed adults playing peek a boo with kids.
>
> Which age group of children do you usually play this with? Why do you specifically play this game with this age group? Have you ever thought about it?
>
> Infants enjoy peek a boo because they are surprised when things come back after being out of sight. When things are out of sight, they are a bit confused and trying to make sense of what is happening around them.
>
> Did you ever realize why?
>
> As babies get older, they switch roles with adults. They start hiding and ask adults to look for them.

To get a deeper understanding of the above activity, watch the video link provided below.

> **Object Permanence and Causality**
>
> This video discusses the two concepts of object permanence and causality in the sensorimotor stage.

Scan the QR code to view this video

Jean Piaget's theory of cognitive development

This leads us further to understand the perspectives of cognitive development as proposed by the great Swiss psychologist Jean Piaget. According to Piaget, children's thinking progresses through a series of four discrete stages. He referred to stages as sequence of thinking patterns with different features. Piaget believed that children develop steadily and gradually throughout the varying stages. He emphasized the child's experiences and its environment along with maturation to cause learning and that the experiences in one stage formed the basis for moving to the next stage. All people pass through each stage before starting the next one, and no stage is skipped.

Piaget based his theory upon observations of his own and other children. Being a psychological constructivist, he viewed learning as a consequence of the interplay of assimilation (adjusting new experiences to fit prior concepts) and accommodation (adjusting concepts to fit new experiences) (Seifert & Sutton, 2009).

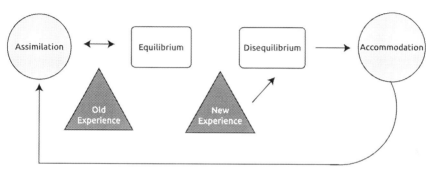

Source: https://en.wikipedia.org/wiki/File:Flow_Chart_of_Piaget%27s_Adaption.png

FIGURE 2.7 Assimilation and Accommodation in Cognitive Development

Piaget considered cognitive development as the development of schemes, or structures. He argued that, as they learn and mature, children develop schemas – patterns of knowledge in long-term memory – that help them remember, organize and respond to information (Stangor & Walinga, 2014). The construction and expansion of schemas occurs through the two processes of assimilation and accommodation. He described assimilation as the process of fitting new information into already existing cognitive schemas or previously learnt ideas to make sense of the new information. On the other hand, he referred to accommodation as a complementary process of modifying the already existing schemas or previous learning to account for new experiences and learning. Piaget believed that both assimilation and accommodation work together, resulting in adaptation, a state of equilibrium between one's schemas and one's experiences by organizing different schemas and grouping them for a broader function (Hansen et al., 2019).

60 Developmental patterns and processes

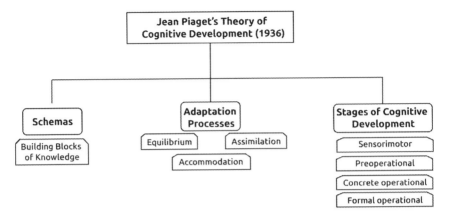

FIGURE 2.8 Theory of Cognitive Development as Proposed by Piaget

Four major stages of cognitive development were proposed by Piaget.

1   sensorimotor stage (birth to 2 years);
2   preoperational reasoning stage (2 to 6 or 7 years);
3   concrete operational reasoning stage (6 or 7 to 11 or 12 years);
4   formal operational reasoning stage (11 or 12 years and throughout the rest of life).

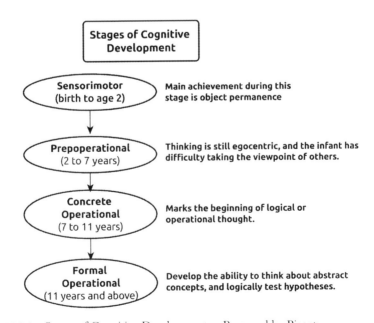

FIGURE 2.9 Stages of Cognitive Development as Proposed by Piaget

Sensorimotor stage

The sensorimotor stage is characterized by children's thinking that is largely realized through their perceptions of the world and their physical interactions with it. Their mental representations are limited (Siegler, 2020). According to Piaget, the infants' actions allow them to learn about the world and are crucial to their early cognitive development.

Piaget's object permanence task is one of his most famous problems related to this stage. An infant younger than 9 months does not understand the existence of objects out of sight, but as the infant grows, s/he gradually organizes the sensations and actions into a stable concept and starts believing that objects exist even if they are temporarily out of sight. This sense of stability, called object permanence, is considered as a belief that objects exist whether or not they are actually present. This progress in development indicates a difference in thinking patterns of older and younger infants about their experiences.

The sensorimotor stage is a very important stage in development and enables children to progress into the next stages of development as they grow. As children enter the next stage, they begin developing symbolic thought allowing them to improve language, imagination and memory skills.

> Try to relate this concept with the peek-a-boo activity provided above. Illustrate a few more examples demonstrating this concept from your own experiences.

The preoperational stage

As infants grow beyond the age of 2, they gradually start showing symbolic representation capabilities, yet focus on single dimension of problems.

To understand this better, try the activity given below with a group of children aged 2 to 7 years.

62 Developmental patterns and processes

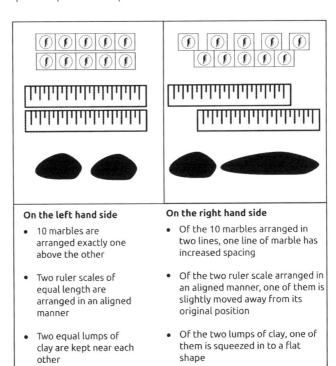

On the left hand side
- 10 marbles are arranged exactly one above the other
- Two ruler scales of equal length are arranged in an aligned manner
- Two equal lumps of clay are kept near each other

On the right hand side
- Of the 10 marbles arranged in two lines, one line of marble has increased spacing
- Of the two ruler scale arranged in an aligned manner, one of them is slightly moved away from its original position
- Of the two lumps of clay, one of them is squeezed in to a flat shape

Activity: Conservation

Arrange the given items in the figure the way it is shown and ask children the following questions-

- Is there more number of marbles on the left or more on the right side, or do they both have the same number?
- Are the rulers same in length on both left and right sides, or is one ruler bigger than the other in either of the sides?
- Is there same amount of clay in both the lumps on the left and the right side or does one lump of clay have more amount than the other on the right side?

Record the responses of each child and tabulate the responses. Try varying the task design and again record the responses. Compare children's responses across different variations of task design. What do you infer from this activity?

Conservation

To understand more about conservation problem in children aged 2 to 7 years, watch the video link provided below.

Developmental patterns and processes   **63**

> **Conservation**
>
> This video reviews the concept of conservation, characteristic of the preoperational stage.

Scan the QR code
to view this video

Children at the preoperational stage use their new ability to represent objects in a wide variety of activities, but their ways of doing it are neither organized nor fully logical, and their thinking is not realistic. Hence children do not start formal schooling until late in this stage.

The term 'operational' refers to logical manipulation of information and this stage of cognitive development largely lacks operations; hence this stage is termed as 'preoperational'. Children base the logic on their own personal knowledge of the world that they have gained till then, rather than on conventional knowledge.

Piaget described two new developments that help setting the stage for more sophisticated thinking. First is the use of symbols that occurs between 2 and 4 years, and the more advanced development is intuitive thinking lasting from 4 to 7 years.

Use of symbols

The ability to use symbols enables children to think about and refer to objects not present in their immediate vicinity and depend on perception. Symbolic thought in this stage is demonstrated through play, language and drawings.

Dramatic play or pretend play is a kind of cognition quite obvious in a dual process of experience, which entails thinking at two levels, one imaginative and other realistic. This kind of experience is an example of metacognition occurring at a very early age in which reflecting and monitoring of thinking is quite evident.

Dramatic play thus finds its way in classrooms with children of very young age till they at least reach second grade.

Development of language is considered important according to Piaget, since children make use of symbols to represent objects that are not present yet concrete.

Drawings Children also make use of symbols when they draw something that they have seen and understand though it may not be directly visible at that moment.

We can see how use of symbols liberates the child from the immediate physical world, yet, their immediate sensory and physical experiences are the main determinants of their understanding of the world according to Piaget.

- *Intuitive thinking*

Now we will look at the second half of the preoperational stage, lasting from 4 to 7 years, marked by greater dependence on intuitive thinking rather than just perception. According to Piaget, children start asking 'Why?' beginning around the age of 3 and want to know reasons for things happening around them. However, they lack logical reasoning and Piaget referred to this as intuitive thought that included transductive reasoning, egocentrism, animism and lack of conservation (Lally & Valentine, 2019).

Transductive reasoning is neither inductive reasoning (from particular to general) nor deductive reasoning (from general to particular), but involves making faulty inferences from one specific to another, creating causal links irrespective of whether any causal link existed or not. Conclusions by children in this stage can be based on a set of unrelated facts and assumptions that things happening simultaneously at a time may cause each other.

For example: if a child sees his/her father take his lunch bag every day before he leaves for wok, every time someone takes the lunch bag, the child will assume that the person is leaving for work thinking that the lunch bag is the cause for one to leave for work.

Egocentrism

Children in this stage are under the impression that others around them see, think and feel the same as they do and hence they are not able to take others' perspectives. This tendency of children to be self-centred in this age is termed as 'egocentrism'.

For example: Imagine a child talking on the phone with an adult on the other side of the phone. The child responds to the person on the other side of the phone by just nodding his/her head, assuming that the person is able to understand the response. The person on the other side of the phone repeats the question, but the child fails to see that the person on the other is not able see his/her nod. The child is able to take only one's own perspective.

Note that: Egocentrism is not the same as egotism or selfishness which means thinking highly of oneself. Egocentrism refers to the child's world, centred around his/her point of view.

Developmental patterns and processes **65**

Link to Learning

Scan the QR code to view this video

Piaget's Three-Mountain Task

Piaget developed the Three-Mountain Task to determine the level of egocentrism displayed by children. Children view a 3-dimensional mountain scene from one viewpoint, and are asked what another person at a different viewpoint would see in the same scene. Watch the Three-Mountain Task in action in this short video (**http://openstaxcollege.org/l/WonderYears**) from the University of Minnesota and the Science Museum of Minnesota

---

Activity: Egocentrism

What is your thought on child's egocentrism in this stage?

Try Piaget's three-mountain task by slightly modifying it to a little lower difficulty level with a group of children around this age and see if children are able to successfully accomplish the task. Is it possible for children in this stage to be less egocentric than what Piaget believed to be?

Several psychologists have attempted to show that Piaget underestimated the intellectual capabilities of the preoperational child. Find out more about this and identify the factors that enable children overcome egocentrism by 4 or 5 years of age.

Animism is another tendency of children at this age to see inanimate objects as possessing life, consciousness and feelings just like humans. It is slightly different from pretend play, where the child pretends to act like someone or something. An example of animism can be when a child gets hurt by a chair or a table, s/he immediately starts scolding the chair for hurting him/her thus attributing a lifelike quality to the chair (inanimate).

Centration

Refer to the activity 'Conservation'. Did you observe that children in this age lack the basic ability to recognize that moving or rearranging matter does not change the quantity?

Their focus on a single dimension of any problem is due to a cognitive limitation called centration as believed by Piaget.

Try a slight variation in the same activity 'Conservation'.

This time, instead of asking them to passively watch the activity and give responses, guide them to do it on their own with their hands. Following this, pose the same questions to this group of children. Observe if there is any difference in the responses of the children in this activity in comparison to the one done earlier.
- What can you infer from this?
- What factors attribute to the change in the responses of this group of children from the earlier one?

This is probably attributed to the concept of embodied cognition, the idea that thinking arises from a combination of brain, body and environmental experiences

Irreversibility is another characteristic of this age, when children do not understand that an operation can be undone to return to its original form.

Classification is another characteristic of this stage. Preoperational children lack the ability of classifying objects on the basis of more than one criterion at the same time due to their focus on one dimension.

The concrete operational stage

The tendency of children to focus on one dimension in the earlier stage is bettered as they continue into elementary school with a more flexible and logical representation of ideas. Piaget believed that children in this stage mentally operated on concrete objects and events unconsciously, using the basic rules of thinking as per adult standards;hence the period was termed 'concrete operational stage'. Children in this stage are not yet able to think systematically about representation of objects.

Let's look at a very common classroom example-

Do you remember your teacher take dictation by reading aloud words to take spelling test? The teacher used to give certain words prior to taking the test and then take the test after a given period of time.

- What are the possibilities of the teacher reading out the words in the same sequence or in a random order?
- Will children in the concrete operation stage be able to complete the task when words are read out in a random order? Why is it so? How is it different from children in the preoperational stage?

The concrete operational stage child is able to decentre, or focus on more than one feature of a problem at a time as compared to the preoperational stage. Thinking in this stage is largely based on objects that are concrete and not on hypothesis which can be reasoned. Children in this stage cannot speculate possibilities, but they can reason in terms of the observable reality in front of them. Most of the shortcomings of the preoperational stage are overcome in this stage.

Concrete operational children are capable of classifying objects or events. They possess the ability to think about steps of process in any random order. The child becomes less egocentric and able to take others' perspectives. A differentiated view of self, distinct from others, is viewed and self-concept emerges. The concrete operational child is able to make use of logical principles in solving problems involving the physical world. The child can understand principles of cause and effect, size and distance.

Classification, identity, reversibility and reciprocity are the cognitive skills that increase the child's understanding of the physical world in this stage. Manipulating representations, a more abstract skill develops later during their adolescence.

The formal operational stage

The final cognitive stage among children is the formal operational stage when they approach 11 years, as proposed by Piaget. According to Piaget, this is the highest level of cognitive development. He believed that children of this age attain the ability to think logically and deal with abstract concepts. It is the period when children can operate on forms or representations, hence the name formal operation stage. This stage is identified as parallel with the period of adolescence by Piaget. Children in this stage are capable of both inductive and deductive reasoning, enabling the adolescent to be creative, inventive, imaginative and original in thinking (Locke & Ciechalski, 1995). Children are more capable of hypothesizing various possibilities to find solutions to problems. This ability has been referred to as hypothetico-deductive reasoning and scientific thinking. This helps adolescents to imagine what *could be* rather than what *is*. Adolescents may become more idealistic, committing themselves to a larger goal. They may also start to question adult authority by challenging the conventional rules by reasoning. They become good at arguments and counterarguments based on evidence (Levine & Munsch, 2016).

Formal operation is said to consist of "thought thinking about itself" while concrete operation is said to consist of "thought thinking about the environment" (Bjorklund & Causey, 2018). It has been observed that lack of exposure to formal education in scientific reasoning may hinder the attainment of formal operational thinking (Siegler, 2020).

Reflect on these questions:

- Do all children reach the formal operations stage?
- Does the achievement of this stage depend solely on maturation?
- Why do some children even after reaching the age beyond 11 or 12 do not attain formal operation thinking?

Identify societies or contexts, in which adolescent children are deprived of formal education. Select a group of children belonging to this age group. Ascertain if they have reached the formal operation thinking stage by posing a problem solving situation or scenario to them. Find out the reasons or factors that may have enabled or hindered their development in this stage.

Preadolescent period: significant for adolescent development

Reiterating the categorization of a child's intellectual development into different stages as proposed by Piaget, the four stages occur in hierarchical order, namely, the sensorimotor, the preoperational, the concrete operations and the formal operational. A child does not automatically progress from one intellectual level to another. Rather, certain mental processes must take place within the child's cognitive framework before progress through these stages occurs. Thus, it is understood that, as a child progresses from one intellectual stage to another, his/her cognitive structure must have been broadened through physical and social interactions with people and objects to the extent necessary to meet the characteristic features of the succeeding hierarchical level. The child's mental framework has therefore been expanded to "contain" the preceding stages he/she has encountered to enable intellectual operations at the higher level. The chronological ages Piaget offers for children's development from one stage to another is subject to the kinds of learning experiences they have undergone. (Smith, 1981).

Studies have shown that children in limited experiential cultures and environments, especially those from the marginalized or the underprivileged sections of the society, may find it difficult to make the intellectual transition from concrete operational thinking to the manipulative cognitive abilities characteristic of the formal operations stage because of limited educationally constructive environmental stimuli (Smith, 1981).

In consequence, it is very crucial for us to have a sound understanding of development that occurs at the earlier stages of development in order to know the underlying factors and experiences that contribute to the development of the adolescent who is in the formal operation stage. It also becomes imperative for educators to facilitate the selection of appropriate kinds of instruction and materials to use in schools at different grades by taking the transitional period into consideration.

Reappearance of egocentrism

As we glance through the four stages of development, we can see the concept of 'egocentricity' repeatedly occurring across all the four stages, yet a fundamental difference is observed between the cognitive egocentricity of a child and the egocentricity of an adolescent (Kalyan-Masih, 1973).

The sensorimotor child is said to be egocentric with respect to objects to the extent that object permanence is confused with object perception. Sensorimotor egocentrism is overcome when children are able to form mental representations of absent objects, an ability that emerges with the symbolic functions of preoperational thought, the next stage of cognitive development. The preoperational egocentrism is overcome by the emergence of concrete operations when the child can hold two mental representations at once and distinguish between them. This form of egocentrism is surpassed at the final stage of cognitive development, i.e. formal operations. The concept of 'egocentrism' evolves with each succeeding stage (Hill & Lapsley). Let us learn more about 'Adolescent Egocentrism' in the following section.

Once adolescents start thinking in abstract terms, they are able to hypothesize a number of possibilities and better able to systematically test alternative ideas to determine their influences on outcomes. This enables them to take decisions on their own. There is a reappearance of egocentrism in this age which is quite different from the preoperational child.

Piaget's concept of adolescent egocentricity was further expanded by David Elkind to explain the consequences of adolescent egocentricty (Lally & Valentine,

Developmental patterns and processes **69**

2019). As we have seen earlier, adolescents are constantly undergoing physiological changes; they become concerned about their physical appearance and tend to believe that others are looking at them. They become self-conscious and are always anticipating reactions from an audience that is supposedly 'imaginary'.

"The imaginary audience is the adolescent's belief that those around them are as concerned and focused on their appearance as they themselves are" (Lally & Valentine, 2019). Especially adolescents of today who are active on social media tend to be far more egocentric than their other counterparts. In this way the adolescent who is like the preoperational child fails to see others' point of view and does not realize that s/he is not the focus of others' world.

For example:

Adolescent girls will usually refrain from going to school with oiled hair, assuming that others will make fun of them.

Adolescent boys usually keep combing their hair at intervals to look good, assuming that others are looking at them.

Another consequence of adolescent egocentrism is the personal fable, a belief that their experiences are unique and different from others and invulnerable to harm. Children in this age feel that they are the only ones who are experiencing a certain feeling or emotion and others cannot understand their feelings (Lally & Valentine, 2019).

Common voices heard from children at this age

FIGURE 2.10 Illustration of Personal Fable in Adolescent Egocentrism

This uniqueness in one's emotional experiences reinforces the adolescent's belief of invulnerability, especially in regard to death. They may even engage in undesirable behaviour like 'drink and drive', or 'smoking', realizing the ill-effects of these actions, and yet feel nothing will happen to them, unlike others. Elkind believed that adolescent egocentricity emerged in early adolescence and declined in middle adolescence, though recent research has also identified egocentricity in late adolescence (Lally & Valentine, 2019).

Imaginary audience and personal fable has been seen as adaptations by adolescents who are dealing with new and important developmental tasks of this age of life. As we have already seen, adolescents are continuously interacting with new environments and are constantly worried about their image as perceived by others in the environment. The imaginary audience enables them to imagine and visualize ideas and ways of coping with conflicting dilemmas. The adolescents' strong desire for individuation or separation from family is further facilitated by the personal fable with its focus on uniqueness of the individual (Levine & Munsch, 2016).

Beyond formal operational thought

Think and Reflect

Compare the thinking of a 15 year old adolescent and adults in their late 30s. Reflect on these questions below-

- What would you infer about their thinking operations?
- Will both the 15 year old and 30 year old think in a similar manner?
- Can decisions be always made on what is idealistic?
- Do you think sometimes decisions need to be based on realistic and practical grounds?
- In what way will a 15 year old and adult in late 30s differ in considering possibilities or taking decisions? Why is there a difference in thinking operations?
- Can the gained experiences of a 30 year old make the adult think differently from the 15 year old, who also is able to think abstractly and consider possibilities and ideas about indirect experiences?

Adults can make adaptive choices basing their decisions on what is realistic and practical, unlike adolescents who are apparently idealistic, and adults don't easily get influenced by others' thinking. This advanced type of thinking is referred to as Postformal Thought (Lally & Valentine, 2019).

To know more about Postformal Thought, scan the QR code below.

Scan the QR code to know more about Postformal thought

> **Beyond Formal Operational Thought: Postformal Thought**
>
> This will take you to the link that explains the difference between formal thought and postformal thought

Consequences of formal operational thought

Due to their ability to think abstractly and hypothetically, adolescents exhibit the capacity to introspect and think about one's thoughts and feelings. Their idealistic behaviour lends them to be critical of others especially adults in their life. They will try to conform to others' expectations by either pretending to be what they may not be or acting like hypocrites. They tend to overlook the obvious at times and fail to make the right choices. This makes them appear stupid even if they are bright, probably due to lack of experience in considering alternatives (Lally & Valentine, 2019).

Cognitive development during adolescence

Adolescence is a period of rapid cognitive development, when changes in the brain interact with experience, knowledge, and social expectations. Along with physical changes, they are also undergoing changes in ways of thinking, reasoning and understanding the world around them. The higher-level thinking attained in the formal operation stage enables them think about alternative possibilities, evaluate alternatives and commit to larger personal goals. The thoughts, ideas and concepts developed at this period of life greatly influence one's future life and play a major role in character and personality formation (Jones, T.).

There are two perspectives on adolescent thinking: constructivist and information-processing.

- The constructivist perspective, based on the work of Piaget, assumes adolescents' cognitive improvement to be relatively sudden and drastic.
- The information-processing perspective derived from the study of artificial intelligence explains cognitive development in terms of the growth of specific components of the overall process of thinking.

Information processing: cognitive processes in adolescents

Attention

Have you noticed that teens usually have their headphones on listening to music while they are studying? Talking on the phone while driving? Texting on the phone while talking or responding to someone?
What are they doing?
Multitasking?

Adolescent children are seen to have improved in selectively attending to a particular task which they may focus on as well as divide their attention between tasks, since they become so confident in their ability to control their attention and believe that that can attend to several tasks at a time by switching back and forth between tasks (Levine & Munsch, 2016). With increased attention, adolescents are able to hold material in working memory while taking in and processing new material. They also become better at response inhibition which enables them to adapt their responses to the situations by inhibiting well-learnt responses when they are appropriate to a situation and thus speeding cognitive processing (Kuther, 2018).

However, neurological research has confirmed that children who took to multitasking ended up with superficial understanding and remembered less as the part of the brain designed for deep processing of information is largely left unused (Levine & Munsch, 2016).

Memory

One can observe improvements in working memory and long-term memory of adolescent children, resulting in quick thinking and learning. Thus, adolescents can retain more information at a time, integrate prior experiences and new information and organize it in more complex ways. This enables them to reason about problems and ideas and the nature of thinking itself (Kuther, 2018). Adolescents are more aware of their own thought processes and can use mnemonic devices and other strategies to think and remember information more efficiently.

We have seen that adolescents' increased facility of thinking results in hypothetico-deductive reasoning. The systematic, abstract thinking allows adolescents to comprehend the sorts of higher-order abstract logic inherent in puns, proverbs, metaphors and analogies. They are quite adept in using language to convey multiple messages such as satire, metaphor and sarcasm. Advanced reasoning and logical processes to social and ideological matters such as interpersonal relationships, politics, philosophy, religion, morality, friendship, faith, fairness and honesty is manifested in their thinking processes (Jones, T.).

Metacognition

Adolescents become more aware of their thought processes and are able to regulate cognitive activities during their thinking processes. As this process of metacognition develops through middle adolescence, teenagers are better able to plan how they take in, manipulate and store information. Their abilities to apply metacognition in real-life settings continue to develop into late adolescence and early adulthood. Metacognition facilitates the development of scientific reasoning because when adolescents keep on trying out strategies and reflecting on those strategies, they come to appreciate logic which they apply to new situations. Although they demonstrate scientific thinking, their reasoning tends to emphasize single solution to problems, as they are not able to coordinate the effect of multiple causal effects on outcomes (Kuther, 2019).

Classroom Activity

Incorporate these tasks in your classroom to promote students' metacognition.

Before you begin to take any session for students, provide them with the name of the topic and the objective of that session. Ask them to assess their current knowledge about the topic that could guide their learning.

After you finish taking the session, ask students to note down the muddiest point of the session, i.e. what was the most confusing part of the session that did not understand clearly. Ask them how the session is influencing their prior thoughts or knowledge about the topic.

Get students to maintain reflective journals to monitor their own thinking processes from their pre-planning to planning to execution to success or failure to evaluating and further re-planning for specific tasks

---

Problem-solving

Problem-solving is demonstrated when children use trial-and-error to solve problems. The ability to systematically solve a problem in a logical and methodical way emerges.

Adolescent decision-making

Adolescents are confronted with various problems and situations in their life and they are capable of taking the responsibility of making decisions on their own based on rational thinking. Even so, we often come across adolescents who make poor decisions and engage in risk-taking.

Why is it so, in spite of their abstract reasoning ability to consider possibilities?

If you have gone through the link on postformal thought, you would probably have an answer to this question.

74 Developmental patterns and processes

We had seen in the previous chapter about the adolescents' tendency to engage in risky behaviours that have a high probability of immediate reward. Research findings supplemented by neurological research suggest that adolescents tend to place more importance on the potential benefits of decisions such as social status or pleasure rather than estimating the potential costs or risks such as physical harm or short- and long-term health according to Kuther (2018).

Smith et al. (2013) claim that, though findings about adolescents' capability of rational decision-making may hold true in ideal situations, decision-making in real life contexts for adolescents is quite complex and influenced by situational, emotional and individual difference characteristics such as peer influences, reward outcomes, excitement, impulsivity and sensation seeking. We have already seen how adolescents act impulsively due to the lag between the development of the emotional parts of the brain and the prefrontal cortex, which is equally responsible for their decision-making too.

Albert et al. (2013), suggests that, in addition to neurological development, psychosocial development also plays an important role in adolescents' decision-making and behaviour. Especially, the presence of peers or even the thought of their peers judging them influences adolescents' decisions and choices of engaging in a behaviour.

Think and Reflect

"What can be the legal implications of adolescent decision making?"

Has this question ever bothered you anytime?
Do you have an answer to this question?

You must have heard about the following cases-
- ❏ Nirbhaya rape case committed by a juvenile,
- ❏ a 15 year old boy kill his brother over PUBG.

Read about these cases and discuss with your peers about what you think.

- Do you favor death penalty for juveniles or a more lenient penalty than that given to adults? What is the rationale behind your opinion?
- What is your opinion about using developmental science for making policy decisions related to adolescent crimes?

How will you explain your argument on the basis of whatever you have learnt about the adolescents' cognitive capacities (formal operation stage), the neurological developments in this stage and the other environmental influences surrounding the adolescents?

The consequences of adolescents' bad decision-making can be quite alarming and serious with a long-lasting effect on their lives. Adult guidance can help adolescents in making the right and appropriate decisions. Experience making decisions and learning from successes and failures in addition to cognitive developments, self-control and emotional regulation can result in adolescent decision-making that is more reflective, confident and successful (Kuther, 2018).

Kohlberg's theory of moral development in adolescents

As adolescents develop the ability to think logically and hypothetically, they can also think about the consequences of their decisions, which can affect the way they think about moral issues (Levine & Munsch, 2016). The onset of adolescence bring with it its independence; their thinking becomes independent and they start making moral judgments about what is right or wrong (Stangor & Walinga, 2014).

As adolescents' cognitive, emotional and social development continue to mature, their understanding of morality expands and their behaviour becomes more closely aligned with their values and beliefs within the culture that they belong to. It is essential to understand moral development in this stage as adolescents become more responsible and make important decisions by applying the guiding principles that emerge during their moral development.

Lawrence Kohlberg built on the work of Piaget and was interested in finding out how our moral reasoning changes as we get older. He wanted to find out how people decide what is right and what is wrong. Kohlberg argued that children learn their moral values through active thinking and reasoning, and that moral development, like cognitive development, follows a series of stages (Lally & Valentine, 2019).

To develop this theory, Kohlberg posed moral dilemmas to children, teenagers and adults. Then he analyzed their answers to find evidence of their particular stage of moral development.

Before we proceed to understand Kohlberg's theory of moral development, watch this video.

Kohlberg's 6 Stages of Moral Development

This will take you to a video that explains the stages of moral development with the help of an example in school.

Scan the QR code to view this video

Activity: 'Heinz's Dilemma Activity'

Towards the end of the video, a task is provided for you to test your comprehension of the various stages of moral development. It introduces you to the best known moral dilemma created by Kohlberg, the "Heinz" dilemma, which discusses the idea of obeying the law versus saving a life.

To facilitate discussion in your classroom, go to the link provided below. This link will open to the 'Heinz's Dilemma Activity' in Chapter 16: The forensic psychologist in the courtroom

76 Developmental patterns and processes

www.iccb.org/iccb/wp-content/pdfs/adulted/healthcare_curriculum/curriculum&resources/context_social_studies/F.%20HC%20Context%20Social%20Studies%20Resource%20File/84.pdf

Kohlberg defined three levels of moral development: preconventional, conventional and postconventional. Each level has two distinct stages.

The individual's sense of morality in the three levels of development are:

- A preconventional level child's sense of morality is externally controlled. Children accept and believe the rules of parents and teachers whom they see as authority figures, and their judgment is based on those consequences;
- In the conventional level, though children continue to accept the rules of authority figures in order to please them or maintain societal order, their sense of morality is based on personal and societal relationships;
- Postconventional level individuals understand the need to question a law, since they possess the ability to think in terms of abstract principles and values.

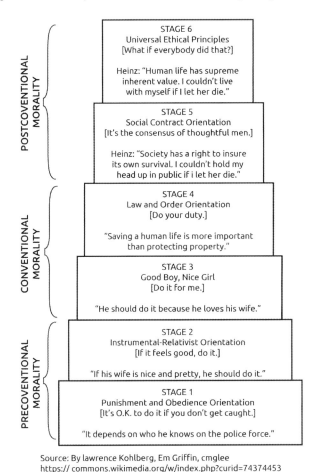

Source: By lawrence Kohlberg, Em Griffin, cmglee
https://commons.wikimedia.org/w/index.php?curid=74374453

FIGURE 2.11 Stages of Moral Development as Proposed by Kohlberg

Adolescents' moral reasoning and behaviour are strongly influenced by their observations within their culture, of the surrounding environment at home, schools and the media. Young children's moral decisions are strongly influenced by family, culture and religion. Early adolescents' moral decisions are extensively influenced by their peers, since friends play a very significant role in their lives. Moreover, the newly gained ability to think abstractly prepares these adolescents to recognize the rules and norms created by the society and also question the authority of these norms and the people who create them. By the time, they reach late adolescence, they tend towards becoming conformists as they begin to establish their own identity, belief system and position in the world.

Nonetheless, life experiences for some of them may impede their moral development. Unpleasant and distressing experiences may cause them to view the world as unjust and unfair. Social learning too impacts moral development. Adolescents often model some adults or significant others in their lives. If these adults make immoral decisions, adolescents observing them develop beliefs and values not aligned with the values of the society. The responsibility for supporting moral development in adolescents rests on adults, particularly parents and teachers by modelling the moral character that we want to nurture in our children. Authoritative parenting as compared to other parenting styles, is more favourable in promoting children's moral development. Encouraging the right kind of peer relations in adolescence by parents is very crucial towards this developmental step (Hoose, N.A.).

According to Kohlberg, few people reach stages five and six; most tend to stay at stage four. Kohlberg professed that women were often at a lower stage of moral development than men, but psychologist Carol Gilligan, one of Kohlberg's research assistants, questioned his findings (Zhou & Brown, 2015). She argued that women are not deficient in their moral reasoning and instead proposed that males and females reason differently: girls and women focus more on staying connected and maintaining interpersonal relationships. She developed an alternative scale, heavily influenced by Kohlberg's scale, which showed that both men and women could reach advanced stages of moral development (Zhou & Brown, 2015).

> **Think and Reflect**
>
> Remember any instance from your adolescent days, in which you were forced to take decision against your will.
> - What guided your decision-making process in that situation?
> - Did you take the decision, thinking what other people will think about your decision?
> - Or did something else influence your decision making?
>
> Consider your decision-making processes in the present stage.
> - What guides your decisions?
> - Do you make choices based on what other people will think about your decision?
> - Or are there other principles that influence your decision making?
>
> How has culture influenced your decision making approach in both times
> 1. When you were an adolescent
> 2. In the present stage (mention the stage in which you are presently)

Significance of developmental theories

Developmental theories enable the understanding of human development through a set of guiding principles and concepts. Development theorists generally draw from a wide range of sources and several perspectives and a developmental phenomenon can be viewed from varied perspectives. One cannot undermine any theory over the other, because each of these theories focus on perspectives based on its own premises and focuses on different aspects of development.

To understand the growth of logical thinking from the stage of childhood to the time they reach the stage of adolescence, it is very crucial to understand the thought processes that the individual has gone through at various stages of life.

To study the development of understanding in an individual, the main focus of attention is the mental activities of the child. The mental activities refer to those processes by which knowledge of outside world is acquired. Piaget termed it as 'cognition'. These processes are further divided into two classes: one that records reality, for example, learning, memory and perception; and the other which transforms reality, i.e. thought. The transformations or operations that the individual has access to, are a function of his level of 'thought' development. Piaget's sensory motor period refers to the infant in pre-thought operations and that which merely records information through ongoing sensory experiences to construct his/her reality. Transformational ability or 'thought' begins to appear with concrete operations, which Piaget describes as interiorized actions which are reversible and can be organized into higher-order structures. The structural reintegration emerging from concrete operations marks the transition from the realm of actual into the realm of the possible. The new powerful operational abilities developed is the formal operational abilities that include hypothetical deductive thought that includes a set of operations such as the inverse, negation, reciprocation and correlation. The formal operational thought stage is hypothesized to be essential to moral reasoning and identity development (Rowe, 1980).

According to Kohlberg, growth through the stages is a function of the interaction of logical analytical abilities with social perception, which develops through the use of higher reasoning in a rich social environment. Eventually, an emergence of a model of development consisting of structural stages of operational logic (Piaget & Inhelder, 1958) allowing advances in stages of social role taking (Selman, 1971) furthers the advances in stages of moral reasoning. Each new stage is considered a reorganization of schemata from the earlier stage. The stages are hierarchically integrative with advancement dependent on ongoing equilibration by the maturing individual (Rowe, 1980).

Kohlberg's cognitive developmental theory proposed that stages of moral judgment correspond to Piaget's stages of logical reasoning. According to Kohlberg an advanced level of cognitive ability assists the process of interpreting situations, thinking abstractly, applying previous experiences and evaluating lines of reasoning. These operations in turn result in mature moral judgments. (Yeh, 2011).

The work of Lawrence Kohlberg focuses on the development of individuals and the ways in which they develop a sense of justice and right versus wrong. Similar to Erikson's 'stage' theory of identity development, Kohlberg also asserts that humans develop their moral sensibility in stages. Kohlberg believes that these stages are not the product of socialization, but they emerge from one's own thinking about the moral dilemmas at hand, and as individuals engage in discussions and debates with others, they find their views and thoughts challenged, thus developing their moral identity. He believed that this process of moral reasoning requires rational thought for resolution of dilemmas or difficult situations. He attributes the succession of every stage to the cognitive operations that are more stable, more reversible and more equilibrated with the progression of each stage (Niedzielski, 2005).

Erikson, Marcia and Kohlberg all present theories of psychosocial development that represent sequencing of stages and a linear progression of rationally finding one's self within a cultural context.

Erikson's view of the biological influence and the contextual influences of the social environment on identity development helps link the psychological and sociological perspectives of identity development. Erikson's concepts of the ego strengths is pivotal to his theory of self-development. He opines that the ego strengths result from the resolution of the various conflicts that come across in life at age appropriate time points in development. The different levels of biological, social and psychological maturation at different point of time in life facilitate the increase in ego strengths over the course of the life. As an individual develops, s/he encounters complex challenges and the increase in ego strengths at previous stages help the individual manage the complexities over the course of the lifetime with identity subsequently being built cumulatively. The lack of resolution of conflicts at a particular stage results in the deficit of one's capacity to manage complexities in life and make them vulnerable in life. However, Erikson also believed that this issue of unresolved stage could be addressed later in life by providing the appropriate opportunities to the individual (Anderson, 2008).

Although Erikson's theory had put forward the concept of identity, the operationalization of the concept was not simplistic because of the interwoven complexities and its nature. Marcia presented the most significant exception to this by translating Erikson's fifth stage of development, the stage of identity formation, into an empirical model (Anderson, 2008). In contrast to Erikson's conception of identity, which presents two opposite poles of identity development, Marcia proposed four identity status classifications. Marcia's ego identity status framework is viewed as an ongoing developmental process in which adolescents progress from diffusion to foreclosure or moratorium, from foreclosure to moratorium, and from moratorium to identity achievement. However, the trajectory of identity statuses can occur in a fluid developmental sequence in which no one status is necessarily a prerequisite for another. Marcia elaborates on Erikson's work by proposing four identity statuses that represent patterns and common issues that adolescents experience during this fifth stage (Yeh, 2011). Marcia chose a section of Erikson's work that was clearly oriented to occupation and finding direction for an occupational role in life (Anderson, 2008). Erikson used the term "psychosocial moratorium" to describe a delay in the adolescent's commitment to personal and occupational choices. James Marcia expands the meaning of moratorium to include the adolescent's active efforts to deal with the crisis of shaping an identity. This is the point when the adolescent begins to employ rational thought by considering alternative choices and experiencing different roles. Rational thought is also reinforced with Marcia's third identity status, "identity foreclosure", wherein the adolescent selects some convenient set of beliefs or goals without carefully considering alternatives (Niedzielski, 2005). Marcia and Erikson both posit identity as a lifelong developmental process. Marcia's model was specific to adolescent identity development, and Erikson's theory terms one particular period of development 'identity'. Marcia's identity status paradigm has been considered very influential in adolescent development especially in area of occupation and interpersonal preferences (Anderson, 2008).

As we navigate through these developmental theories, there is a common thread that runs across all these theories. The individual as an active learner in varied social and cultural contexts is highlighted in all the theories. There are theories of development that have taken into consideration the social and cultural aspects of the learner. We will further gain an understanding of these theories to deepen our knowledge of children's development.

Another recent approach of understanding development is the 'Sociocultural Theory of Cognitive Development'.

Vygotsky's sociocultural theory of cognitive development

Russian psychologist Lev Vygotsky built on Piaget's theoretical idea of the child as an active learner but expanded the idea with emphasis on the influence of culture and social interaction on children's thinking. He proposed that different cultures and societies play varied roles in the cognitive development of children.

He posited that cognitive growth occurs in a sociocultural context and children's cognitive skills evolve from social interactions with their parents, teachers, peers and significant others. He also pointed out that human cognition, carried out in isolation is also inherently sociocultural since it is affected by beliefs, values and tools of intellectual adaptation transmitted to individuals by their culture. He argued that it is the language, writings and concepts arising from the culture that elicit the highest level of cognitive thinking. His idea of intellectual growth was opposed to Piaget's idea of a universal pattern of growth.

He proposed that the mental functions of attention, sensation, perception and memory possessed by children are eventually transformed into higher mental functions by the culture in which the individual resides and interacts with. The sociocultural perspective describes learning as a social process, wherein children interact with more skilled and competent partners who provide them with new challenges and guide them through the difficult tasks and thus stimulate their cognitive development. Vygotsky believed everything is learnt on two levels. First, through interaction with others (interpsychological), and then integrated into the individual's mental structure (intrapsychological) (Allman, 2018).

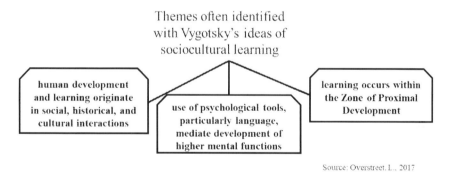

Source: Overstreet, L., 2017

FIGURE 2.12 Themes Identified with Vygotsky's Ideas of Sociocultural learning

Vygotsky's best known concept is Zone of Proximal Development (ZPD). Vygotsky defined ZPD as "the distance between what a learner can do without help and what he or she can achieve with adult guidance and encouragement or from a more knowledgeable peer." (Allman, 2018).

The more knowledgeable other (MKO) refers to someone who has a better understanding or a higher ability level than the learner, with respect to a particular task, process or concept.

The notion of scaffolding is closely related to the idea of ZPD. It refers to the support or guidance given to a learner by a More Knowledgeable Other (MKO) that enables the learner to perform a task until such time that s/he can perform the task independently.

82 Developmental patterns and processes

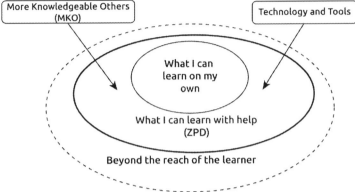

FIGURE 2.13 Zone of Proximal Development and Scaffolding

Beyond culture and social interactions, language was another important concept that Vygotsky associated with thinking. Communication is considered a prerequisite to the child's acquisition of concepts and language. He suggested that thinking leads to the use of language and vice versa, thus implying the reciprocal relation between language and thinking. He believed that children talk to themselves and they learn to think in words. Over time, the child internalizes the language. The child's talking to oneself was termed by Vygotsky as "private speech" or "inner speech", while the same talking was interpreted by Piaget as egocentric speech. Vygotsky believed that thinking ability grows with the growth of language (Lally & Valentine, 2019).

Children in many cultures or contexts do not acquire formal education. Parents of these children are either not educated enough to teach their children or they are too busy earning a livelihood.

How do these children learn and develop cognitively?

They learn through guided participation by actively participating in culturally relevant activities alongside more skilled partners who provide necessary aid and encouragement (Shaffer & Kipp, 2010, p. 284).

Guided participation is an informal 'apprenticeship in thinking' in which children's cognitions are shaped as they partake, alongside adults or other more skilful associates, in everyday culturally relevant experiences. Barbara Rogoff believes that cognitive growth is shaped as much or more by these informal adult – child transactions as it is by more formal teaching or educational experiences (Shaffer & Kipp, 2010, p. 287). Jerome Bruner further developed Vygotsky's concept of ZPD to describe the process of adult guidance to help children learn (Levine & Munsch, 2016).

Social cognitive theory: an agentic perspective

Albert Bandura focused his work on modelling, which is learning through observation. He believed that children learn by imitating others. Especially adolescents struggling to form an identity rely on their peers to act as role models. Social cognitive theory extended from social learning theory proposes that personality results from the interaction of an individual's thoughts with inner qualities, self-beliefs, and environmental cues. According to Bandura (2005), social cognitive theory takes on an agent-like perspective to change, development and adaptation. An agent is described as someone who intentionally influences one's functioning and life circumstances; "In this view, people are self-organizing, proactive, self-regulating, and self-reflecting. They are contributors to their life circumstances not just products of them" (Bandura, 2005, p. 1) mastering new skills to adapt to the adult society. Their activities are extended to a larger social community unlike childhood involvements. They take the agency of their own functioning and developments

Adolescents have to manage major biological, educational and social role transitions all at the same time. Adolescents start taking adult-like responsibilities, take decisions regarding their career and start in life.

Notwithstanding the common notions of adolescence as a period of stress and discontinuity, social cognitive theory emphasises personal growth through mastery and other enabling experiences as the more normative developmental process. Given the interdependence of personal, cultural and social developments in adolescents, a study of the evolving social systems to understand the changes in adolescent functioning and well-being is inevitable.

Self-efficacy beliefs play a key role in cognitive development and accomplishment of children. Bandura defines self-efficacy as beliefs in one's capabilities to organize and execute the courses of action required to manage prospective situations (Bandura, 2005, p. 2).

Situated view of learning and identity formation

While cognitive learning process involves a selective transmission of comparatively abstract knowledge from one context to another, Lave and Wenger's situated learning theory, drawing from Vygotsky's theory of social learning, views learning as a sociocultural phenomenon rather than the action of the individual acquiring general information from a decontextualized body of knowledge. Lave and Wenger viewed situated learning as participatory in nature and as a process of social participation, a process of growth through which learners dialectically construct their identities (Besar, 2018). Knowledge acquired through this process includes knowing oneself, and in a broader sense, knowing one's identity. Since identity originates through daily activities and "experience of engagement" in social practices, reviewing lived experiences and activities within daily life plays a critical role in understanding the concept of identity and examining the process of identity construction (Park, 2015).

We will discuss the situated view of learning and identity formation in detail in the following chapter, in which will attempt to explore the various contexts of adolescents and the role played by these contexts in their identity formation.

Aspects of self-functioning: self-concept, self-esteem and self-efficacy

Identity is a set of beliefs, defined as self-concept, self-esteem and self-efficacy, which are interrelated and in continuous development (Rodriguez & Loos-Sant´Ana, 2015).

Self-concept

While developmentalists like Brown and Meltzoff believe that newborn infants possess the capacity to distinguish their self from the surrounding environment, there are others like Mahler et al., who believe that infants are born without a sense of self (Shaffer & Kipp, 2010, p. 480).

At a certain level of cognitive development and social experiences, both are necessary for self-recognition. One social experience that contributes to self-awareness in humans is a secure attachment to a primary caregiver.

Parents usually keep telling their children about 'what they are', 'what their behaviour should be or should not be', and this slowly contributes to the child's expansion of his/her self-concept. Povinelli and Simon suggest that autobiographical memories about oneself co-constructed with the help of adults help children to illustrate that the self is stable over time, thus contributing to a growing sense of extended self (Shaffer & Kipp, 2010, p. 482). Evidences of cultural differences in parenting styles' influence on toddlers achievement of self-recognition has also been observed. As toddlers grow, they start categorizing other people based on the differences in age, gender, etc. and incorporate these characteristics into their self-concepts.

Children between 3 to 5 years, when asked to describe themselves, usually describe themselves with respect to their 'physical attributes' or 'what they possess' or 'what activity they did and they are proud of'. Their descriptions seem to lack any psychological self-awareness. Eder's research has, though, observed basic psychological conceptions of self in this age children, long before they can express this knowledge. It is believed that, as children grow, their descriptions of self advance to representation of their inner qualities such as their traits, values, beliefs and ideologies. This exhibits a shift towards a more abstract and psychological description of self (Shaffer & Kipp, 2010, p. 484).

In addition to a psychological description of self, adolescents come to understand that their roles are multifaceted depending on situations and people. A study was done by Susan Harter and Ann Monsour to understand adolescents' reactions to the inconsistencies in their selves with different people: (1) parents, (2) friends, (3) romantic partners, and (4) teachers and classmates. The findings revealed that beginner adolescents aged around 13 are less concerned about their different selves with different people; adolescents around the age of 15 were confused about their several different selves inside them and were concerned about finding the 'real me'; older adolescents around the age of 17 were not much concerned about their multiple selves as they had integrated them into a higher-order, more coherent view of themselves (Shaffer & Kipp, 2010, p. 485).

One's self-concept is more psychological, more abstract, and more of a coherent, integrated self-portrait from childhood throughout adolescence. This development of self-concept derives from research conducted in societies that value independence and personal attributes of one's character (Shaffer & Kipp, 2010).

Does self-concept development follow the same path in all cultures and societies?

Individualist societies that value competition and individual autonomy tend to emphasize ways in which people differ from each other. Whereas collectivist societies like India value social cohesion and interdependence. Triandis asserts that their identities are closely tied to the groups to which they belong (e.g. families, religious organizations and communities), rather than to their self-achievements and personal characteristics (Shaffer & Kipp, 2010, p. 486). Traditional values and beliefs of one's culture strongly influence the kinds of self-concepts that emerge. The differences in ways of looking at achievement behaviour, aggression, moral development and many other aspects of development in different cultures and societies impact the way of looking at self and the formation of identity in the respective cultures.

Self-concept is defined as an organized cognitive structure covering attitudes, beliefs and values that cut across all facets of experience and action, organizing a variety of habits, abilities, ideas and feelings that a person displays. This structure is not stable through time, and its development occurs from experience, self-reflection and feedback from others (Rodriguez & Loos-Sant´Ana, 2015).

Task for the Learner

The Context

Research on this concept has been exclusively conducted in developed countries and evidences are usually derived from these contexts. Whether the existing research is relevant to the vast amount of majority residing in a diverse set of developing countries is yet a question that needs to be explored.

Explore the path of the development of self-concept

Identify settings in developing contexts, like India. Find out how the development of self-concept takes shape in these contexts.

Guiding questions
- How is self-concept related to adolescents' education and work status in their transition to adulthood?
- What role does gender play in the experiences of adolescents with respect to the relation between self-concept and adolescents' education and work status?
- Do adolescents from higher and lower castes experience a similar relationship between their self-concept and education/work status in the transition to adulthood? If no, what are the factors that are responsible for a difference in their experiences?

Self-esteem

As children develop, they not only construct identities, but also evaluate their qualities as they perceive, determining a sense of self-worth. This aspect of self is called self-esteem. High self-esteem enables an individual to recognize their strengths and weaknesses and feel positive about what are their characteristics and competencies, whereas low self-esteem drives the individual to dwell on perceived inadequacies rather than on any strengths that they may possess.

Self-concept refers to how a child views his or her qualities and sense of self while self-esteem is evaluative and refers to the child's satisfaction with those qualities comprising his or her sense of self.

Allen and Land, suggest the importance of secure attachments with parents in adolescence for promoting their identity and self-development. Allen et al., believe that the increased autonomy from parents gained by adolescents is established not at the expense of strong relationships with parents but in the context of secure relationships with parents. This task of separation-individuation reflects the differentiation of the individual self-concept during the former years of the life of adolescents. Allen and Land, infer that secure attachments provide adolescents with a "secure base" to explore identity issues and promote aspects of self-development, especially self-esteem (Laibel et al., 2004).

Bowlby (1982) & Bretherton (1991), extend the tenets of attachment theory to assert how the construction of rudimentary models of the self (and others) is in response to the availability and sensitivity of caregivers in toddlerhood and how these representations are reworked across the life span. Researchers have identified links between secure attachments with parents in infancy, childhood, adolescence and positive representations of the self, including high levels of self-esteem and self-efficacy. Besides, peers are also found to influence adolescent self-development and shape an adolescent's global self-esteem (Laibel et al., 2004).

According to Harter, 4- to 7-year-olds, tend to rate themselves positively in all domains, and their ratings are modestly correlated with those given by their teachers on the same competency domains. Starting at about age 8, children's ratings of their self closely reflect other people's evaluation of them, specifically, social self-esteem based on their peers' rating of them. Harter, believed that, children's feelings of self-esteem depend both on how they think others evaluate them (i.e. the social looking glass) and on how they choose to evaluate themselves (Shaffer & Kipp, 2010, p. 488).

Individual's perceptions of self-worth become increasingly centred on interpersonal relationships by the time they enter adolescence. Susan Harter and her colleagues found that adolescents often begin to perceive their self-worth somewhat differently in different relational contexts (e.g. with parents, with teachers, with male classmates and with female classmates). This feeling of self-esteem within a particular relationship context was termed 'relational self-worth'. This contributes to a difference in the extent of self-esteem in varied contexts, which indicates that adolescents' self-esteem depends not only on how others evaluate them but also on how they evaluate themselves. This underscores the importance of the kinds of relationships and aspects of relational self-worth for the formation of self-concept. Late adolescence beholds new relationships with romantic partners or close friendships; these relationship-oriented dimensions are observed to contribute to adolescents' global self-esteem. However, gender differences are observed in the way self-esteem is manifested in adolescent boys and girls. Girls' high self-esteem is more concerned with supportive relationships with friends, whereas boys' high self-esteem is stemmed from their ability to successfully influence their friends. Girls' low self-esteem has been strongly associated with a failure to win friends' approval, whereas, boys' low self-esteem is linked to failure in romantic relationships (Shaffer & Kipp, 2010).

Smith and Lovin defined self-esteem as a reflexive emotion that has developed over time in social processes of invention, that individuals learn to experience and to talk about, that arises in predictable social circumstances and that is subject to social control. Based on this definition, Hewitt viewed self-esteem more as a socially constructed emotion grounded in mood rather than a universal psychological and motivating force (Abdel-Khalek, 2016).

> **Think and Reflect**
>
> **Is self-esteem stable through adolescence?**
> Imagine as a child, you held very high self-esteem. Did you feel the same as an adolescent? Explain the reasons for your answer.

Erik Erikson believed that adolescents often become confused and show some attrition in their self-esteem in the onset of adolescence when they are just beginning to search for identity. Decline in adolescents' self-esteem is particularly noticed for some domains (e.g. academics, sporting competence) early in adolescence, probably due to the realization of their lack of competency in certain domains (Shaffer & Kipp, 2010, p. 489).

Trzesniewski et al. have affirmed that the temporal stability of self-esteem is lowest in childhood and early adolescence and becomes much stronger later in adolescence and early adulthood. Children's varying experiences during their transition to adolescence accounts for this instability in self-esteem across their pathway to adulthood through adolescence. Diminished self-esteem is likely to be observed in adolescents who are encountering multiple stressors and are struggling to cope with too many changes occurring at the same time (Shaffer & Kipp, 2010, p. 490).

Robins et al. have argued that adolescent girls tend to show lower self-esteem than adolescent boys, presumably due to reasons that they mature faster than boys do; are more likely than boys to be dissatisfied with their bodies and physical appearance during the adolescent years; are more concerned with maintaining others' approval; are bothered more by hassles with family members and peers than boys are (Shaffer & Kipp, 2010).

Trzesniewski et al. (2003), strongly claim that self-esteem does show some meaningful temporal stability during the adolescent years. Self-esteem of adolescents with a good sense of self-worth in their childhood is likely to persist or gradually rise with successful negotiation of the developmental challenges of young adulthood (Shaffer & Kipp, 2010, p. 490).

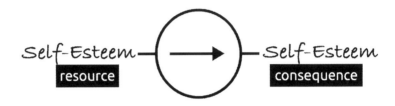

Donnellan et al. assert that a solid sense of self-esteem is a positive resource that facilitates productive achievement experiences and offers some protection against mental health problems, substance abuse and antisocial behaviour (p. 490). Research conducted in the Indian context suggests that socio-emotional problems such as loneliness, adjustment difficulties with parents and interpersonal conflicts may contribute to impaired feelings of self-esteem in adolescents. Individuals with low self-esteem were likely to feel rejected and disapproving of others. They may also lack self-confidence and social skills required for initiating and developing relationships, which are factors related to loneliness (Dhal et al., 2007).

High self-esteem for some children can have adverse effects on the child's behavioural outcomes. A longitudinal study by Medhavi Menon and colleagues found that aggressive preadolescents with high self-esteem came to increasingly value the rewards they gained by behaving aggressively and to increasingly belittle their victims – cognitions known to perpetuate or even intensify future aggression and antisocial conduct. High self-esteem derived from prosocial and adaptive life experiences are preferable for positive development as compared to self-esteem derived from antisocial or maladaptive conduct (Shaffer & Kipp, 2010, p. 491).

Adolescence is the critical period for the development of self-esteem and self-identity, and low self-esteem may endanger adolescent's emotional regulation. The level of self-esteem is reflected in the adolescent's attitude and behaviour, both at home and at school. Hence it is the responsibility of adults, especially parents and teachers, to encourage the formation of self-esteem in adolescents (Abdel-Khalek, 2016).

Self-efficacy

We have already seen in the earlier part of the chapter that self-efficacy beliefs play a key role in cognitive development and accomplishment of children. It is referred to as the individual's level of confidence to achieve a desired outcome. These beliefs are also related to the evaluation of self-concept elements.

Self-efficacy is grounded in the larger theoretical framework of social cognitive theory. The social cognitive theory proposed by Bandura marks human functioning as the product of a dynamic interplay of personal, behavioural and environmental influences. Academic performance of children or even their career choices can be determined by understanding the individual beliefs of his/her own capabilities and looking at the outcomes of their efforts (Tsang et al., 2012).

Self-efficacy is a very important construct of social cognitive theory, which highlights the four major psychological processes that encompass the concept.

Information used to assess self-efficacy is acquired from four primary sources: actual performances, vicarious experiences, forms of persuasion and physiological reactions (Schunk & Meece, 2005).

Evaluation of an individual's self-efficacy can be determined more by the individual's own performances than the effects of other sources. Gaining mastery in a specific task or being successful in a task boosts the individual's level of confidence in performing that task, thus increasing his/her self-efficacy.

Children learn by observing their parents, teachers or significant others who may have successfully performed certain tasks. They also look at their peers as role models who successfully perform certain tasks and make them believe that they too can learn it. These kind of experiences gained through social comparisons generates a strong sense of self-efficacy. But it is also found that self-efficacy gained through vicarious experiences can be nullified through subsequent failure in performance of those tasks.

Words of encouragement by parents, teachers and significant others can heighten the self-efficacy of the child, if s/he truly possesses the capabilities of doing that particular task. However, if s/he fails to perform that task successfully based on false expectations displayed by adults, self-efficacy beliefs of the child is susceptible to risks.

Self-efficacy information can also be acquired through physiological indicators or affective processes. Mental readiness of the individual to perform a task, fatigue factor, indecisiveness to continue or discontinue a task – such states of the individual influence the ways in which the individual reacts to a situation. Learners who experience fewer emotional symptoms may feel more self-efficacious.

Children's beliefs about the anticipated consequences of their actions or the value they place on certain activities or tasks directs them to engage in those activities, resulting in favourable outcomes.

Adolescents encounter varied experiences in the social contexts of family, school and peer environments. These experiences strongly influence the adolescents' beliefs about their capabilities of succeeding in and out of school (Schunk & Meece, 2005).

Families are the primary source of children's efficacy. Differences are observed in the capital resources of families in terms of financial resources, human resources with respect to educational background and social resources with respect of social networks and connections. Families can augment children's self-efficacy by providing them with rich experiences, motivating them to take challenges and achieve, teaching them strategies to cope with difficult situations and modelling the desirable behaviour (Schunk & Meece, 2005).

Adolescents' experiences at school have a great impact on their self-efficacy. Instruction methods, ease or difficulty of learning, assessment methods, student-teacher relationships, feedback from stakeholders, competitive conditions, transitions to different levels – all these elements can either raise or lower the self-efficacy of the adolescents depending on the kind of experience. Peer influences are very strong in adolescence. They tend to imitate their peer's behaviours to prove themselves and show their capability without even being familiar with the kind of tasks their peers perform.

Conclusion

The life-span perspective on identity presented in this chapter draws widely from diverse disciplines of social and personality psychology, cognitive – developmental studies, motivational psychology, life-span psychology, humanistic psychology and the narrative study of lives.

We have also attempted to provide a view of identity as an inherently reflexive, internalized patterning of psychological individuality. Through different theories, we have attempted to look at the development of identity from different perspectives such as the psychoanalytical, cognitive, social cognitive, situated cognition and psychosocial perspectives. To depict the essential subjectivity of human selfhood, psychologists and other social scientists have used terms such as 'self-esteem', 'self-concept', and 'self-efficacy', which have been discussed.

We have also seen gender differences and the role of social media in the formation of identity. However, these sections have been brought in with the aim of creating discernment so that necessary interventions can be thoughtfully implemented by adolescents and other stakeholders. With a growing number of children with special educational needs and the effect of the complex interplay of challenges to their learning, concepts such as identity, self-concept, self-esteem and self-efficacy needs to be reimagined. We hope that these discourses would help provide the necessary knowledge base to initiate action and focus attention on how to do so.

This chapter comes with a deep conviction that "Many individuals die before they have been born"; Erich Fromm (1942). This resounds the urgency for looking at education as a part of socialization, where culture plays a prominent role in identity formation. We look at culture as a crucial and critical context in the development of identity from the perspective of movements that the individual needs to make from 'Identity with' to 'Identity in'. The following chapter will discuss in detail the different contexts of adolescents and the interplay of these contexts in influencing their growth and development.

It is our hope that in the life long quest, individuals are able to broaden their consciousness to encompass a wide range of life goals and eventually narrow consciousness so as to focus on and commit to those goals most worth pursuing. When it comes to identity, we need to remember that you can be many things, but you cannot be everything.

So, in our quest of seeking identity, which is often lost and regained, we hope as educators or adolescence alike that we will be seekers of this truest, strongest, deepest self. Reviewing the list of choices that society throws before us, we need to carefully work on the self, to evolve that *unique self* by identifying 'with others' and 'in others'. In this quest of defining oneself, we will also accept our failure – our real failures, its triumphs, real triumphs, carrying shame and gladness with them.

Key terms: identity, adolescence, development, identity development, role confusion, identity status, gender, social media, culture, psychosocial development, cognition, cognitive development, socio-cultural development, situated learning, moral development, self-concept, self-esteem, self-efficacy,

---

Bibliography

Abbassi, N. (2016). Adolescent identity formation and the school environment. In *The Translational design of schools: An evidence-based approach to aligning pedagogy and learning environments* (Vol. 1, pp. 83–103).

Abdel-Khalek, A. M. (2016). Introduction to the psychology of self-esteem. In F. Holloway (Ed.), *Self-esteem perspectives, influences and improvement strategies*. New York, NY: Nova Publishers.

Albert, D., Chein, J., & Steinberg, L. (2013). The teenage brain: Peer influences on adolescent decision making. *Current Directions in Psychological Science, 22*(2), 114–120. doi:10.1177/0963721412471347.

Allman, B. (2018). Socioculturalism. In R. Kimmons (Ed.), *The Students' guide to learning design and research*. EdTech Books. Retrieved from https://edtechbooks.org/studentguide/socioculturalism

Anderson, K. (2008). *Who am I? The experience of subjective identity*. Doctoral theses, Swinburne University of Technology. Retrieved from https://researchbank.swinburne.edu.au/file/f90ce168-b90d-4e05-917c-3631e355cc72/1/Kathryn%20Anderson%20Thesis.pdf

Bandura, A. (2005). Adolescent development from an agentic perspective. In *Self-efficacy beliefs of adolescents* (pp. 1–43). Information Age Publishing.

Besar, P. H. (2018). Situated learning theory: The key to effective classroom teaching? *International Journal for Educational, Social, Political & Cultural Studies, 1*(1), 49-60.

Bjorklund, D. F., & Causey, K. B. (2018). *Children's thinking cognitive development and individual differences*. Thousand Oaks, CA: SAGE Publications. Retrieved from https://ebin.pub/childrens-thinking-cognitive-development-and-individual-differences-6nbsped-9781506334356.html

Buckingham, D. (2008). "Introducing identity." Youth, identity, and digital media. In D. Buckingham, D. John, & T. Catherine (Eds.), *MacArthur Foundation Series on digital media and learning* (pp. 1–24). Cambridge, MA: The MIT Press. doi:10.1162/dmal.9780262524834.001

Dhal, A., Bhatia, S., Sharma, V., & Gupta, P. (2007). Adolescent self-esteem, attachment and loneliness. *Journal of Indian Association for Child and Adolescent Mental Health, 3*(3), 61–63.

Golubović, Z. (2011). An anthropological conceptualisation of identity. *Synthesis Philosophica, 26*(1), 25–43.

Graf, S. C. (2003). *Cross-cultural study of adolescent identity formation and autonomy within the context of parent-adolescent relationships*. Doctoral thesis, Florida State University, FL. Retrieved from http://purl.flvc.org/fsu/fd/FSU_migr_etd-4076

Hammack, P. L. (2015) Theoretical foundations of identity. In K. C. McLean & M. Syed (Eds.), *The Oxford handbook of identity development*.

Hansen, B., Bretl, B. L., & Amini, B. (2019). *Adolescent development in context: Social, psychological, and neurological foundations*. University of Kansas Libraries. Retrieved from http://hdl.handle.net/1808/27707

Hill, P. L., & Lapsley, D. K. Egocentricism. In E. Anderman & L. Anderman (Eds.), *Psychology of classroom learning: An encyclopedia*. University of Notre Dame Jones, T. Cognitive Development in Adolescence. Retrieved from https://courses.lumenlearning.com/wmopen-lifespandevelopment/chapter/cognitive-development-in-adolescence/

Hoose. (n.d.). *Moral reasoning in adolescence*. Retrieved from https://courses.lumenlearning.com/adolescent/chapter/moral-reasoning-in-adolescence/

Kalyan-Masih, V. (1973). Cognitive egocentricity of the child within Piagetian developmental theory. *Transactions of the Nebraska Academy of Sciences and Affiliated Societies, 2*. Retrieved from https://digitalcommons.unl.edu/cgi/viewcontent.cgi?article=1382&context=tnas

Kuther, T. L. (2018). Cognitive change: Information processing approach. In T. L. Kuther (Ed.), *Lifespan development in context: A topical approach*. Thousand Oaks, CA: SAGE Publications.

Laible, D. J., Carlo, G., & Roesch, S. C. (2004). Pathways to self-esteem in late adolescence: The role of parent and peer attachment, empathy, and social behaviors. *Journal of Adolescence, 27*(6), 703–716.

Lally, M., & Valentine, S. (2019). *Lifespan development: A psychological perspective* (2nd ed.). Grayslake, IL: College of Lake County. Retrieved from http://dept.clcillinois.edu/psy/LifespanDevelopment.pdf

Levine, L. E., & Munsch, J. (2016) *Child development from infancy to adolescence: An active learning approach*. Thousand Oaks, CA: SAGE.

Locke, D. C., & Ciechalski, J. C.(1995). Basic theoretical models applicable to teaching. In *Psychological Techniques for Teachers* (2nd ed.). Taylor and Francis Modification of Kohlberg's Stages of Moral Development. Retrieved from www.boundless.com/psychology/textbooks/boundless-psychology-textbook/human-development-14/theories-of-human-development-70/kohlberg-s-stages-of-moral-development-268–12803/

McAdams, D. P., & Cox, K. S. (2010). Self and identity across the life span. In M. E. Lamb, A. M. Freund, & R. M. Lerner (Eds.), *The handbook of life-span development, Vol. 2. Social and emotional development* (pp. 158–207). Hoboken, NJ: John Wiley & Sons, Inc.

McElhaney, K. B., Allen, J. P., Stephenson, J. C., & Hare, A. L. (2009). Attachment and autonomy during adolescence. In R. M. Lerner & L. Steinberg (Eds.), *Handbook of adolescent psychology: Individual bases of adolescent development* (pp. 358–403). Hoboken, NJ: John Wiley & Sons. https://doi.org/10.1002/9780470479193.adlpsy001012

McLean, K. C., & Pasupathi, M. (2012). Processes of identity development: Where I am and how I got there. *Identity, 12*(1), 8–28. doi:10.1080/15283488.2011.632363

McLeod, S. A. (2018). Erik Erikson's stages of psychosocial development. *Simply Psychology*. Retrieved from www.simplypsychology.org/Erik-Erikson.html

Myin, E., & Zahnoun, F. (2018). Reincarnating the identity theory. *Frontiers in Psychology, 9*, 2044. doi:10.3389/fpsyg.2018.02044

Niedzielski, J. J. (2005). *Psychosocial theories of development: Socializing future educators in modernity*. Master's theses, Western Michigan University. Retrieved from https://scholarworks.wmich.edu/masters_theses/3331

Park, H. (2015). Learning identity: A sociocultural perspective. *Adult Education Research Conference*. Retrieved from https://newprairiepress.org/aerc/2015/papers/41 (Part II: Educational Psychology. Retrieved from https://courses.lumenlearning.com/teachereducationx92x1/chapter/piagets-theory-of-cognitive-development/)

Rao, M. A., Berry, R., Gonsalves, A., Hastak, Y., Shah, M., & Roeser, R. W. (2013). Globalization and the identity remix among urban adolescents in India. *Journal of Research on Adolescence, 23*(1), 9–24. doi:10.1111/jora.12002

Rodriguez, S. N., & Loos-Sant'Ana, H. (2015). Self-concept, self-esteem and self-efficacy: The role of self-beliefs in the coping process of socially vulnerable adolescents. *Journal of Latino/Latin American Studies, 7*(1), 33–44. doi:10.18085/1549-9502-7.1.33.

Rowe, I. S. (1980). *Ego identity status, formal operations and moral development.* Master's these, Simon Fraser University. Retrieved from https://core.ac.uk/download/pdf/56368126.pdf

Sandhu, D., Singh, B., Tung, S., & Kundra, N. (2012). Adolescent identity formation, psychological well-being, and parental attitudes. *Pakistan Journal of Psychological Research, 27*(1), 89–105.

Schunk, D. H., & Meece, J. L. (2005). Self-efficacy development in adolescences. In *Self-efficacy beliefs of adolescents* (pp. 71–96). Information Age Publishing.

Seifert, K., & Sutton, R. (2009). *Educational psychology* (2nd ed.). Winnipeg: University of Manitoba. Retrieved from https://home.cc.umanitoba.ca/~seifert/EdPsy2009.pdf

Shaffer, D. R., & Kipp, K. (2010). Cognitive development: Piaget's theory and Vygotsky's sociocultural viewpoint. In D.R. Shaffer & K. Kipp (Eds.), *Developmental psychology childhood and adolescence* (8th ed., pp. 281–290). Belmont, CA: Wadsworth Publishing.

Shapiro, L. A., & Margolin, G. (2014). Growing up wired: Social networking sites and adolescent psychosocial development. *Clinical Child and Family Psychology Review, 17*(10), 1–18. doi:10.1007/s10567-013-0135-1.

Siegler, R. (2020). Cognitive development in childhood. In R. Biswas-Diener & E. Diener (Eds.), *Noba textbook series: Psychology*. Champaign, IL: DEF Publishers. Retrieved from http://noba.to/8uv4fn9h

Smith, A. (1981). Piaget's model of child development: Implications for educators. *The Clearing House, 55*(1), 24–27.

Smith, A. R., Chein, J., & Steinberg, L. (2013). Impact of socio-emotional context, brain development, and pubertal maturation on adolescent risk-taking. *Hormones and Behavior, 64*(2), 323–332. doi:10.1016/j.yhbeh.2013.03.006.

Sokol, J. T. (2009). Identity development throughout the lifetime: An examination of Eriksonian theory. *Graduate Journal of Counseling Psychology, 1*(2), Article 14. Retrieved from http://epublications.marquette.edu/gjcp/vol1/iss2/14

Stangor, C., & Walinga, J. (2014). *Introduction to psychology – 1st Canadian edition.* Victoria, BC: BC Campus. Retrieved from https://opentextbc.ca/introductiontopsychology/

Stroud, R. (2011). Moratorium and work in adolescence. *Didache: Faithful Teaching, 10*(2). Retrieved from http://didache.nazarene.org/index.php/volume-10-2/823-didache-v10n2-09-moratorium-and-work-adolescence-stroud/file

The self is multilayered: Freud. Retrieved from https://revelpreview.pearson.com/epubs/pearson_chaffee/OPS/xhtml/ch03_sec_08.xhtml

Tsang, S. K. M., Hui, E. K. P., & Law, B. C. M. (2012). Self-efficacy as a positive youth development construct: A conceptual review. *The Scientific World Journal, 2012*, Article 452327. doi:10.1100/2012/452327

Watson, A. (2014). Who am I? The self/subject according to psychoanalytic theory. *SAGE Open, 4*(3).

Yeh, L. (2011). *Moral reasoning and ego identity status in academically gifted adolescents.* Doctoral theses, University of New South Wales. Retrieved from http://unsworks.unsw.edu.au/fapi/datastream/unsworks:10345/SOURCE02?view=true

Zana, B. H., Pakstan, M., & Karwan, K. (2019). Piaget's cognitive developmental theory: Critical review. *Education Quarterly Reviews, 2*(3), 517–524.

Zhou, M., & Brown, D. (2015). *Educational learning theories* (2nd ed.). Education Open Textbooks. Retrieved from https://oer.galileo.usg.edu/education-textbooks

3
SOCIAL CONTEXTS IN ADOLESCENCE

CHAPTER 3: Social Contexts in Adolescence

Overview

After reading this chapter, you will be able to achieve the following objectives

- Acknowledge the multiple dimensions of change involving the adolescents and their immediate and broader social contexts using Uri Bronfenbrenner's bioecological systems theory

- Apply the perspective of social cognitive theory to address the determinants and mechanisms of adolescents' personal agency operating within a broad network of sociostructural influences

- Take cognizance of the different theoretical perspectives to the socialization of adolescents

- Recognize and appreciate the role and importance of the four key contexts of adolescents' life- family, school, peer and media vis-à-vis a layered structure of society and its influences on adolescents

- Appraise the implications of the contextual influences and its impact on adolescent outcomes across various cultural settings, specific to India and around the globe

Social contexts in adolescence

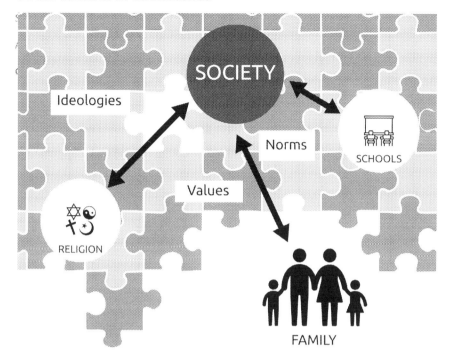

FIGURE 3.1 Social Contexts in Adolescence

Determinants of choice of trajectories in adolescence (self, agency and social milieu)

Every stage of life has its typical challenges and requirements for successful functioning. Changing aspirations, time perspectives and societal systems over the course of the life span alter how people structure, regulate and evaluate their lives (Bandura, 2006). As individuals navigate through the different stages of life there are different trajectories that each one of them chooses. There are no preordained steps to a psychosocial development sequence. The one belief that all development psychologists would agree with is that development happens in a social milieu or a context in which the individual is immersed. Another perspective is that beliefs that an individual holds related to their capabilities to produce results by their actions are an influential personal resource in negotiating their lives through the life cycle. These beliefs are nothing but beliefs of self that we have seen in the previous chapter.

Social cognitive theory analyzes developmental changes across the life span in terms of evolvement and exercise of human agency. When we view development through this perspective, the paths that lives take are shaped by the reciprocal interplay between personal factors and diverse influences in ever-changing

96 Social contexts in adolescence

societies. There is much that people do wilfully to exercise some control over their self-development and life circumstances. We also see that there is a lot of literature to support the fact that there is a lot of fortuity in the courses that lives take (Bandura, 2006). People often enter into new life trajectories through fortuitous circumstances. To operationalize the term, fortuity does not mean uncontrollability of its effects. In our discussion of the term in this chapter we mean the ways that people capitalize on the fortuitous character of life. They make chance happen by pursuing an active life. It is assumed that the more active life one leads, it increases the fortuitous encounters that individuals will experience. It also has another feature. It includes the individuals capacity to make chance work for them by cultivating their interests, enabling beliefs and competencies. These capacities are the personal resources of people. These personal resources enable them to make the most of opportunities that arise unexpectedly. Therefore, the environment in which people live their lives should not be considered as a situational entity that ordains their life course. Viewing adolescence though this perspective, we see that there are three different concepts that are crucial for understanding development through the social cognitive perspective, namely social milieu, beliefs of self and human agency.

In this chapter, we will deal with each of these three concepts. We have briefly seen the importance of society in the defining and development of adolescents. The various terms associated with the understanding and development of self for an adolescent has been dealt with in Chapter 2. We will now look at the rather complex, yet interesting relationship between the three constructs of social milieu, beliefs of self and human agency.

Let us look at an example to understand the fortuitous character of an adolescent's life.

Context of the Situation
Two friends - Sehul and Vihaan have completed their tenth grade and awaiting their results. Sehul has been an average student all his years of schooling and Vihaan has always been a bright student. Both of them aspire to become doctors. Their teacher has different expectation from each of them. She encourages Vihaan to pursue his aspirations of becoming a doctor, while she discourages Sehul to aspire to become a doctor. She advices him to choose any other professional of his capability.

The Day of Results
The day of tenth result declaration has arrived. The grade cards will be distributed to students at 3.30 PM.

Let us have a peep into the conversation between Sehul and Vihaan that depicts their character and their dreams and aspirations.

Social contexts in adolescence **97**

The day of result declaration – 10 AM Sehul is standing and daydreaming.

FIGURE 3.2 Adolescent Daydreaming

It is 2PM in the afternoon. Both the friends are going to school to receive their report cards. They are talking to each other on their way to school.

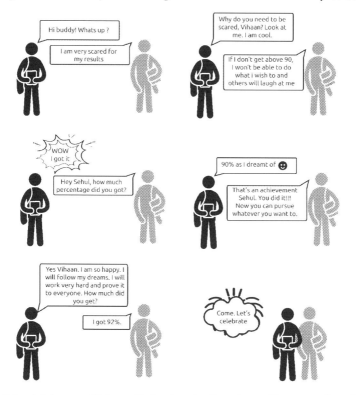

FIGURE 3.3 Adolescent Dialogue Indicating the Fortuitous Character of an Adolescent's Life

Attempting to capture the concept of human agency

The present chapter views adolescent agency from a psychological and a sociological perspective. This section addresses adolescent development from an agentic perspective. In this conception, people are self-organizing, proactive, self-regulating, and self-reflecting. They are contributors to their life circumstances, not just products of them. To be an agent is to influence intentionally one's behaviour and life circumstances. There are four core features of human agency that we will briefly discuss. The first feature is *intentionality*. People form intentions for their own lives. By 'intentions' we mean action plans and strategies for realizing their goals. The second feature involves *forethought*. It is the capacity of the individual to be able to be forward looking. This includes more than future-directed plans. It is beyond visualizing a future for themselves. It involves moving from intentionality to setting goals to anticipate likely outcomes of their prospective actions to guide and motivate their efforts anticipatorily. Agents are not only planners and forethinkers; they are also self-regulators. They adopt certain standards for themselves. They monitor and regulate their own actions in the direction that leads them to their goals. They engage in activities that give them satisfaction and a sense of self-worth and refrain from embracing actions that bring self-censure. All these abilities help them to be motivators to themselves. This is the third feature, which is termed as *self-reactiveness*. Thus, a person who exercises agency will be in control and will be an agent of their own action. This includes a variety of skills such as the ability to be reflective about their own actions, thoughts and pursuits. Based on self-awareness and reflection, they are willing and make necessary adjustments in goals or behaviour or even processes and trajectories used to reach their goals. This brings us to the fourth feature, which is *self-reflectiveness*, leading to self-influence, which is an important part of the causal structure.

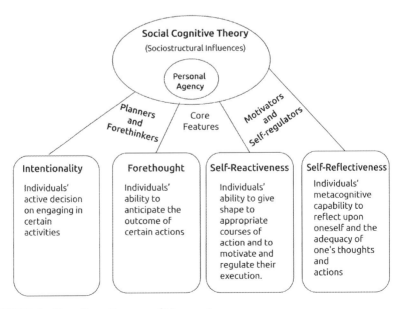

FIGURE 3.4 Four Core Features of Human Agency

Thus far, we have seen agency as crystallized in the psychological literature. This is delineated towards focusing more on the individual with a sense of personal agency demonstrating many capacities, assuming agency as a motivational drive or an inborn psychological trait. Though agency can be thought of as a "universal capacity", it is treated as a "variable" that individuals differentially possess as reflected in sociological works (Hitlin & Johnson, 2015).

In addition to the mental processes underlying human agency, there is a need to pay attention to the environmental factors over which the individual has to act upon. The psychological perspectives emphasize more of the individual's perception of and response to that environment rather than the environment by itself.

Sociological literature on the other hand attempts to focus on environment and society as the causal agent in individual's life. This perspective leads us to look at how the dynamic network of the nested social institutions influence individual's life by reinforcing the social norms. Mayer highlights societal forces such as institutionally defined careers or role sequences, historical conditions and policies that govern individuals' entry into and exit from social roles and statuses (Crockett, 2002).

In its broadest sense, agency refers to "something that causes something else". Thus, agency not only resides within the individual but also lies in social forces and institutions. Bandura believes that agency may be expressed collectively by groups of individuals working together for a common cause. Examples of collective agency in adolescents' life course can include influence of family contexts, school and peer influences, and political influences. Additionally, the agency of individuals or groups may be extended by the use of tools and technology (Crockett, 2002). Thus, human agency can be considered within a wide range of individual and group efforts and involve larger collectives such as the environment and societies. It is thus essential to view the individual as a developing agent embedded in a dynamic social environment within a changing sociohistorical context.

Social contexts often afford not only opportunities and resources for action but also obstacles and constraints. The individual-environment interaction results in a particular biography, which explicates how an individual changes and develops over time rather than how a developing individual shapes a clear-cut well-defined path through a particular social context (Crockett, 2002).

Hitlin and Long assert that agency involves both actual capacities/resources and individuals' perceptions of those capacities/resources. Clausen makes a mention of variations existing in individual's capacities. Structural advantages and psychological development facilitate more agentic options (Hitlin & Johnson, 2015).

Let us try to understand the varying nature of 'agency' which is represented as a continuum, moving from 'severe constraints' towards the 'totally devoid of constraints' situation.

Age-related configuration of social roles and norms also creates normative transition points when major role changes occur, and the person moves into a new social status or life phase. Examples include adolescent's transition from middle school to high school, or from schooling to entering the workforce, schooling to marriage or parenthood, etc. Within the different contexts of family, school, peers, etc., adolescents move through a sequence of linked states that form the trajectory of development. Each status and context comes with both opportunities for action as well as constraints or barriers, leading to diversity in agentic actions. Adolescents exercise their agency by making specific choices that relate to social roles, the timing of role transitions, structure of society, cultural norms, etc., and these choices shape adolescents' behaviour and actions, thus creating unique biographies (Crockett, 2002).

The diverse nature of society in the Indian context furnishes opportunities and constraints differently for different individuals who may belong to distinct social groups defined by gender, class, colour and caste, among others. Thus, adolescents with very low socio-economic status may have limited opportunities compared to those belonging to the urban middle class with higher socio-economic status. Adolescent girls may be at a lesser advantage than boys from the same society if they hail from rural and marginalized communities or if they lived in the 19th century or before. These kind of differential opportunities and roles available to adolescents result in varying degrees of agency.

Crockett and Silbereisen talk about dramatic changes in political, technological or economic systems as having the potential to alter developmental paths and social norms or expectations to which individuals are exposed and the social relationships and resources for coping. Adolescents' choices are impacted by cultural, economic and historical forces in addition to their personal dispositions, ideals and beliefs about what works for them. This gives a sense of agency as constructed by individuals through the choices and actions they take within the opportunities and constraints of history and social circumstances as Elder, suggests. Elder also refers to these choices as the building blocks of an individuals' evolving life course. When an individual feels strongly about one's ability to have a considerable degree of control over any situation, then the perceived influence of agency is likely to be high. However, if one's feeling of self is low in terms of having control over the situation, the individual may not be able to exercise the desired degree of agency. This make it very critical for all the environmental contexts in providing the appropriate and relevant opportunities for adolescents to be able to make the right choices and decisions and exercise a higher degree of agency (Crockett, 2002).

Structure and agency, hereby, cannot be treated as separate or isolated terms. Agency can be represented as a continuum, moving from "severe constraints" towards the "totally devoid of constraints" situation which is apparently unrealistic (Rudo, 1996). A dialectical relationship exists between structure and agency. While social structure shapes individuals, individuals (and groups) also shape social structure. Nonetheless, individuals have the ability or *the agency* to make decisions and express them in behaviour.

Situating adolescence in a social milieu: Bronfenbrenner's bioecological systems theory

The transition period of adolescents from childhood to adulthood is not simplistic, but is subject to the various changes that occur across settings in which the adolescents are situated. These changes can be visible across and within societies, communities, cultures and families.

We have seen various identity theories from the perspectives of psychosocial development, cognitive development, sociocultural development and moral development in the previous chapter. We also have understood that identity cannot develop in a vacuum; rather it is a complex multidimensional concept that is highly context-dependent.

Uri Bronfenbrenner's bioecological (1998) systems theory conceptualized the context in which the adolescent develops as a set of nested structures each embedded in the other. This theory poses that every individual in a society is layered in distinct patterns that can be individually observed. Supportive or disruptive factors specific to that environment can either enhance or disrupt the well-being of the individual over time. The theory identifies five layered systems and presents the lens through interaction between these layers to understand the coexistence of the individual within these layers and availing the resources in a particular context (Anagurthi, 2017). The five systems are the microsystem, mesosystem, exosystem, macrosystem and chronosystem. The microsystem is the immediate setting in which adolescents live, which comprises their family, school, peers, community, etc. The mesosystem consists of the relations microsystems have with one another; it is in the relationships where the contexts interact in adolescents' lives. The exosystem covers the more distal environments referring to connections between social settings in which the adolescent does not have an active role, but the adolescent is directly affected by the changes in the system. For example, parents' workplace, media, government, family friends, etc. The macrosystem includes the larger sociocultural context and comprises the culture, attitudes and ideologies of the culture in which the adolescents live. The chronosystem emphasises historical time and the changing and consistent characteristics over a period of time, both of the individual and the environment in which the individual resides.

102 Social contexts in adolescence

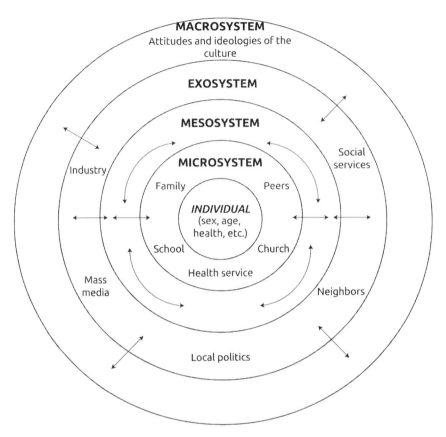

FIGURE 3.5 Bronfenbrenner's Ecological Theory of Development

Source: https://commons.wikimedia.org/wiki/File:Bronfenbrenner%27s_Ecological_Theory_of_Development_(English).jpg

Scan the QR code to view the video

Bronfenbrenner's ecological theory

This short video from Professor Rachelle Tannenbaum of Anne Arundel Community College explains and gives examples of Brofenbrenner's theory.

> **Activity:** Classify the given examples into the different system according to Bronfenbrenner's ecological theory. Give reasons for your answer and justify.

Sarah's mother loses her job and keeps complaining at home that she doesn't have money to spend on anything including Sarah's needs. Sarah's mother is too depressed about her condition. Sarah too is very sad and worried. Her life is very much affected	Veena is a Hindu Brahmin by birth. But her family, since two generations have been residing in a Jain society. Her beliefs and practices almost reflect Jainism. She follows all the religious rituals of Jains and moves along with her other Jain friends
Joseph's parents divorced when he was just 9 years old. After two years, his mother remarried and they shifted to a new city. This major transition provided new experiences for Joseph	Vishwa studies in the eighth grade. She has been having some trouble with her academics. She needs some extra attention. The parent-teacher meetings held regularly in her school enables her to deal with her troubles by ensuring that she gets the desired assistance at home and at school
In the period of lockdown due to Covid-19, many employees lost their jobs. Raheem's dad was one of them, who couldn't get his salary since the last three months. It affected both Raheem and their household	Jalal grows up in a very rich family. He is raised by his nanny and not by his parents. He gets whatever he wishes for. He is also able to pursue his career due to his family affluence. He is not a very well-raised child. He is too spoilt and doesn't know how to connect with other people
Angel is studying in th seventh grade. She has many friends in her class. But her parents dislike her friends and openly criticize them. They persuade her to not keep relations with her friends. Angel experiences very conflicting emotions and she is in a state of confusion	Natalie's family is very traditional and orthodox in nature. Females in her family are not supposed to work outside home. Their sole responsibility is to stay at home and take care of the children at home. Natalie's mother has enough time to spare for Natalie. Mothers of Natalie's friends are all employed and they have hardly any time to spend with their children. Natalie's development is a bit different form her other friends' development
Subrojit's parents did not share a good relationship with each other. His father used to drink a lot and abuse his mother very often. Some days, he never showed up at home. His mother used to be away for work to make their ends meet. She hardly spent any time with Subrojit. The violent behaviour by his father at home influenced him a lot. He used to hit others in his class for no reason, tease girls and harass them and dealt in all undesirable behaviours outside home	Wilson had to relocate to another city during his high school days. He lived with his cousin, who stayed close by to school. For the first time, he stayed away from home and family. He dated one of the girls in his neighbourhood. She belonged to a different religion. He desired to marry her in future. He feared that his family wouldn't accept her. He also did well in school. His parents wanted him to study undergraduate in the US. He left for his further studies to the US. His experiences are quite different as compared to his friends'

The relevance of this theory lies in its capacity to provide a theoretical and analytical framework to understand adolescents' development as a function of the individual, context and time. The theory highlights the agents of socialization that influence the identity formation of adolescents – family, peers, school and the media.

Adolescents' socialization in terms of four mechanisms: channelling, selection, adjustment and reflection

Socialization begins right in the cradle, without any conscious awareness. As the child grows, conscious efforts in terms of actions, behaviours, dressing, eating, talking and other habits, become crucial, considering the norms of the context in which the child grows. Social contexts include the family where they are born into, the schools where they go to learn, the teachers who teach them, friends both in and out of school, peers in their classroom, the neighbourhood where they live, the farther society, community and the widespread media. Socialization represents a set of social processes that influence the expression of agency.

Let us look at how this dynamic interaction between various contexts relates to the adolescents' development by using the four key mechanisms presented by Nurmi, J. (p. 86) in describing adolescents' socialization – Channelling, Selection, Adjustment and Reflection

104 Social contexts in adolescence

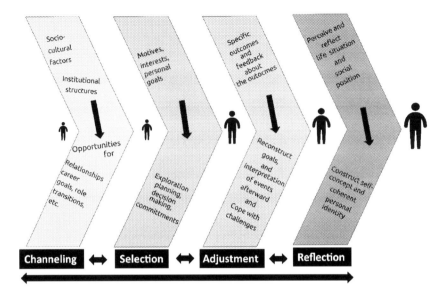

FIGURE 3.6 Channelling, Selection, Adjustment and Reflection as Mechanisms of Adolescents' Socialization

Channelling mechanisms in adolescents' socialization

Adolescents grow up in environments that consist of a variety of social expectations set by their parents, teachers and peers. We are aware how the parent and home play as a crucial determining factor in the formation of a child. In most of the discourses on the relationship between school and adolescents, we see that the school stands out for the impact that it makes on the adolescents' choice of trajectory that they choose with regard to careers and coping with social demands. They provide a variety of opportunities through the school curriculums, teachers, and classmates to participate as productive citizens of society. It has been suggested that these age systems are important for adolescent development because they create predictable, socially recognized road maps for human lives (Hagestad & Neugarten, 1985). One major feature of such environments is that they are closely related to a person's age. Parental expectations get woven with educational standards at school and opportunities for educational decisions, making the school a very potent agency of socialization. Another striking feature of the school is the opportunity provided to the adolescent to receive, give and mix with peers of the same age as well as receive opportunities which are age-related. Although these kinds of age-graded environments are in most part similar to adolescents of a particular age living in a certain society, they also differ along many factors, such as gender, social stratum, cultural background and family characteristics. Perhaps because psychologists interested in adolescence have been committed to individuals' thinking and behaviour, they have often overlooked the role of such environmental structures.

Selection mechanisms in adolescents' socialization

Adolescence is characterized by many challenges, demands and options (Caspi, 2002). Based on this assertion of the variety of challenges, demands and options, we also are aware of the fact that there are restricted individual resources, such as time and energy, that adolescents must focus on in dealing with some of the future challenges available for them. Selection process according to (Baltes & Baltes, 1990) has been described in previous literature in terms of a variety of psychological mechanisms such as goal construction, planning, exploration and commitment. School as a social institution actively engages and connects with the adolescent in these areas there by fostering adolescent identity. Family and peer contexts also influence adolescents' decisions in choice of careers and formation of identity. Media also plays its unique role in adolescents' decision-making and selection process. However, we need to be mindful that these connections and engagement may not always be experienced with positivity by the adolescent.

Adjustment mechanisms in adolescents' socialization

Family, schools, peers, media and other environmental influences play a significant role in the development of the selection process. We would all agree that in the course of the selection process, adolescents may attain the goals at which they were aiming, be it, long-range career goals or short-term objectives that they have set for themselves. In many situations, adolescents fail to reach their goals or do not succeed to the extent they expected. Young people may also face unexpected events in their lives that may alter some important aspects of their future lives. When adolescents face problems in goal attainment, adjustment to a new or previous goal, cognitions or behaviour is required. The kind of environment and ways in which they foster the adjustment process may sometimes even be a source of maladjustment and is described in the next section.

Reflection mechanisms in adolescents' socialization

The way individuals perceive and look at themselves and reflect on their own characteristics, behavioural outcomes and social positions contribute in the construction of self-concept and identity (Erikson, 1959; Harter, 1990). This self-concept and identity in turn forms an important criterion for determining adjustment and well-being of the individual. Three different conceptualizations that have been used to describe this self-reflection process are discussed below. These conceptualizations are identity, self-concept and narratives. To simplistically define the term 'identity', we can say that it is the way in which an adolescent perceives him/herself across time and space (Baumeister & Muraven, 1996; van Hoof, 1999). Narratives are ways individuals construct and tell stories about themselves as a way to create an identity (McAdams, 1999). This is because the main feature of human cognition is that its contents can be shared by language; telling stories is an important means to increase positive self-concept and high self-esteem. The concept of self was expanded in Chapter 2 to refer to a wide variety of mechanisms. The definition of self-concept for this section refers to the relatively stable schemata of oneself that are generalized to the extent that they refer to an individual's view of him/herself across different situations. Self-esteem is defined as the ways in which individuals evaluate themselves according to normative or self-related standards.

Having understood the dynamic interaction between various contexts as they relate to the adolescents' development, we cannot ignore the culture-specific influences on adolescent development.

Culture-specific influences on 'Adolescence'

Culture is the most significant system within which human development occurs. Culture can be highly varying, defining the ways in which one should act, behave or partake in a particular social context conforming to the norms of that context. The modern definition of culture is referring to culture as "inventing meanings" from symbols (e.g. language) and then behaving as though these meanings are the truth (Hansen et al., 2019) Human's biological structure, especially, the brain, enables both learning from and creating culture which is widely imparted through socializing. Our thoughts, emotions, behaviours and traditions are woven in the cultural realm.

Adolescence acquires special significance in the course of life span development. It serves as a conceptual continuity between childhood and adulthood. Socially and culturally, this translates into wide variations in what may be described as the stage of adolescence in the Indian context.

Recognizing the cultural variability in the construction of adolescence, adolescent development can be viewed within the broad characterization of societies as individualist and collectivist in their psychological orientations. For more collectivistic societies like ours, the self is defined relative to others; is concerned with belongingness, dependency, empathy, and reciprocity, and is focused on small, selective in-groups at the expense of out-groups (Kapadia, 2008).

Families do not exist in isolation, and family dynamics are often best interpreted in the context of their societal and cultural background. The dynamic nature of adolescent characteristics as a function of the complex and differential family structure, roles and relationships and the culture in which the families are embedded needs to be understood in a collective society like India, where relationships are based on interdependence.

Studies have shown that Indian adolescents were found to spend more time with families and feel positive in doing so most of the time. There seemed to be hardly any sign of conflict between the adolescents and their parents, and even when they disagreed on issues, it was more towards a compromise as a result of the belief that parents had the best interests for their children. Indian adolescents are generally inclined towards family ethos, are more likely to subordinate individual needs to family needs and restrain their decisions to those made by the family in order to maintain harmonious relationships and family values. This again depends on the context and is likely to change with times.

Parent-child relationships develop within the context of routine family activities (Kuther, 2018). The daily routines and rituals of family fosters a sense of identity, self-esteem, family cohesion in adolescent children. Indian family routines usually include common meal times, frequent family gatherings, frequent interactions with members of family, helping each other in difficult times, festive gatherings, traditionally performed rituals and other moments specific to a culture or region. The practice of these routines provides adolescents opportunities for positive development by creating a sense of identity, promoting socio-emotional development, improving their social skills and elevating other aspects of their development.

Socialization of adolescence: theoretical perspectives

The role of culture in socialization of adolescents and their functioning has been discussed in two major developmental theories in the previous sections.

Ecological theory (Bronfenbrenner & Morris, 2006) emphasizes culture as a context or as a part of the socio-ecological environment and posits that cultural beliefs, values and practices reflected in social norms and perceptions shape the quality and characteristics of social interactions and relationships. Recapitulating the conceptualization of Bronfenbrenner's (1979) ecological theory, culture forms the outermost layer of the macrosystem that successively impacts the child through a series of transitional systems and microsystems.

Vygotsky's (1978) sociocultural theory also proposed that different cultures and societies play varied roles in the socialization practices of children, thus impacting their development. The theory also attributes culture to the channelling of competencies such as language and concepts, drawing our attention to the internalization of cultural systems that comes about from the interpersonal to the intrapersonal levels. Coinciding with the tenets of this theory, results of cross-cultural debates reveal possibilities of variations in the cognitive processes of individuals in societies arising out of the changes in sociocultural structures and related practices. Peer interactions too are very much shaped by the cultural values and norms within the context or culture in which they occur.

108 Social contexts in adolescence

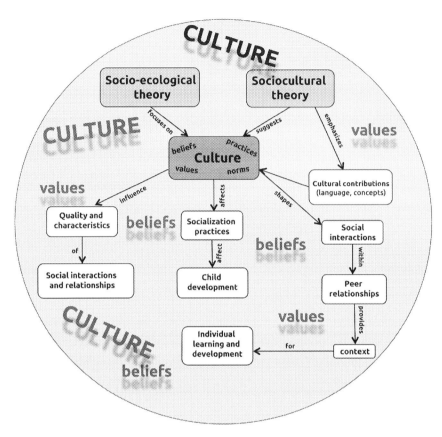

FIGURE 3.7 Socio-ecological and Sociocultural Framework of Socialization Processes

Chen and colleagues (e.g. Chen, 2012; Chen & French, 2008) proposed a contextual – developmental perspective, based on socio-ecological and sociocultural theories, focusing on the role of social interactions mediating between cultural values and children's socio-emotional functioning. According to this perspective, different societies place different values on children's specific behaviours – behaviours that can be characterized largely by the fundamental dimensions of social initiative (the tendency to initiate and maintain social interactions, often indicated by children's reactions to challenging situations) and self-control (the regulatory ability to modulate behavioural and emotional reactivity). This developmental perspective asserts that social interactions, particularly the evaluation and regulation processes, are important mediators of the links between cultural values and individual development (Chen, 2012). Peers and adults may perceive and evaluate children's behaviours according to cultural norms and values in the society and express corresponding acceptance or rejection of the behaviour of the social behaviours in social interactions. Social evaluations and responses, in turn, may regulate children's behaviours and their developmental patterns. Therefore, children actively engage in social interactions through displaying their reactions to social influence and through participating in constructing cultural norms for social evaluations and other peer-group activities (Corsaro & Nelson, 2003). Thus, the social processes are bidirectional and transactional in nature.

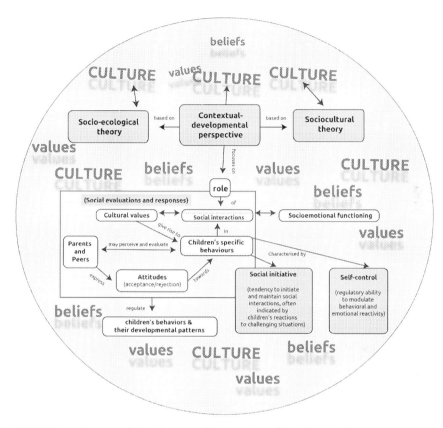

FIGURE 3.8 Contextual-developmental Perspective of Socialization Processes

Developing on this framework we see that the individual-culture interface contributes to the development of self and the identity of the individual. Within the cultural space of any individual lies the social interaction that makes and develops the self of the individual.

Framework of self and identity for understanding adolescence

McAdams and Cox in their article 'Self and Identity Across the Life Span' have presented a view of people's internalized life stories that are layered over their characteristic goals and values, which are, in turn, layered over their core dispositional traits. Later, in this chapter we attempt to integrate disparate themes, findings and theories regarding the influence of peers and media on self and identity in terms of three broad metaphors: the self as actor, agent and author. These three metaphors specify three fundamentally different and progressively more complex standpoints from which the human self can be seen to operate (McAdams & Cox, 2010).

As seen in the various development theories in the previous chapter, whatever the perspective to development we adopt, all would agree that we begin life as social actors, even before a self emerges. The self's first and most fundamental role is that of a social actor. Human beings begin their journeys in the social world in their families and then move on to interact in other social institutions. Tracing human civilization too, we see that humankind evolved to live in small groups, competing and cooperating, seeking to get along and get ahead in the environment of evolutionary adaptedness (Buss, 2008; Hogan, 1982). As one socializes, we see that being actors is a skill that we need to survive in any social group starting from the family. Therefore, we are fundamentally oriented towards social performance. This extends in social institutions such as schools, religious organizations and so on. In these agents of socializations, we see that family, educational institutions, peers and mass media play a significant role. We know ourselves as social actors before we know anything else about who we are. Self-development begins in the early childhood years and continues through our entire life span, reflecting the elaboration and maturation of an actor-self who performs on a social stage. As we progress in life, we see that the role of a motivated social agent comes next. It is in this stage that humankind desires, plans, schemes and strives to achieve ends in the social world – an actor with a forward-looking purpose. Even infants are goal-directed in some sense. As we move from infancy to childhood and then adolescence, we become more resourceful in planning, self-conscious, and goal-oriented. Slowly by adolescence we become more self-agentic. Self-esteem begins to play a role. The agent self-assesses the mismatch between his/her desires, hopes and plans on one hand and his/her current beliefs at that point in time on the other hand. The greater the mismatch, the lower the self-esteem. The individual is then able to mobilize resources to move towards their desires and convert plans into pathways to reach their goals.

Eventually, the self becomes an author, too, seeking to tell a story – for its own and others' understanding and enlightenment – a story regarding how I came to be (the past) and where I may be going (the future). The author-self develops in the background for much of childhood and early adolescence, only to make a developmentally grand entrance in the emerging-adulthood years.

In a fundamental sense, we can say that the actor exists in the performative present; the agent extends the timeline forward, to look to, to plan towards a motivated future; and the author extends the timeline even more, backward and forward, bringing coherence to the reconstructed past and the imagined future by composing, and then living, a story of self (McAdams & Cox, 2010). In the adult years, all three guises of self – actor, agent and author – are fully operative.

Though we discussed these stages as progressive, we need to understand that first, they are not stage specific in the sense that as one stage is crossed, the previous one ceases to exist. Second, this journey is a lifelong process of development of self and identity. Third, it is based on the interaction of the individual with the environment or social milieu that they come from.

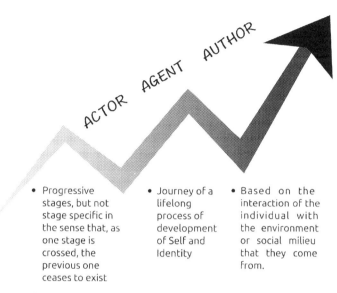

- Progressive stages, but not stage specific in the sense that, as one stage is crossed, the previous one ceases to exist
- Journey of a lifelong process of development of Self and Identity
- Based on the interaction of the individual with the environment or social milieu that they come from.

FIGURE 3.9 Self as Actor, Agent and Author and Its Features

We see the fully operative self of an individual where all the guises are operational. As an actor-self, the adult is able to identify and reflect on his or her action traits, aware of himself or herself as an actor who plays characteristic roles and expresses characteristic action patterns ("I am an extravert"; "I talk less when I see the person is intimidating" etc.). As an agent, they are able to reflect, mobilize and regulate their actions to reach long-term goals that they set for themselves. "I am doing all this so that one day I will own a house", "I am looking for a man who will love me and cherish me". As an author self, the young adult is able to say that my life's story is that of "Coming up from zero to something". "I My life has been a struggle but a joyful journey".

Thus far, we have tried to view adolescent development through the social cognitive perspective in alignment with the concepts of social milieu, beliefs of self and human agency.

Further, let us understand the development of adolescents through the lens of various social contexts in general and specific to the Indian context.

112 Social contexts in adolescence

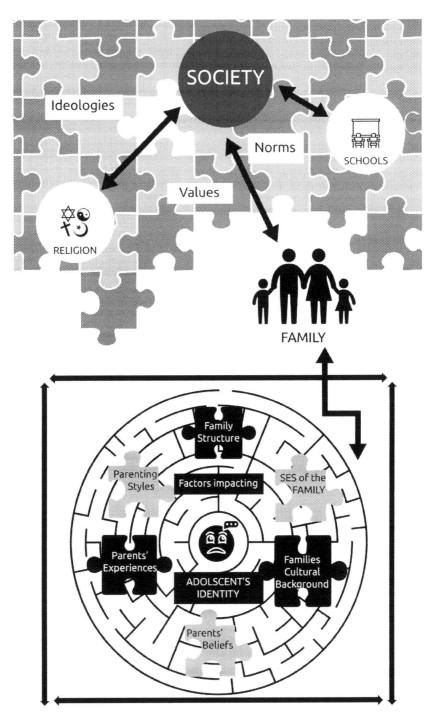

FIGURE 3.10 Family Factors Impacting Adolescents' Identity (Social Contexts in Adolescence)

Family context

Family context is most primarily the first point of socialization of the child. Family socialization fosters a collective identity in which the individual is viewed as important yet best understood in relation to close and significant others. Research on family relationships has focused predominantly on the parent-adolescent relationship (Steinberg & Morris, 2001).

Family structure

In families, where the hierarchy relations between the parent and adolescent is minimal, there is a possibility of reciprocal dependency and friendly relationships between the parent and adolescent. This results in more autonomy for the adolescent thus being responsible towards the family. This gained sense of responsibility enables the adolescents to acquire competence and mastery in performing tasks and become aware of the trust their parents show in them. Gender differences can be observed in terms of taking responsibilities. Girls are more likely to take on responsibilities as compared to boys. Also family structure may show varying results. Adolescents in single-parent, step-parent or poor families may end up being forced to take on more responsibilities due to undesirable reasons. This may not necessarily influence in positive ways as seen in the earlier case.

Adolescents born into families with lower socio-economic status where parents' household income may be low usually tend to take on more adult responsibilities compared to their advantaged peers. These children not being able to rely on their parents for economic or social capital start behaving like adults at a very early age and have adult-like interactions with their parents and other adults. Thus, the transition from childhood to adulthood may be devoid of adolescent characteristics as compared to the normal transition phase (Benson & Johnson, 2009).

Parental involvement

Parental involvement has been found to play a major role in the lives of their adolescent children to help them cope with stress and maintain physical and mental health. Parental involvement significantly impacts adolescent behaviour (Graf, 2003). A study that examined the association between parental involvement and mental well-being of India's nationally representative adolescent sample in 2007 suggested parental involvement as an important factor for positive mental health for both boys and girls. Parental involvement in this study included checking their children's homework, understanding their problems and worries and knowing what their children did with their free time.

To get an insight into the perceptions of parents and adolescents about parental involvement in adolescents' lives, we will look at a very recent study in 2020 that explores the dimension of parental involvement in the lives of their adolescent children in rural and urban areas of Udupi and Brahmavara taluks. Adolescents in the study stated that the amount of time they spent with their parents has decreased as they matured from childhood into adolescents due to more academic work and hence prevented them from engaging in activities centred on the family; parents perceived the same. In addition to this, parents perceived technology as a deterrent to parent-child communication. Adolescents perceived the family values instilled by parents as controlling them, resulting in a generation gap, thus inclining them to share their concerns with peers whom they thought were less judgmental. Yet, adolescents believed that their parents influenced them positively. Parents believed that establishing open routes of communication should begin at an earlier age of the child before they enter the stage of adolescence. Parental involvement in this study centred around two important themes of guiding the adolescent: towards their educational goals and towards instilling family values.

Indian family system

Considering the importance of academic achievement in Indian families and the stressful period of adolescents' transitioning from school to college to further their education and careers, family factors and family environment needs to be appropriately addressed in an adolescent's life.

Given the pluralistic nature of Indian society, generalizations about Indian families cannot be simplified. The patriarchal, collectivist nature of Indian families has as its oldest tradition a joint family system that has survived through ages and has influenced strongly the life of its members. The Indian joint family system constitutes at least three generations. including grandparents, parents, aunts, uncles, siblings, cousins and usually follows the traditional patriarchal system, where lines of hierarchy are clearly drawn within collective responsibility. This is undergoing transformation, replacing the joint family system by the nuclear family especially in urban India, wherein people prefer to stay with their own family for providing better educational and health facilities for their family members. At the same time, parents are working hard to fulfil the desires of their children and hardly giving quality time for their social development. These differing family structures have great implications for the growth and development of adolescents.

It is often assumed that the joint family helps in promoting and maintaining better psychosocial adjustment skill among the generations. It is also understood that in a nuclear family, the opinions and decisions of adolescents are given some consideration as compared to adolescents in a joint family. Experiences of support within joint families reduces stress and mental health problems as compared to nuclear families, but at the same time, dynamics of joint families cause mental strain. Joint and nuclear families give rise to distinct parental styles. Joint family's emphasis on cooperation for its survival leads to more authoritarian parental styles, whereas the individualism of the nuclear family is associated with democratic parenting styles (D'Cruz & Bharat, 2001).

Let us take a look at the different family structures vis-à-vis adolescents' adjustments in different Indian contexts.

A study conducted by Rehman and Singh (2015) conducted on family type and adjustment level of adolescents in Ghaziabad showed that adolescents of joint families were more adjusted, and reportedly girls were better adjusted than boys. This study highlights the role of grandparents and the quality time spent with them for better emotional and social adjustment of adolescents and fewer behavioural problems.

Another study by Kurup et al. (2016) on the effect of changes in the family system on the psychosocial adjustment of adolescent children in the southern part of Kerala in 2016 revealed slightly differing results from the previous study. The results indicated that more than half (57.7%) of the respondents from joint families showed a low level of psychosocial adjustment than that from the nuclear family, and a large percentage (77%) of children belonging to the nuclear family showed moderate level of adjustment with educational situations than that among the children from the joint family (22%). It was also observed that self-esteem of adolescents was generally high among the children of nuclear families, especially girls from nuclear families exhibiting a higher level of self-esteem than boys; whereas in joint families, children had a moderate level of self-esteem among males and low levels among girls as a result of the dependency and lack of decision-making skill. Parental care factor in the study was found to be at a moderate level among adolescents of the joint family in comparison with a high level in the nuclear family. Autonomy was more felt in adolescents from nuclear families as compared to joint families, and it emerged that parents and adolescents show better care and friendship in the nuclear family than that in the joint family. The relationships of adolescent with mother and father was observed to be almost the same in nuclear families and not in joint families. It was deduced that parents act in a closely rational way with their children in nuclear families while on the other hand, each member of the big joint family holds their own views and perceptions, and they try to exert it on the adolescents of the family, which creates adjustment problems among adolescents.

In the earlier part of this chapter, we had seen how parents from nuclear families hardly have quality time to spend with their children. However, this study revealed that the conversations, discussions, opinion making etc. were more frequent in nuclear family than the joint family environment. This strongly impacted the parent-adolescent relationship. Another significant finding from the study disclosed an increasing level of psychosocial adjustment of respondents from the joint family according with their educational level as against a sharp decrease in the nuclear family. Trouble with school and education was found to be considerably less among the children from joint families as compared to nuclear families. But at the same time it was found that a higher percentage of adolescents (72%) from nuclear families discuss their future aspirations with the parents (mother 70.24%, father 73.88%). The autonomy in decision-making of adolescents from nuclear families encourages them to develop romantic relationships, which is not very common with adolescents from joint families.

Further, a study carried out by Rani and Khajuria (2017) on the adjustment problems of adolescents of joint family and nuclear family in an urban locality of Karnal district of Haryana in 2017, showed no significant difference in the emotional, social or educational adjustment of adolescents of joint family and nuclear family. Similar to this study, a study conducted in the same year to investigate the impact of family on the adjustment of adolescents in Darbhanga town in Bihar showed concurrent findings.

A study conducted by Singh et al. (2017) on family structure and social and emotional maturity of adolescents in Pantnagar town in Uttarakhand revealed that adolescents from joint family were more personally, interpersonally and socially adequate and thus, socially mature than those from nuclear family and hence the adolescents from joint family were significantly higher on emotional stability, emotional progression, social adjustment, personality integration and independence component of emotional maturity.

Results of these studies in different contexts point out to conflicting and inconclusive results. This is quite indicative of disparity in the customs, traditions and ways of life prevailing over different regions and the uniqueness of the characteristics, customs and traditions of state or locality of a country like India.

Even with family patterns in transition, certain traditional norms and values operate dominantly, with roles of men as providers and women as homemakers, even if the women are employed. With the coexistence of traditional and modern values during the period of transition of family systems, inconsistency in parental handling leading to behavioural problems in adolescents are quite common. Mothers played both the role of providing love and authority, a contradiction that induces anxiety in the child. With limited members in a nuclear family, adolescents have fewer role models. This may reduce diffused identification, but also reduces the possibility of a variety of role models for the adolescents. Moreover, many other institutions have shouldered the shared responsibility of socialization of adolescents.

Alternate family forms in India

Families in India are also undergoing vast changes as a result of personal or socioeconomic conditions such as increasing migration patterns, socio-economic changes, work participation of women and adoption. This alternate family pattern has come into existence predominantly out of forced circumstances beyond control. A few of the different family variations observed in India today are singleparent families, dual earner families and adoptive families.

Single-parent families can be as a consequence of death of any one parent, divorce/ separation, migration for employment or unwed motherhood. Marital separation commonly involves major emotional distress for child relationships (Tijani & Ogunbanwo, 2009). Father absence is reported to have a negative impact on cognitive and intellectual functioning, resulting in poor school performance, especially among boys. Paternal deprivation is frequently found to be associated with juvenile delinquency, anxiety and low self-esteem. These concerns are partly rooted in the Freudian theory that emphasized the significant role of both mother and father in shaping the child's personality, and partly in theories that regarded the father to be the only appropriate sex-role model for sons and an important link between the family and society (Bharat, 2008).

Children from two-parent families tend to view their mothers as caring and affectionate more often than do children from fatherless homes. Children from divorced families tend to perceive their parents and themselves less favourably than do children from intact families. They also found that upon remarriage of the mother, children's perceptions of themselves and their absent fathers become negative (Colyard, 1986). At times a single parent may not be able to cope with double responsibilities due to lack of time and money, thus resulting in lesser attention to the needs and well-being of the child. Some findings indicate that adolescents from disrupted homes perceive their parents and themselves more positively than adolescents from intact homes, while other findings indicate the opposite. Researchers argue that the negative impact may not be due to the 'structural deficit' in the family, that is, absence of the father, but due to the associated impoverished conditions such as a decline in the income, poor living standard and lack of resources (Bharat, 2008).

Whether children in single-parent families are necessarily at psychological risk is yet a question to debate. Adolescents in single-parent families may be quite well adjusted. The risk may be just in our minds either because of our preconceived notions of a 'broken family' being ineffective in taking care of children (Bharat, 2008).

A study (Bhat & Patil, 2019) of single-parenthood families and their impact on children in India has documented the literature about family issues and found that disputes between parents as causing a negative impact on children's psychological well-being more than any other major disease. Typically belonging to a patriarchal society, fathers were seen to be tougher as compared to mothers, with whom children are able to share and get support. In terms of accommodating the expenses, children's education, lifestyle maintenance and meeting the emotional needs of children, single parents find it difficult as compared to intact families. Due to time constraints, a single parent is not able to devote an appropriate amount of time to nurture the child's development. Expressions of anger and conflict are often seen in children of dual parenting as compared to children with single parents, indicating that children of single parenting families are encouraged to be assertive and self-sufficient to make their own decisions. Comparatively, children of single-parenting families are not socially and emotionally expressive because they are quite likely to be turned down socially.

Today, with a rapid increase in consumerism and the rising cost of urban living as a result of industrialization and modernization, women have joined the work force in large numbers to meet the needs and requirement of their families. The cultural norms of India position the working women as supplemental earners rather than providers, due to which women are yet seen as homemakers and hence receive little or no help in their domestic roles despite having taken on the economic role.

This leads to more strain and stress on the part of the mother's role in parenting of the adolescent child. Employed mothers may be less effective parents if they are dissatisfied with their jobs, are not highly committed to being a parent or receive little support in their parenting role. This situation may result in children becoming more argumentative and difficult due to the impatient and restrictive nature of the mother who is employed. Mothers having stimulating jobs and who receive adequate social support from their husbands and other close associates are highly committed to being a parent and generally have favourable impressions of their children, rely less on power assertion to control their behaviour and are inclined to take an authoritative approach to child-rearing – precisely the parenting style so often associated with favourable cognitive, social and emotional outcomes (Deb & Walsh, 2010).

The study conducted by Deb and Walsh on adolescents in Kolkata, India, revealed that adolescents having working mothers showed more anxiety than that of adolescents having non-working mothers, which is in contrast to an extensive body of previous research conducted in developed countries revealing neither positive nor negative effects of maternal employment on children's development. Rather, it has been observed that children of employed mothers often experience favourable developmental outcomes and appear to be socially mature since their mothers are more inclined than unemployed mothers to grant their children independence and autonomy when their youngsters are ready for it. Adolescents of working mothers have not been found to be more delinquent or more academically handicapped than children of unemployed mothers. It was also suggested that daughters tend to benefit more than sons from their mother's employment, in terms of their academic and vocational achievements. In India, women's employment rates vary substantially across the country (Deb & Walsh, 2010).

Hence, to better understand the role of maternal employment or dual earner families in adolescent development in a developing country such as India, it is important to examine the interconnected family and contextual factors that influence adolescent development.

Parent-adolescent relationships

Parent-child relationships have always been seen as important social and emotional resources for childhood and beyond. Research suggests that parents serve as a key force that can either push youth towards or pull youth away from maturity and adult development (Benson & Johnson, 2009). Familial relationships have far-reaching implications for adolescents' relations with peers, teachers, and other adults; for romantic relationships; for school performance; and for eventual career choices and degree of success.

Drawing on principles from a diverse range of fields including psychoanalytic theory, developmental psychology, evolutionary biology and ethology, John Bowlby's attachment theory described attachment as a unique relationship between an infant and his caregiver that is the foundation for further healthy development. But the nature and function of the attachment system over the course of the life span, with a particular focus on adolescence has gained further attention.

With increased maturity, adolescents tend to be less likely to depend on their parents or caregivers as they attempt to manage their environments with minimal support from parents or their caregivers. This concept of autonomy development is integrally embedded within the theory regarding the nature and function of attachment relationships. There appears to be a continuous balance between dependence on family and exploring the environment. Ainsworth suggests that both the attachment system and the exploratory system cannot coexist. The more dominant exploratory system in adolescence corresponds to a decrease in dependence on attachment figures. Bowlby suggested that in adolescence it is the combination of autonomy – relatedness that is most linked to optimal outcomes in the parent-child relationship (McElhaney et al., 2009). Bi, X. et al. refers to autonomy as actions arising from the agency of self in contrast to forced behaviour. When parents or any attachment figures support adolescents emotionally and also encourage autonomy, the adolescents are able to focus on developing relationships, regulating their emotions and behaviour and developing the capacity to confidently approach tasks and situations by themselves and at the same time are also able to ask parents or any other attachment figure for help if needed. Adolescents who are both secure and autonomous behave like agents within their capacities while relying on others in times of need. This indicates that autonomy in adolescence is not totally synonymous with independence from parents or caregivers but reflects the nature of interpersonal context in which adolescent autonomy develops as influenced by the intra-individual traits of the autonomous adolescent (McElhaney et al., 2009.

The parent-adolescent relationship plays an important role in developing identity process (Pellerone et al., 2015). As it has been stated earlier, patterns of parent-child relationship undergo changes taking the form of conflicts within adolescents in construction of their identity. Such parent – adolescent conflicts may not be acceptable in collectivist cultures like India, where major emphasis is placed on interdependence. Thus, a parental-adolescent attachment needs to be understood as a function of the cultural perceptions and interpretations of adolescents' needs, including competence, autonomy and relatedness, which are the basic psychological needs of an individual (Sondhi, 2017).

Although this developmental process is considered normative and a significant part of adolescent development, the quality of the relationship between parents and adolescents plays a very important role in determining the type of adolescent autonomy development. Adolescents may feel lost and confused at times with their new-found independence, and they could depend on their parents to support them at these times. Close relationships with parents can help them overcome such moments of anxieties and enable them to develop a sense of autonomy. Children who had warm relationships with their parents during preadolescence are likely to remain close and connected with their parents during adolescence, even though the frequency and quantity of positive interactions may be somewhat diminished (Collins & Steinberg, 2006).

Adolescents employ their autonomy and begin to exercise their own agency in taking responsibilities for their successes and failures while evaluating choices for themselves. Early adolescents express a preference for spending time with peers over parents. Older ones are more likely to identify romantic partners for support. Healthy parent-adolescent relationships enable both parents and adolescents to recognize the need for adolescent autonomy and support them while maintaining the relationships.

> Context: Parent adolescent relationships can be either pleasant or unfriendly depending on the kind of interactions that exist between parents and their adolescent children. These interactions in the adolescent years may take the form of quarrels, disagreements and arguments that may prompt presence of conflicts

Think and Reflect

Cite from your own experiences, examples that feature parent-adolescent conflict.
Revisit Erikson's theory of psychosocial development and review adolescent's autonomy development vis-à-vis parent adolescent relationships/conflicts with respect to the questions raised below.
Record your opinions and comments with respect to the adolescent's conflicting stage, adolescent's gained autonomy, parent-child interactions and parenting practices.

- Are these conflicts considered as negative events or can they perceived from a positive standpoint?
- Conflicts provide means for expressing both concern and dissatisfaction. Explain.
    - Can these bring about opportunities for adolescents' development?
    - Can these hinder the adolescents' desire for autonomous exploration?
- How does the extent of conflicts differ as adolescents typically move from elementary school to middle or junior high school and then to senior high school?
- Does gender play a role in differential parent-adolescent conflicts? Give an example to supplement your response.
- Discuss the various possible strategies used for re-negotiation of parent-adolescent relationships in conflict resolution of adolescent. (Focus on the conflict resolution styles - negotiation, dominance and withdrawal, that adolescents usually use with their parents)

Extra Reading: Go to the link provided below to read through a study that sheds light on changes in conflict resolution styles in parent-adolescent relationships.

Developmental Changes in Conflict Resolution Styles in Parent-Adolescent Relationships: A Four-Wave Longitudinal Study https://link.springer.com/content/pdf/10.1007/s10964-010-9516-7.pdf

Parent-adolescent conflicts

Early and middle adolescence are marked by a considerably lesser number of parent-adolescent conflicts, but of higher intensity and according to Smetana these conflicts most of the times occur because of the adolescents' capacity to reason and question parental authority. The conflicts are over matters which are considered as morally or socially acceptable by parents as against adolescents who define it as a personal choice and justified, thus challenging their parents' authority (Collins & Steinberg, 2006).

Social contexts in adolescence **121**

Research findings convey that parent–adolescent conflicts during adolescence are equally normative and important as warm relationships with parents for healthy psychosocial development. Though there is not much consensus about the conflicts in relations leading to positive outcome, it is argued that it does facilitate parental detachment and independence or autonomy. On the other hand, it has been argued that detachment, especially early detachment, may have negative consequences for youth and can lead to more distress and greater susceptibility to peer pressure. It has been observed that divorced single-parent and step-parent families have higher levels of conflict and detachment between parents and children than two-parent, intact families and female adolescents who experience high conflicts with their parents are likely to self-identify as adults as compared to male adolescents (Benson & Johnson, 2009).

The very foundations of the functioning of a family as a social institution keep changing with social transformations. Various factors such as the parenting styles, parents' beliefs and experiences, family structure, socio-economic status of the family, cultural background and many more factors impact on the development of adolescents' identity.

FIGURE 3.11A Parent–Adolescent Interaction (Mother Understands Her Adolescent Child)

FIGURE 3.11B Parent–Adolescent Interaction (Adolescent Values Friends' Company than Family Gathering)

FIGURE 3.11C Parent–Adolescent Interaction (Father is Irritated with His Adolescent Child's Behaviour of Isolating from Family)

Parenting styles

For a long time, parenting has been typified in terms of global, consistent and stable parenting styles. However, do these parenting styles mean the same in different groups and whether they actually represent the contextual variations are yet issues unsettled. This has resulted in novel, granular and 'domain-specific' models of parenting that can be perceived as situational and flexible. Studies have mostly focused on parent-to-child effects, yet, in actual fact, studies have exhibited bidirectional association between parenting styles and adolescent behaviour (Smetana, 2017).

Cultural influences and beliefs moderate the effects of parenting on children's development. In response to the cultural critiques of parenting styles, distinct dimensions of parenting enable greater specificity in understanding the effects of parenting in a specific context. Dimensions premised on psychological control, behavioural control and parental monitoring have been widely used to study parenting styles. Further, domain-specific models look at parenting as a multifaceted and situational concept (Smetana, 2017).

In this chapter, though we will be focusing on the widely used Baumrind's work on parenting, let us be aware of the fact that there are other models of parenting which have other ways of looking at parenting styles. Lemasters and Defrain's model of parenting interestingly looks more closely at the motivations of the parent, suggesting that parenting styles are often designed to meet the psychological needs of the parent rather than the developmental needs of the child (Laff & Ruiz, 2019).

Parenting styles

This resource defines parenting style, explores four types, and discusses the consequences of the different styles for children.

Scan the QR code to access the resource

Literature shows evidence of the influence of parenting behaviours and parenting styles on adolescent outcomes, though there are still gaps in research. Three parenting styles, authoritative, authoritarian and permissive, were derived from the classification of Baumrind's work on parenting based on the dimension of parental control. Parenting behaviours included parental monitoring and parental discipline practices that may operate on identity development through innumerable pathways. Additional dimensions of parenting added by Maccoby and Martin were: parental responsiveness constituting parental warmth, parental support, parental involvement and uninvolved parenting. It is important to take note that one cannot categorize parents as strongly dominant on any dimension but can be either high or low on each dimension.

Authoritative parents display a supportive nature and encourage mutual give and take. This parenting style is most often associated with positive adolescent outcomes and has been found to be the most effective and beneficial style of parenting among most families. Studies have shown that adolescents whose parents are both authoritative or having at least one authoritative parent promotes desirable outcomes as compared to those with no authoritative parent. These adolescents display higher well-being such as higher self-esteem and life satisfaction (Hoskins, 2014).

Authoritarian parenting is often associated with traditional parenting whereby parents expect children to obey and conform to their instructions without questioning them. It is more often related to lack of trust towards the child and strict control over the child. Specifically, though authoritarian parenting style has consistently been associated with negative developmental outcomes, such as aggression, delinquent behaviours, somatic complaints, depersonalization and anxiety

(Kuppens & Ceulemans, 2019), the effects of this parenting style is found to vary based on the communities in which the adolescent lives.

Differences in cultural orientation furnish varied meanings and interpretations of parental control and its nuances. For example, adolescents raised in an individualist culture may perceive parental control as interfering and unwelcome to their autonomy, as opposed to adolescents raised in a relatively collectivist culture, who may perceive parental control as a manifestation of love, care and sensitivity through parental involvement. Nonetheless, the changes evolving in a value system as a result of increasing Westernization and widened cultural awareness through education and social media can in due course influence the way adolescents perceive parental control (Sondhi, 2017).

Permissive parenting identifies with an affirmative behaviour of parents towards the adolescents' desires and actions. This style of parenting is devoid of strict rules for adolescents or any kind of engagement in behavioural control. Interestingly, permissive parents show steep decrease in monitoring once their children reached adolescence, and these children increased their levels of externalizing behaviour. This often results in undesirable outcomes – substance use, school misconduct, delinquency – and is associated with low self-esteem and extrinsic motivational orientation among adolescents.

An uninvolved parenting style has been found to have the most negative effect on adolescent outcomes when compared to the other three parenting styles. This is associated with lack of any kind of control or supervision of the child's behaviour and is considered less demanding as compared to the other styles. It is observed that parents who are largely disengaged from responsibilities of child-rearing and not much concerned about the child's needs tend to share a very distant relationship with their children. Researches have also found that adolescent children of these kind of parents fall to various unpleasant and undesirable behaviours of the society as compared to their peers who lived in authoritative households (Hoskins, 2014).

Interestingly, it has been observed that monitoring varies among parenting styles. Extreme levels of monitoring by being too overprotective or exercising too much authority by not allowing adolescents to take their own decisions has been found to hinder independent identity formation. Concurrently, too low levels of monitoring may result in adolescents engaging in and exploring undesirable and inappropriate behaviours. This also has could have implications on family structure, wherein studies have shown that single-parent families provide less monitoring than two-biological-parent families, which may operate through differences in monitoring and control (Benson & Johnson, 2009)

Parental experiences and beliefs

The general beliefs parents carry about the developmental processes of adolescents are derived through both cultural transmission and personal experiences. These experiences constitute the period of adolescence they have gone through themselves or with

Social contexts in adolescence **125**

their own children or any other adolescent child. Here again, it has been observed that mothers and fathers have different experiences with adolescents. Mothers spend more time than fathers with children before adolescence. Mothers who have exposure to one or more adolescents compared to those who do not may consider the individuality of the adolescent rather than generalizing adolescent characteristics. Fathers act more as playmates while mothers act more as caretakers and nurturers to their children. The quality of such parent-adolescent relationships poses different expectations for the adolescent period. The roles of mothers and fathers also differ, thus influencing the interaction pattern. The roles of father being more instrumental and the mother being more emotional and expressive tend to result in behavioural differences of both parents. Mothers tend to be more empathetic and supportive towards adolescent children as compared to fathers. Contrary to this, conflict in adolescence is more common between adolescents and their mothers than adolescents and their fathers (Montemayor, 1982; Montemayor & Hanson, 1985), and mothers are more likely than fathers to associate disagreements over rules with a nature of revolt on the part of the adolescent. The above discussion suggests discordance in a qualitative role and a quantitative role played by adults, especially parents in dealing with adolescents (Buchanan et al., 1990).

> Take a look at these four examples given below. These examples exhibit different experiences of adolescents' interactions with their mother and father. Review these examples and analyse the implications of these kinds of dissimilar experiences with their parents, on adolescents' behavioural outcomes.

EXAMPLE 1

126 Social contexts in adolescence

Whattt!! Have you gone crazy! Wear that dress which I got you recently. And don't ask me again. I am not going to allow any such thing.

I don't think it's a good idea. Your father will not like it. You can wear such dresses after you grow up, darling. I will buy you a nice trendy dress that you can wear for your friend's birthday party.

Can I buy an off-shoulder dress to wear for my friend's birthday party? All my friends are going to wear an off-shoulder dress.

EXAMPLE 2

A 16 year old comes home with the report card showing below-average marks in her examinations.

Why are you even going to school? Am I sending you to coaching classes for this result? Now onwards, you will not go for any parties or playing till your next exam. You will only study. You better obey my orders.

What is the problem? Where did you lose marks? Do you think you need some assistance with studying? If you wish to attend a good college, you need to get good marks to get admission. Study hard and do better in your next exam.

He gets very angry and starts yelling at his daughter

She sits down by her side

EXAMPLE 3

Daughter goes for a late night movie with friends and returns very late in the night.

> Late night movies are okay sometimes, but you shouldn't do it often. We were never allowed to be out of the house late in the night. Times have changed. But you see, it is for your own good that we are against these late night movies. Nowadays it's too unsafe for anyone to be on the streets late in the night. Your mother and I are concerned about you. We are worried for your safety. Try to avoid such actions in future.

> These late night movies and all, just not acceptable. In our days, we were supposed to be home by 9 Pm in the night from wherever we went. What do you get by being out late in the night? Why can't you go to watch a movie in the day time?

EXAMPLE 4

Sociocultural influences on adolescents' identity formation

The psychological impact of different kinds of family structures and the patterns of interaction and communication within the family such as parent-parent, parent-child and sibling engagements differ invariably with respect to contexts resulting in distinct parenting styles. The contexts shape adolescents' experiences which play a significant role in their identity development. According to Erikson, the final identity is consolidated at the end of adolescence when the adolescent embraces all significant identifications from the past and makes independent judgments in forming a unique and coherent sense of self. Arnett observed that adolescent identity formation is promoted by close family relationships, particularly in terms of commitment to a set of beliefs, values and goals. Marcia indicated that adolescents may undergo increased guilt- and anxiety-ridden exploration in the absence of parental support. Higher levels of separation anxiety limit adolescent identity exploration; moderate levels of separation anxiety may promote development of commitment. Smollar and Youniss emphasized individuation as an important characteristic of adolescent development because it initiates children towards exploring and developing a sense of self that is separate from parental identity. Noller suggested that the best approach for families to promote identity exploration during adolescence is by emphasizing individuation without downplaying familial closeness and vice versa. Researchers have referred to adolescent identity formation as a product of both separateness and connectedness with family. Researchers have suggested that identity is better developed during adolescence when parents themselves encourage youngsters to be autonomous and independent within the context of secure parent-child relationship; families in which adolescents are encouraged both to be connected to their parents and to express their own individuality. Erikson contended that identity was a fit between the culture and the individual (Graf, 2003).

Distinctly different family structures have culturally context-specific influences in the life of an adolescent. Class, caste, gender and socio-economic status are other factors that may interact with different family patterns and structures in influencing the process of adolescents' identity exploration. Contexts other than the family – schools, peers, community – concomitantly function alongside families in identity development of adolescents. Thus, adolescent identity formation determined by the sociocultural milieu of adolescents can be linked to different psychosocial outcomes for adolescents.

A study conducted on adolescent identity formation, psychological well-being and parental attitudes in the city of Amritsar in Punjab, India, reported that maternal acceptance was positively related to identity achievement in both boys and girls. It also was observed that girls commit themselves to life choices and making decisions without exploring opportunities when they are controlled by parents. It was inferred that lack of societal and family support hinders adolescent girls to explore their identity. Boys usually were more privileged than girls in exploring opportunities as usually happen in a male dominant society.

However, literature shows that youth in the Indian context might benefit from parental control and overprotection for the achievement of identity (Sandhu et al., 2012). In a culture where parental control is a traditionally accepted norm, control is perceived more as a security rather than authority. Restrictive and normative parenting in collectivistic cultures is not necessarily associated with parents being rejecting or lacking in warmth (Sondhi, Ch 5, 2017). We had earlier referred to authoritarian parenting style as being associated with negative developmental outcomes, but we also see how control and restrictions can result in positive outcomes.

Though it is agreed upon that exposure to external factors has brought about huge transformations and transitions along with decline of traditional values and norms in the collectivist Indian culture, there are evidences of instances where family values are quite strong enough to influence the adolescents' development. Cultural factors play independently within families, thus having significant implications for adolescents' development. Hence characterization of a culture cannot be generalized for implications on child development.

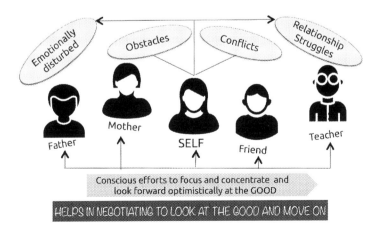

FIGURE 3.12 Key Constituents in Adolescent Identity Formation

Parent-adolescent communication

Open communication between parents and children was significantly and positively associated with the development of adolescents' moral reasoning, academic achievement and self-esteem Adolescents' perceptions of the openness of the communication with their parents are associated with their emotional disclosure to parents. Few studies that examined the relationship between perceived parental-adolescent communication from the perceptions of both parents and adolescents demonstrated a high rate of discordance between parents and adolescents in the interpretations of their conversations. This discordance has been frequently attributed to the generation gap existing between parents and children. The generational stake theory argues that parents and children, as two contrasting generations in the life cycle, have different psychological needs and different investments in establishing the generational bond. Parents are keener on maintaining intergenerational continuity, whereas children are more focused on the lookout for a separate identity for themselves and being withdrawn from the family (Xiao et al., 2011).

In India, notwithstanding the recognition in policies and programmes of the need to actively engage parents in enabling adolescents to make safe and healthy transitions to adulthood evidence about parent-child interaction and communication, particularly with regard to sensitive matters such as the physical changes associated with puberty, sex, pregnancy and sexually transmitted infections/HIV is sparse. For example, village-level studies have identified parents' own lack of awareness and their perception that their children were not at risk of HIV as key factors limiting communication; other studies have noted parental discomfort and perceptions that informing their children about sexual matters would lead them to engage in sex (Svodziwa et al., 2016).

A study on adolescents in India revealed that young urban women were more comfortable in talking to their mothers about menstruation (77%) and more urban women than their rural counterparts were likely to have discussed growing up matters with their mothers ((Population Council & UNICEF, 2013).

Adolescent girls usually find it difficult to talk about sexual problems or menstrual disorders with their mothers. Baseline findings of an intervention evaluation undertaken by the Population Council in 2006 show that girls aged 13–17 years reported limited communication with their parents, specifically mothers, about sexual and reproductive-health related matters.

This sexual communication is highly influenced by traditional gender norms wherein both parents and adolescents find it quite embarrassing to talk about. Adolescents then rely on their peers or the social media for information related to these matters, which may be unreliable and misleading. This necessitates the need for sex education for both adolescents and their parents to facilitate better communication between them on such matters.

The adolescent period is characteristic of romantic relationships. In the Indian context, studies majorly focus on sexuality-related issues and premarital sexual relationship. There is very minimal literature on adolescent girls in romantic relationships. Marriage being considered a sacred institution in India, the concept of romantic relationships or dating is very unusual. There is a total lack of communication with their parents regarding such matters due to the fear of losing their partner or bringing dishonour to the family.

Another important barrier to verbal communication between parents and adolescents is the influence of multimedia technology. This we will see in detail in the last section of this chapter.

Adolescents and parents: cause or effect?

Parent-adolescent relationships have been among the most examined topics in adolescent development. Although family relationships have been theoretically conceptualized as a two-way interaction between the adolescent and his or her parent, empirical researchers seem to make a strong assertion that it is parenting that influences adolescent development. However, many researchers have challenged this view and suggested that children also impact their parents' child-rearing patterns (Nurmi, 2004, p.95). This brings us to the key question of the extent to which parents' attitudes, behaviours and child-rearing patterns influence their adolescents' development or whether it is adolescence's thinking and behaviours that have an impact on their mothers' and fathers' parenting.

On one hand we can see at least three possible ways of parents' influence on adolescents. First, parents may direct the development of their children's interests, goals and values by communicating expectations and setting normative standards; second, they may influence the ways in which their adolescent child deals with various developmental demands by acting as role models and providing tutoring; and finally, they may contribute to the ways in which adolescents evaluate their success in dealing with these demands by providing support and feedback. On the other hand, the adolescent's success in dealing with the key demands of his or her age-graded environments may well influence his or her parents' expectations concerning their child's future; adolescents' competencies and coping skills may evoke the use of certain parenting styles among the parents; and adolescents' behaviour may cause extra stress for parents, which then influence their thinking, behaviour and even well-being (Nurmi, 2004, p. 96).

Social contexts in adolescence **131**

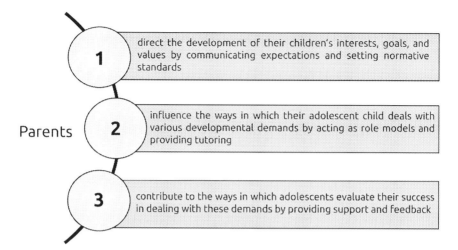

FIGURE 3.13A Parents' Influence on Adolescents

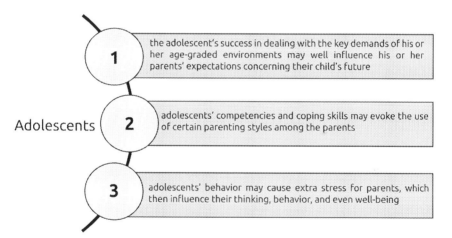

FIGURE 3.13B Adolescents' Influence on Parents

> Think
>
> Parenting influences not just a child's development, but also the development of the parent
>
> - Can Parenting be bidirectional?
> - Can children's behaviour influence their parents' parenting style?

School context

Understanding the relationship between schools and adolescent development requires a conceptual framework for thinking simultaneously about schools as contexts in which development takes place and about the changing developmental needs of students as they move through the school system. In our visualizations of schools we often think of schools as a place where most of the years of childhood and early adolescence are spent. Agbenyega (2008) has attempted to define this space as a place that contains goods and services of both animate and inanimate nature which interact in a symbiotic fashion to create these meanings. The nature and types of goods and services available in a particular school place are directly related to the culture and value systems of the society which creates these places, and the goods and services in turn shape the culture and value systems. The goods would usually encompass the teacher's classroom resources such as books, learning technologies and the classroom architecture. Services may include medical facilities, administrators and cleaners. The main thing that distinguishes one place from the other is the difference of their objects (goods and services), which implies that the function of the classroom place is driven by the goods and services within it. Therefore, according to this perspective, goods and services are a reflection of the culture and value system of the society that creates and uses them as well and goods and services that transform and shape the values system of that society.

Drawing from the above perspective of understanding a school, the nature of the goods in a classroom place affects teachers' pedagogical behaviours and their relationship with students. Suppose a school place with a high student-teacher ratio and insufficient books; the teacher in this place is more likely to use a unidirectional form of instruction which would invariably affect students' way of learning. Ashcroft's (2001) position that the continuous cohabitation of individuals and the goods of their place is "intimately bound up with the culture and identity of its inhabitants." (p. 156). In a classroom situation, individuals bring in unique identity forms which include teachers' and students' values, behaviours and perceptions based on their cultural backgrounds. These individual identities of teachers, students and administrators are in turn influenced by the culture and values of the place they cocreate. Ellis argues that the entire experience of schooling results from the way people inhabit a place. How they inhabit it is influenced by identities they have already created in other places such as homes, playgrounds, religious affiliations or former schools. This is particularly critical for student and teacher relationships – to be mindful of these identities as they are constantly at play in the individual's life though they now belong to a common space called as 'school'. It is the identities that the individual has developed outside school as well as in relation to the interaction within the school that drive the type and nature of teaching strategies that are planned for students in a particular classroom place (Agbenyega, 2008). Therefore, the understanding of the influence of the school is not a simplistic understanding of what do the players or social actors in the schools do in the life and development of the adolescent.

Eccles and Roeser (1999) had proposed a framework for thinking about school influences that dissected the school context into a series of hierarchically ordered interdependent levels of organization. To begin with, at the most basic level is the classroom, then moving up in complexity to the school as an organizational system embedded in a larger cultural system.

Based on this framework of understanding schools, following assumptions were made.

1   schools are systems characterized by multiple levels of regulatory processes (organizational, social and instructional in nature);
2   these processes are interrelated across levels of analysis;
3   such processes are usually dynamic in nature, sometimes being worked out each day between the various social actors (e.g. teachers and students);
4   these processes change as children move through different school levels (elementary, middle and high school); and
5   these processes regulate children's and adolescents' cognitive, social-emotional and behavioural development.

In this chapter we will focus on the interface between these theoretical frameworks. We begin with a summary of Eccles's and Roeser's multilevel description of school contexts.

At the classroom level, we need to understand and focus our attention on teacher beliefs and teaching learning practices, teacher-student relationships, the nature and design of tasks, assignments and instruction, and the nature and structure of classroom activities and groups. At the level of the school building, there is a need to focus attention on organizational climate and such school-wide practices as academic progress strategies, school timings and the provision of co-curricular activities. At the next level of the school, one needs to look at how transitions are made within one level or grade to another and how they create a particular unique transition experience for students. Finally, at the level of schools embedded in larger social systems are issues as school resources as well as the linkages of schools with parents and with the world of work. Eccles and Roeser (1999) further assumed that in any given school setting these multilevel processes are interwoven with one another. Relations between different levels of organization in the school may be complementary or contradictory and may influence students either directly or indirectly or may influence positively or negatively (Eccles, 2004, p.127).

Adolescents in school contexts

In adolescence, identity formation is enabled through such capacities as increasingly complex socio-emotional regulation and advanced cognitive functioning. Cognitive and emotional capacities can be enhanced by school contexts by offering curriculum-based activities and varied forms of social engagement within and outside the context (Erentaitė et al., 2018).

As adolescents drift away from parents and family, they start exploring aspects of their own personal identity though their needs for belonging, acceptance and social support are quite strong at this age. At such times, schools, where they spend most of their time, serve as very important sources for meeting this critical developmental need for young adolescents. Finding their place and constructing an identity within the school context may be quite unchallenging for some adolescents, while a few of them may struggle to do so due to its demanding nature. There are quite a number of factors and practices that may succeed or fail to promote a sense of belonging in adolescent students towards their school, having implications on their behavioural outcomes (Stumpers et al., 2005).

Considering Ashcroft's (2001) position of cohabitation, schools can be considered as a place of continuous cohabitation of individuals, dynamically relating to one another and also contributing to the identity of the individuals.

Further we will discuss the following dimensions of school context woven with the mechanisms of socialization discussed in page 103 of this chapter_____

- School Climate
- Adolescents' Personal Beliefs in the Realm of School Context
- Classroom Climate
- School safety
- Teacher Beliefs
- Nature of Academic work
- School Culture

School climate

A school environment encompasses its physical, social, pedagogical, organizational and other key components. Adolescents' identity formation is not just a result of separation from parents and gaining autonomy, but Marcia reports it to be a complex interplay of intrapsychic processes and interpersonal experiences. Marcia communicates that the school contexts may provide opportunities for exploration to adolescents by fostering their decision-making skills, exploring their aspirations, providing counselling and offering flexible curriculum (Abbasi, 2016).

Adolescents spend maximum time in schools, where they are engaged in a number of activities and programs, which aids them in discovering their interests and abilities and developing those abilities. Many of these exploratory tasks and mechanisms are embedded in the social interactions and interpersonal relationships with peers at school. Nakkula, affirms that adolescents living in poor and working class urban communities and deprived of enough opportunities for exploration outside schools benefit from these opportunities at school (Abbasi, 2016).

Adolescents' decision-making with respect to choosing a career option, gender orientation, life values and attitudes reflect their identity formation, giving rise to their commitment towards their choices and achieving an initial sense of identity. School climate, student-teacher interactions and peer interactions within school contexts provide social and emotional experiences with possible long-term implications for identity. Students' identity formation is usually of greater intensity as the school year progresses. Socio-economic status of students is found to influence the extent of identity exploration and commitment with higher SES displaying more impact than lower SES. The type of school that an adolescent attends also determines identity status. For example, a study by Roker and Banks found a considerable number of girls from private schools in foreclosure status compared to those from state schools who tended to be in moratorium and identity achievement statuses (Abbasi, 2016). They opine that private schools generally include a homogeneous group of students with lack of exposure to a wide variety of ideological viewpoints, thus coercing students to take decisions; whereas state schools may facilitate more exploration of alternatives and making commitments by providing them exposure to a wide range of ideological viewpoints and belief systems (Abbasi, 2016).

Building upon Erikson's emphasis on the experience of "psychosocial moratorium" as an important period in the life of an adolescent for the development of identity, the prime responsibility of devising adequate opportunities for the adolescents' exploration of diverse values, roles and relationships rests on schooling. Dreyer argues that educational environments that stimulate exploration and commitment encourage adolescent identity formation (Abbasi, 2016).

School curriculum that facilitates abundant choices for adolescents through a wide variety of alternatives in areas of life such as occupation, religion and politics enhances adolescents' identity by promoting their identity achievement. In this regard, schools should essentially provide real-world or authentic experiences and mentoring programs for career decisions through linkage with industry. School learning environments have to transcend beyond physical boundaries through either physical or virtual partnerships with the multiple world outside. This facet of the school context can be made possible through Information and Communication Technologies (ICTs), which bear the potential of providing virtual practical experience to students for engaging in learning activities; encouraging personalized learning and assessment and opening up new avenues for exploration (Abbasi, 2016).

Reiterating the role of different social contexts in promoting adolescents' identity, 'relationship building', which is at the heart of all these contexts, cannot be underestimated. As we proceed further, we will be able to discern the different relational aspects of school context in adolescents' development.

According to Nakkula, connectedness to school and engagement in school activities also play an important role in fostering adolescent identity. Adolescents who form positive connections with their school are more likely to engage in a variety of prosocial behaviours, achieve up to their potential academically, and less likely to engage in problem behaviours such as fighting, bullying, truancy, vandalism and substance use. School bonding is referred to as attachment to prosocial peers; commitment to academic and social activities at school; and belief in the established norms for school behaviour (Simons-Morton et al., 1999).

The feeling of belongingness to school is dependent on the kind of relationships teachers nurture with their students. The caring, empathetic, understanding and sensitive nature of teachers towards adolescents can not only strengthen their identity formation but also support their connection to the identities of their families, communities and peers. This can further assist the adolescents' relationship to learning. School curriculum inclusive of extracurricular programs present adolescents with innumerable challenges and opportunities with limitless choices of networking with the world, inside and outside, and experiencing meaningful relationships with others through participation in activities, freedom of expression, generation of social and human capital and exploration of the self. Additionally, the impact of schools on this developmental task of adolescence can extend beyond these programs by adopting community service learning and cooperative learning approaches. These approaches can facilitate an increase in social awareness of adolescents and promote multicultural relationships, inclusivity, prejudice reduction, self-esteem, peer support for academic goals, empathy and more (Abbasi, 2016).

Cotterell views physical organization of institutions as equally significant in providing the appropriate settings for socialization, informal interactions among peers, students and teachers, and also accessibility of teachers for students. Such a supportive school culture confronts adolescents' individuation and social integration needs, which in turn offer students a secure base for exploration of identity alternatives and making meaningful commitments.

Findings of studies have revealed positive impacts of small-size schools on self-concept of students, and positive correlations between small-size schools and strong interpersonal climate. However, one needs to be cautious in perceiving these correlations, as researches have denied any automatic assurance of school success attributed to small school size (Abbasi, 2016).

Task for the Learner:

In a diverse country like India, there are different types of school. The Indian school education system can be segregated by means of levels of education, ownership of educational, educational board affiliations. Other than these different categories, there are divides in schools on basis of the geographic location, rural and urban, availability of resources, religious segregation, political ideologies and many other aspects.

With such vast diversity, explain the function of a school culture in confronting adolescents' individuation and social integration needs and offering them opportunities for exploration of their identity with respect to the following aspects of a school culture?
- Teacher qualifications
- School infrastructure
- School's access to computers and internet
- Class size
- Teachers' overload

Attempt any one of the tasks given below with respect to the above question:

- Identify any two categories of schools that are different from each other, make a comparison chart with respect to the aspects given above.
- Choose any two aspects from the ones given above and discuss these aspects for the different categories of schools that you can identify. Make a small group presentation in your class and discuss the alternative possibilities with your peers.
- Design a school with the above aspects of a school culture that can shape positive adolescent experiences in a tribal area. Represent your idea through a graphical organizer using photographs, text, or any other form to explain your school design and its specifications.

Adolescents' personal beliefs in the realm of school context

In addition to various external factors that shape adolescents' experiences and influence their development, adolescents' own constructions of meaning and interpretations of events within the school environment are strong determinants of students' feelings, beliefs and behaviour.

As adolescents enter middle school, they don't have a single-class teacher as in their previous classes, but come across a number of teachers teaching different subjects and maybe different classmates too in higher grades, especially post ninth grade. At such times, adolescent students shoulder the responsibility of managing their diverse learning environments on their own. A major portion of their academic activities such as reading, completing homework and assignments and preparing for examinations, takes place out of classrooms; these activities grow in difficulty level as they progress in school. Not all adolescents are able to fulfil these demands successfully due to various factors hindering their attempts. These students' grades are affected very poorly, often resulting in diminished self-efficacy of their success in school. Adolescent students' lowered self-efficacy propels them towards peers who devalue the importance of school. Contrary to this, Bandura et al. posit that adolescents with a strong sense of efficacy for learning exhibit more resilience in resisting the unfavourable academic influences of low-achieving peers than are those with low self-efficacy. Adolescents' school success is determined by their development of self-regulatory skills such as goal setting, self-monitoring, time management and self-evaluation. These skills empower the adolescents in regard to their beliefs about their personal capability and inculcate a sense of personal agency for effectively and responsibly managing their behaviour and acting in the world (Zimmerman & Cleary, 2006).

The social cognitive perspective proposes that school-related context variables and academic variables along with non-academic variables are responsible for students' academic functioning. Students, who fail to nurture positive social relationships with peers or are unable to self-regulate their behaviour don't succeed in academics or social and personal functioning. Adolescent children's prosocial behaviour is seen to be influenced by parents' academic aspirations for their children, which is observed to be dependent on the families' socio-economic status.

Adolescents' degree of prosocial behaviour impacted their peer preferences which in turn controlled their engagement in problem behaviours. Adolescents with low--level efficacy about their capacities resulted in cultivating reduced aspiration levels and less prosocial behaviour and are more likely, in the long run, to close the doors of opportunities and exploration, thus being in the foreclosure identity status (Zimmerman & Cleary, 2006). On the other hand, adolescents' increased self-efficacy, while taking personal decisions during transition from one education level to another, enables them to not only carry out new and different types of school tasks and adapt to new study contexts, but also has a positive effect on their school academic performance and orientation towards their future career (Pedditzi & Marcello, 2018).

Classroom climate

The classroom is the most proximal environment to the student in school. Classroom climate is reflected by the kind of academic engagement, peer relationships and student-teacher relationships in the classroom. Students' engagement in classroom activities, freedom to voice their feelings or opinions, the feeling of being accepted and valued in classroom by peers and teachers fabricate a positive classroom climate. A positive classroom climate promotes the emotional, social and psychological adjustment of students at school and is related to their self-concept (Povedano-Diaz et al., 2020).

Student-teacher relationships are a very significant part of classroom climate. Healthy and positive student-teacher relationships foster adolescent students' academic motivation, school engagement, academic success, self-esteem and socio-emotional well-being. Adolescent students' perceptions of caring teachers enable them to engage and persist on academic learning tasks and develop positive achievement-related self-perceptions and values, thus enhancing their feelings of self-esteem, school belonging and positive affect in school (Eccles, 2004, p. 129).

As adolescents move from elementary school into secondary schools, their perceptions of emotional support from teachers becomes low, and their transition becomes a bit difficult and unmanageable. Teachers at school are considered to be one of the important and immediate sources of non-parental role models for adolescents. Besides, teachers' roles can buffer unfavourable or non-supportive conditions in adolescents' families and communities by providing the right guidance and assistance for promoting developmental competence in adolescent students.

Classroom management with regard to procedures for monitoring student progress, providing feedback, enforcing accountability for work completion, and organizing group activities, impact students' achievement and conduct in classrooms. Teachers' easy-going attitude in managing classrooms and provision of less systematic control over instructional procedures may account for relatively low performance of students in school (Eccles, 2004, p. 130).

Motivational climate created by teachers in the classroom affect students' motivation; however, certain classroom practices – groups made on basis of ability, giving feedback in front of the whole class and focus on competition between students – lay emphasis on extrinsic motivators and ego-focused learning goals, which may lead to prevalence of social comparison behaviours, unhealthy competition and lowering the quality of students' motivation and learning, especially the low-performing students. Building on the premise of goal theory, classroom practices that focus on mastery-oriented goals enables students' sustained school engagement and better achievement as compared to those practices which focus on performance orientation. Students with performance orientation generally are committed towards performing better than their peers in class, rather than focusing on learning the material and their own improvement over time. Though performance-oriented goals may not always have negative consequences, the fear of failing may hinder school performance. Teachers' efforts to foster positive outcomes for adolescents' academic motivation, endurance on difficult learning tasks and socio-emotional development should be devoid of classroom practices associated with performance feedback, social comparative grading systems and ego-focused, competitive motivational strategies in classrooms (Eccles, 2004, p. 131).

Adolescents' preferences for different types of learning contexts vary depending on gender, and at times these differences also lead to varied interest in different subject areas. For example, if you carefully observe the choice of elective courses in ninth grade, one can discern the differences in interest of girls and boys for a particular course. The 'Arts' class has a maximum of female students, while 'Computer Science' class has a maximum of male students enrolled. This apparently happens due to the misfit between the teaching styles, the instructional focus and students' values, goals, motivational orientations and learning styles. It is generally found that students' motivation is at its peak if their learning situations are in alignment with their interests, skill level and psychological needs, and the learning material is challenging, interesting and meaningful. On that account, one essentially needs to understand group differences in achievement and achievement choices of adolescent students as a broad set of classroom characteristics related to motivation to minimize poor performance and high dropout rates (Eccles, 2004, p. 131).

School safety

School safety is understood in terms of violence occurring in schools, harassment of the underprivileged and peer influences in school. Unsafe environments in school can have direct effects on adolescents' health through low levels of psychological adjustment, school engagement and academic achievement. Bullying is a quite common form of violence that takes place in schools. Students who fear violence in school are likely to drop out of school. The probability of suffering from depressive symptoms such as loneliness and difficulty in making friends is high in adolescents who are bullied. Gender or sexual orientation, disabilities, race, culture, religion, socio-economic status, under-represented groups – these are major factors based on which students get victimized (Marin & Brown, 2008). School climate, especially, bonding with teachers and receiving their support can aid in reversing the effects of school violence and make the students feel safe at school by increasing students' self-esteem and lowering the levels of depressive symptoms. In addition to this aspect of school culture, schools with a prevalence of consistent authoritative discipline also can impede the negative effects of bullying (Eccles & Roeser, 2011).

Peer norms and culture within a school context can determine the adolescents' social position in terms of their peer network with which they share the same classroom or hangout in school. These norms and cultures are found to influence students' identity formation, short- and long-term goals and aspirations plus educational choices during the secondary school years. The formation of adolescents' personal and social identities emerging from the influence of peer groups are consequences of school-wide characteristics and policies that shape the peer group structures that emerge within the school building (Eccles & Roeser, 2011). Moreover, centre-wide and statewide government policies and characteristics that reflect local political and cultural beliefs and economic conditions govern many aspects of within-classroom and within-school interactions.

Students' performance in any context is generally perceived as a fit between their contexts and students' development, culture and psychological needs. Adolescents' own individual efforts towards development, along with the inbuilt support system and the barriers within the settings, contribute to their development. This emphasizes the agency of adolescents in creating their own identities for all aspects of their intellectual and social-emotional development through their social interactions, the nature of which are influenced by their social milieu, which is further impacted by the external structures of the broader society. Notwithstanding these, one needs to pay attention to the unique challenges faced by different kinds of schools and communities in urban, rural and suburban settings in contemporary times and adolescents' individual differences to understand the reciprocal relationships between their between identity formation and experiences in school.

Teacher beliefs

Teachers' own beliefs affect their pedagogical decisions and their interaction with students. Teachers' tacit beliefs about gender, religion, castes and class reflect the stereotypic convictions of society and lead to discriminated treatment of adolescent students resulting in differential outcomes and decline in their academic self-concept. Adolescent students' perception about the emotional support of their teachers impact their self-esteem, belongingness to school and positive affect in school. As adolescents progress from elementary to secondary schools, they generally perceive decreased levels of teacher care and sense of belonging in the classroom, which is likely to affect their academic motivation, engagement and learning, and social-emotional well-being in school (Eccles & Roeser, 2011).

The level of expectations teachers hold for their students influence students' behaviour in school. When teachers expect high performance and achievement from students, these students also feel the same and attempt to work hard towards the expectations; they experience a high sense of self-worth as learners; develop a feeling of connectedness to their teachers and school; and avoid problem behaviours. Teachers' high level of general efficacy also boosts students' confidence and efficacy in achieving the best. When teachers exhibit confidence and beliefs in their ability to shape students' experiences in a positive manner, students put in more efforts to keep up to their teachers' expectations. Vice versa, teachers with low confidence in their teaching efficacy communicate feelings of incompetence and alienation in their students, resulting in these students exhibiting lower confidence in learning, depressive emotions and disengagement in academic activities. This highlights the important role of teachers' general beliefs for adolescents' development in school (Eccles, 2004, p. 128).

Teachers' differential treatment of students within the classroom is also quite evident in many schools.

Time to Think and Reflect

"Teachers' differential treatment of students within the classroom is also quite evident in many schools."
Read this statement and think of instances when you have encountered such a situation.

- Why is differential treatment meted out to students studying in the same class? Is it justified? What is your opinion and what are the reasons for the same?
- How do you perceive the relation between teachers' differential treatment and differential expectations for students within the same classroom?
- What factors according to you are responsible for teachers' differential treatment to students within the same class?
- What are the anticipated consequences of this differential treatment on adolescents' academic performance or their behaviour in school?
- Can you think of ways and strategies to reduce the effect of differential treatment on students?
- How will you as a teacher try to create awareness among teachers who resort to differential treatment for students?

Teachers' differential treatment is accompanied with teachers' differential expectations from students within the same class. Teachers, whose expectations differ for different students structure academic activities differently and interact differently with students, thus influencing the way students perceive these differences. In the Indian context, such factors as gender, socio-economic status, religion, social class and colour are obviously responsible for teachers' differential expectations and treatment of students.

This form of differential treatment can result in students' disengagement from school and dis-identification (low self-esteem in school context) to maintain their self-esteem otherwise. The psychological processes associated with the implicit labelling of stereotypes by teachers regarding the intellectual strengths and weaknesses of different social groups can either promote or hinder students' performance on standardized tests (Eccles, 2004, p. 129).

Rich and Schachter state that perceiving teachers as role models and studies as meaningful is associated with higher identity exploration and more confidence in identity commitments in middle- and late adolescence (Erentaitė et al., 2018).

Teacher qualifications, content specialization, years of teaching experience – all these factors influence the development of adolescents through varied learning experiences. Quality of teachers may differ in different contexts determined by socio-economic status, accessibility of resources and demographic characteristics, thus having huge implications on the intellectual development of adolescents.

Nature of academic work

The sociocultural and socio-constructivist perspective affirms schools as "communities of practice" where participants are actively involved in the process of knowledge construction and learning (Pedditzi & Marcello, 2018).

The nature of academic work influences the way students understand 'self' and the world around them, and their capacities to pay attention, their interests and passions, and their morals and ethics. Academic work is generally characterized by the content of the curriculum and the design of instruction which may or may not align with the developmental needs and capacities of adolescent students from different cultures and backgrounds. As students advance to their secondary years of schooling, they encounter boredom in school due to passive instruction strategies used in schools. Academic work lacking challenge and meaning comparable to adolescents' cognitive and emotional needs may result in diminished motivation in some adolescents during the transition to secondary school years. Relevant and meaningful ways of academic work boosts adolescents' motivation to learn and nurture positive relationships with others at school; lack of interest and perceived irrelevance of academic work results in adolescents' disengagement in learning and school. Particularly, adolescent students belonging to under-represented groups get affected by curriculum that fails to address developmentally and culturally meaningful aspects relevant to their groups. The nature of instruction can foster a strong personal identity in adolescent students through ways of providing appropriate instructional materials that induce interest and engagement in tasks, influencing their motivation and learning. The design of academic tasks that can scaffold learning need to be responsive to diverse cognitive operations of students and offer materials that provide appropriate level of challenges to students (Eccles & Roeser, 2011).

School culture

Schools as a community vary in their interpersonal, moral and academic cultures. School cultures that facilitate academic engagement and learning for all students and those linked to school safety have its effects on adolescents' development. Bandura et al. suggest that schools vary in the climate and general expectations regarding student potential, and such variations affect the development of both teachers and students in very fundamental ways. A school or school climate may or may not value academics, have high expectations from students regarding their learning and affirm the actual vision of the school. Differences in between-school climate in terms of teachers' sense of their personal efficacy and their confidence in their ability to teach translate into teaching practices at their respective schools, and this may partly result in between-school differences in adolescents' high school performance and motivation (Eccles, 2004, p. 134).

Schools too like classroom practices, give rise to different achievement goals through unique policies and practices, affecting students' academic beliefs, affects and behaviour. The academic goal focus of a school is strongly correlated with adolescents' perceptions of the school's social climate and also has important implications for their mental health. School culture with more diverse goals and emphasis on non-academic needs, school attachment (valuing of school, liking teachers), foster school bonding and less delinquent activity in adolescents (Eccles, 2004, p. 135).

Extracurricular activities in school too have an important role to play in adolescents' development. Participation in school-based extracurricular activities can facilitate positive developmental outcomes as good academic performance, increased school engagement and high educational aspirations, deterring adolescents from engaging in high-risk behaviours. Participation in sports, in particular, is associated with reduced school dropout and higher rates of school attendance.

Results of studies have also negated the positive effects of participation in sports, suggesting that organized extracurricular activities can have both positive and negative effects.

Think and Reflect

- What factors may have resulted in studies showing contrasting results with respect to influence of participation in extracurricular activities?
- Review a few school contexts and identify some negative influences of sports participation on adolescents' behaviour.
- How will you explain the link between peer group values and norms, adolescents' personal identity, and the kinds of activities they participate, in shaping the nature of their developmental pathway into adulthood?
- Schools differ in the extent to which they provide positive extracurricular activities for their students. How can you explain the variations of these school characteristics? (Refer to the aspects under **'Task for the Learner' under 'School Climate'**)

Social agents: moving to peers and mass media

To exercise some measure of control over one's developmental course requires, in addition to effective tools of personal agency, a great deal of social support. Social support comes from social resources provided by various social institutions, not only home and school, but also peers and mass media which will see in the next sections. This support which comes from social agencies are especially important during formative years when preferences and personal standards are in a state of flux, and there are many conflicting sources of influence. To overcome challenges and obstacles that adolescents face in their life's journey, such social agents as family, school, peers and messages from mass media help in not only developing agency but also help the adolescent to operate from the Author "I" guise of identity, whose foundation is laid and strengthened by the social milieu. Let us understand the interaction of peers and mass media with the development of the adolescent through this perspective.

In the following section, we will look at two major social interactions – peers and mass media – that have a bidirectional and transactional relationship with the adolescent through the framework of Actor, Agency and Author guises of self.

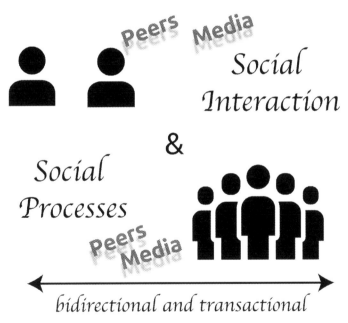

FIGURE 3.14 Bidirectional and Transactional Nature of Social Processes and Interactions

Social contexts in adolescence **145**

Peer context

Assumptions for adolescents' socialization in peer context

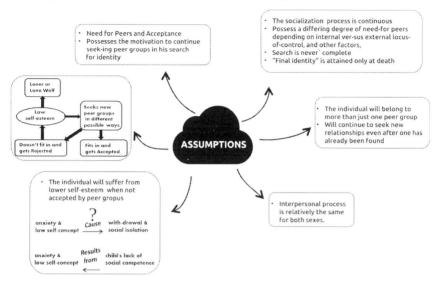

FIGURE 3.15 Assumptions with Respect to Interpersonal Processes of Adolescent Identity in Relation to Peer and Peer Groups

Source: (Asbridge, 1984)

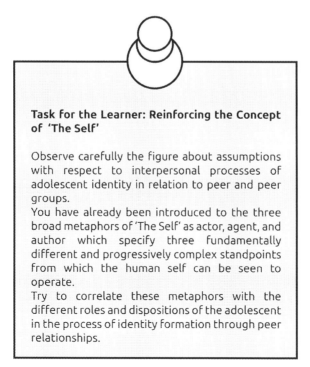

Task for the Learner: Reinforcing the Concept of 'The Self'

Observe carefully the figure about assumptions with respect to interpersonal processes of adolescent identity in relation to peer and peer groups.

You have already been introduced to the three broad metaphors of 'The Self' as actor, agent, and author which specify three fundamentally different and progressively complex standpoints from which the human self can be seen to operate.

Try to correlate these metaphors with the different roles and dispositions of the adolescent in the process of identity formation through peer relationships.

> Consider a specific example of an adolescent-peer relationship and review the process of identity formation of the adolescent in that relationship in terms of the three guises that the adolescent dons at different times.
>
> Attempt any one of the tasks given to you

1

Identify few expereinces of the adolescent in relationships with peers. Recognize the metaphor or guise donned by the adolescent in those experiences. Critically analyse them correlating with the assumptions given above.

2

Reflect on the following questions along the assumptions given above. Supplement your responses with specific instances from your example.

- What kind of variations do you find in the guises or images that adolescents put on in the interpersonal processes of peer relationships?
- Explain using examples, how these variations can be related to adolescent's formation of identity in terms of self-concept and self-esteem?

Adolescents and peers

The relationship between an adolescent and its peers is a two-way relationship where they derive their sense of worth and identity from the peer as well as where they actively and unconsciously also modify and influence their peers. The stages are blurred but nevertheless conspicuous in the identity formation stage of the adolescent. Various research studies discussed below have shown that adolescents modify their behaviour based on peer group influence, which could be positive or negative.

Studies have shown that peer groups serve a number of important functions throughout adolescence, providing a temporary reference point for a developing sense of identity. They start identifying with their peers, compare themselves with their peers and begin to take moral decisions strongly influenced by their peers. They also attempt to define how they differ from their parents (APA, 2002). Peer group as a source of emotional support for adolescents and an indicator of social status necessary for his/her identity development through the process of identity exploration within the groups (Rageliené, 2016).

Adolescence is the prime time when self-concept is shaped by peers in specific. Spending time with peers is valued a lot and influences the adolescent's behaviour. Changes in self-concept might contribute to behavioural phenomena typical in adolescence, such as heightened self-consciousness and susceptibility to peer pressure (Sebastian et al., 2008). Findings from studies suggest that a peer's observation of any task or performance influences adolescents' decision-making irrespective of whether the peer is anonymous and physically absent. Studies have reported that adolescents took more risks in the presence of their peers as compared to times when they were alone by increasing the subjective value of immediately available rewards. Analysis of adolescents' neural activity during the decision-making epoch constitute the evidence that peer presence accentuates risky decision-making in adolescence by modulating activity in the brain's reward-valuation system (Albert et al., 2013).

Adolescents are highly influenced by their peers in ways of thinking and feeling. The interpersonal challenges faced in friendships are quite unique to this age, and this formative context facilitates adolescents' acquisition of certain social knowledge and skills (Bukowski et al., 2011). It is through their peers that adolescents get to know information about the world outside the family and about themselves. Peer groups serve as major sources of popularity, status, prestige and acceptance for the adolescents. Acceptance in a peer group enables adolescents to develop a positive identity for themselves and perform and achieve better in their lives, whereas isolation and rejection from peer groups affected adversely on the adolescents and incline them towards negative behaviours (Tome & Matos, 2012).

Social interactions with peers enable the adolescents to understand different perspectives and clarify their own world views. Peer group interactions provide them a cordial social environment, thus giving them the scope for free discussions about their 'self' or what they aspire to be, without any apprehensions or fear. This, in turn, drives the adolescents to commit to their goals and beliefs and thus boost their self-esteem (Ragelienė, 2016). Peer networks reflect vast similarities and boost peer influence. Adolescents' self-efficacy is also at its high, since they judge their own capabilities in comparison with their peers due to lack of familiarity with the tasks they perform (Schunk & Meece, 2006). The adolescent's act of debating with oneself and reflecting on the correctness of any information or performance for assessing one's own abilities is a constant ongoing process in the perception and belief of their self-efficacy during peer interactions. Bandura's theorizing about self-efficacy beliefs exhibit clear indication of reflective thoughts and cognitive processing and highlights the agentic role of adolescents in the formation of self-efficacy in peer interactions (Nyman et al., 2019). Adolescent attachment with peers is observed to positively affect their academic self-efficacy, whereas victimization and aggression are seen to be negatively related to academic self-efficacy (Llorca et al., 2017).

However, adolescents may also become vulnerable to peer pressure while trying to be accepted by the group and be part of it; this may have adverse effects if they fall prey to antisocial or deviant activities such as smoking, drinking, substance abuse, bullying or any other undesirable behaviour (Ragelienė, 2016). At such times, parents' involvement and support can aid to manage the social lives of adolescents. However, strained parent-adolescent relationships may encourage adolescents to resort to friends' advice for decision-making, which in turn can be associated with compromised behavioural and emotional health. Interventions aimed at improving the parent–child relationship may provide an avenue towards preventing health risk behaviours in youth (Khan et al., 2015).

As opposed to the typical assumption of negative influences of peer influence, it is a complex phenomenon that needs to be understood within the specific context. Adolescents generally liked to be associated with peers who shared the same interest as they enjoyed. Adolescents get quite influenced by peer groups in discerning their intrinsic value for school and achievement. Khan et al. (2015), in their study found peer pressure to be a prime factor to promote improvement in academics (96%), skill and personality development (96%) and improved self-confidence (80%) of adolescents. Exploration of the pathways of adulthood results in many close friendships and often belongingness to multiple groups but of similar demographics and interests. The duration of these friendships also keep on changing, some of which may be of longer term than the others. An analytical cross-sectional study of peer pressure on adolescents revealed that about half of the adolescents preferred to have long-term relationships (47 %), and with peers of similar economic status (48 %); the majority (66%) of them preferred to have friendship with the opposite gender (Khan et al., 2015).

I was that nice girl who used to obey my mom and also my teachers. My school had this rule of tying hair in two plaits for girls. I always used to go to school with two plaits and sometimes in oiled hair. My mom always used to tell me oiled hair reflects discipline. I never cared about what others felt or talked about me. Suddenly when I entered the eighth grade and I started noticing my classmates around me talking about others and cared about what other people did or what other people thought. I kind of got frightened and scared and started worrying, what others would talk about my oiled hair and two plaits. I started verbal fights with my mom against my wish. I didn't like to fight with her; I loved her a lot and didn't wish to hurt her. But I started going to school with one plait and avoided oiled hair in school. Now when I look back, I feel like laughing at myself for doing such a silly thing.

An experience of a teen as she changed her hair style in her eighth grade due to peer influence

FIGURE 3.16A Adolescent Vulnerable to Peer Influence

Social contexts in adolescence **149**

FIGURE 3.16B Adolescent Influenced by Positive Peer Pressure

Involvement with a peer group differs in nature and intensity at different stages of adolescence. Early adolescence identifies with a more intense peer group affiliation and conformation. In this stage of adolescence, when they are aged about 10 to 13, adolescents are ready to do any task or engage in activities which they would otherwise refrain from in order to belong to a peer group that they are a part of. This stage is a very crucial period when their strong belonging to a peer group can neither be ignored, nor can the adolescents be left completely unsupervised by adults who can guide them to withstand peer pressure and help them maintain healthy peer-group relations.

The stage following this, when the adolescents are aged about 14 to 16, is characterized by their increased maturity and higher tolerance of individual differences in appearance, beliefs and feelings. The groups tend to be more gender-mixed replaced by intimate dyadic relationships and romantic relationships with partners of the opposite sex (APA, 2002).

Sullivan argued that adolescent friendships satisfy needs of intimacy and consensual validation. Friendships in adolescence entail such interpersonal dynamics as loyalty or commitment to friends, intimacy in relationships and similarity in the type of personalities they characterize. Friendships in adolescence feature talks that allow self-exploration, and these talks include confidential self-disclosure and gossip to explore and evaluate similarities and differences between self and peers, building abstract ideals (Bukowsly et al., 2011, p. 166).

The number of friends adolescents have or the quality of time spent with friends is greatly influenced by the dynamics of culture, society, religion, socio-economic status, sexual orientation and contexts that could affect values and expectations about peer relations. It is thus necessary to understand the nature of peer relationships by describing the nature of peer attachments, peer group attitudes and peer problems as experienced by adolescents in different contexts.

Radmacher and Azmitia talk about the nature of gender differences in friendships exhibiting a manifestation of higher quality, more intimate relationships in female adolescents as compared to males (Robinson, 2014). Girls, especially during middle- and late adolescence, interact more with each other than boys, and they report more intimate self-disclosure than boys. But the core features of adolescent friendships remain the same irrespective of sexual orientation or cultural differences. Friendship with the other gender, which may start in childhood and become increasingly intimate, is a very common characteristic of late adolescence. McDougall and Hymel assert that these other-gender friendships need not be always sexually motivated, but may have many common features of the same-gender friendships as well. Dexter Dunphy suggests that there is a progression across adolescence, starting with same-gender friends' group called cliques, advancing to an intermingling of boys' and girls' cliques in big groups, culminating during late adolescence by moving to smaller, mixed-gender cliques that often include romantic relationships (Bukowsly et al., 2011, p. 166-167).

> ### Activity.
>
> You have already read through a few of the research findings provided to you in this chapter.
>
> - Identify similar studies that have been done on adolescent peer relationships
> - Analyze the findings of these studies with respect to the 'actor' and 'agent' guises of self through the interpersonal processes of adolescents.
> - Identify the social players in the adolescents' environment, which influence the variety of guises in facilitating the adolescents' identity formation.

Peer influences and adolescent well-being

Referring back to Chapter 1, we had discussed the emphasis on the importance of exploratory system as relatively more activated and developed in adolescents resulting in adolescents building relationships with peers, romantic partners and managing their own emotional states and behaviour.

Social contexts in adolescence 151

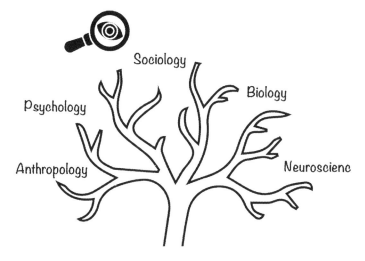

Look Back and Reflect

- Try to recollect the various developmental characteristics of adolescents through this multidisciplinary lens.
- Attempt to study adolescent development in peer contexts by considering adolescents' developmental characteristics and the multidisciplinary aspects that influence adolescent development.

Studies demonstrating maturational changes in brain structure and function occurring across the second decade of life have emphasized the salience of peer relations in adolescence. Puberty-related increases in gonadal hormones and oxytocin-receptor density contribute to changes in a constellation of social behaviours observed in adolescence. Brown and Larson assert that adolescents are found to spend more time interacting with peers, reporting the highest degree of happiness in peer contexts and assigning the greatest priority to peer norms for behaviour (Albert et al., 2013). Laible et al., (2004) records that peers become sources of emotional support and comfort, serve as safe havens and secure bases, even becoming sources of separation distress. This is the time when they are developing autonomy from their parents and lean towards peers for social and emotional support. Strong peer attachments have been associated with better psychological well-being. However, it can also result in a range of positive and negative influences of behavioural, social-emotional and school outcomes depending on the quality of attachment with friends and attitudes of their friends. (Gray et al., 2018). Secure attachments with peers foster the adolescent's self-development and his/her global self-esteem through the development of empathy as they learn to take other's views and perspectives (Laible et al., 2004).

Peer relationships provide a context not only for making friends, but also for the development of various skills such as social skills, social problem-solving skills, resilience, empathy and many more. Usually it has been observed that, adolescents' potential friends are more likely to be those who share similarities with regard to demographic characteristics, the type of school they attend, education and economic characteristics or peers who are around in a classroom, neighbourhood, sports team, religious group or any other group they belong to. Beyond these facets of friendships, others may include common interests, abilities, preferences, social status and so on (Janardhana & Manjula, 2018).

Social influences and adolescence

Indian culture and Western culture have unique and different norms, attitudes and customs surrounding marriage. The concept of dating in adolescence is not very welcomingly accepted in Indian society. Caste, religion, socio-economic status and educational qualifications are important factors that determine eligibility for marriage. Hence, parents constantly supervise and monitor their adolescent children till their marriage, controlling their children's network of relationships, especially with the opposite sex. In India, globalization, urbanization, rapid economic growth and the wide exposure to media has changed the outlook of people towards these concepts, particularly in urban areas. The declining age of puberty and the increasing age of marriage have provided adolescents with ample opportunities to engage in romantic relationships (Janardhana & Manjula, 2018).

The romantic relationship is considered one of the important developmental tasks in adolescence and to influence the course of other developmental tasks. Romantic relationships contribute to adolescents' identity formation, changes in family and peer relationships, and adolescents' emotional and behavioural adjustment. The quality of adolescent romantic relationships strongly influences the self-esteem of adolescents. Adolescents can benefit from healthy romantic relationship but also are likely to be affected negatively by such relationships if they turn unhealthy. Negative outcomes may include deviating from the norms of society, dysfunctional relationships with family and others, poor academic outcomes and deprivation of other opportunities, eventually affecting their developmental process. Alcohol in parents, disturbed family routine, parental discord, poor parental supervision and monitoring, poor quality of relationship between parents and children, poor communication between parents and children, and rejection of girls by their parents are some of the family factors associated with adolescents in romantic relationships. The role of family and school gains primary importance in recognizing and being responsive to the issues and problems of adolescents in romantic relationships to enable healthy navigation to adulthood (Janardhana & Manjula, 2018). Parent's knowledge about their adolescent children's activities, their friends and their whereabouts can safeguard adolescents from risky behaviours such as substance abuse or sexual behaviours, though it may vary with respect to age, gender or the culture to which they belong (Tome & Matos, 2012).

In addition to all this, romantic relationships are centrally connected to adolescents' emerging sexuality. Sexual orientation refers to whether a person is sexually and romantically attracted to others of the same sex, the opposite sex or both sexes. Russell et al., record that adolescence is often the period of revelation when they perceive themselves as who they are – lesbian, gay, bisexual or transgender. Thus, romantic relationships are a domain in which adolescents experiment with new behaviours and identities. Many adolescents may choose to come out during this period of their life, satisfied with the formation of an identity; while others may still be in a state of exploration by experimenting with both homosexual and heterosexual experiences. Coming to terms with and creating a positive identity for adolescents who may perceive oneself as gay, lesbian, bisexual or transgender can be very stressful when they are surrounded by normative peers who may question their sexuality or gender identity (Overstreet, 2020).

Even today, in times of worldwide awareness, homosexuality in the Indian context is largely considered as an unnatural phenomenon and a legitimate crime; hence, social exclusion of these communities has been quite evident (Sahni et al., 2016).

The extent and nature of peer group influence on adolescent achievement beliefs and behaviours is quite complex. Peer influence is also likely to occur through the process of modelling. Observing a friend's commitment towards certain tasks or acknowledging a friend's belief or view about something, may encourage the individual to behave in a certain manner and construct viewpoints for oneself. Other elusive ways of communicating undesirable behaviour may include gossip, teasing, making fun of someone and humour. These different ways of interactions among peer group members result in the formation of a peer group context with regard to norms, values and standards that influence academic motivation and engagement in school (Ryan, 2001).

Although peer group influences may be positive during adolescence, adolescents who are not too dependent on their peer groups are resilient against the influence of the peer group. The ability to resist the influences depends on the maturity of adolescents, and it is observed to increase with age. Adolescent girls are perceived to be more resilient than adolescent boys. The quality of friendships also determines the kind of influences on adolescents. A reciprocal close friendship of quality exerts greater influence on adolescents (Tome & Matos, 2012).

While peer culture is a universal characteristic of all cultures, there is a great deal of variability in the nature and the degree of peer relationships. Compared to Western culture, adolescents in Indian culture continue to depend on their families for support or decision-making, thus engaging less with their peers and friends. Much of their time is spent with family, limiting the role of friends and peers in adolescents' lives. Extensive relations with peers in collectivistic cultures tend to impede adolescents' obligations to the family and their obedience to adult authority. However, there is evidence to support the increasing incidence of what may be termed 'peer culture' among middle- and upper-class urban youth as affluence, mobility and consumption become common. In families where both parents (including the mother) are working, the adolescent tends to spend more time with peers. While peer relationships or peer groups in early adolescents may be largely supervised by parents, late adolescents are likely to evade adult supervision. It is generally observed in the Indian context that adolescent boys tend to spend more time with their peers and friends as compared to adolescent girls, primarily due to the greater mobility that boys are allowed (Chaudhary & Sharma, 2012, p. 108)

Research has indicated that problematic parenting or troubled parent-child relations in childhood can lead children to associate with deviant peers, which in turn promotes their own engagement in antisocial activities. On one hand, we have seen that family members, especially adults, facilitate adolescent adjustment by enabling healthy and conducive peer experiences; on the other hand it has been observed that the quality of peer relationships can buffer the ill effects of family characteristics on adolescent outcomes (Brown & Larson, 2009). This underscores the importance of the reciprocal relationship between family and peer contexts for adolescents; however, this depends on cultural factors and norms for peer relations in a particular context.

Adolescents today are the most avid users of social networking sites. Social media provides a unique interpersonal context to shape individuals' thoughts, behaviours and relationships. This portion of the chapter will exclusively focus on how social media impacts peer relations. Peer victimization has very drastic effects through different forms of cyber bullying or cyber aggression. Though this is not anything very different from traditional bullying, it leads to feeling of powerlessness, leaving no scope for the adolescent to escape from bullying experiences since it occurs with no boundaries of time and space. Online victimization can happen outside of school or within home at night outside of adult supervision. This can induce feelings of hopelessness and fear in adolescents. Social media platforms can elevate the experience of peer status by attracting attention of friends and peers who post likes and comments on pictures or any tasks posted on social media. At the same time, adolescents feel pressured to manage these relations and keep up with these relations in the fear of missing out on these experiences. This makes them construct an imaginary social identity that allows them constantly to be in the loop of these experiences by careful selection of photos of social events to post on social media. On the other hand, social media also provides access to social opportunities, conversations and events, which they are unlikely to miss out on. This eventually can exacerbate their efforts to change their actual behaviour offline through unrealistic expectations and demands. Deviating from the socially acceptable behaviour may lead to negative feedback from peers and reputational repercussions. Social media can also provide ample opportunities for such adolescents who, despite rejection or alienation, can explore new possibilities of identity formation through different social media platforms. We will look at the other influences of social media on adolescence in the following section.

Social contexts in adolescence **155**

> ### Activity: Reinforce your Learning
>
> We have already learnt about the three frameworks – socio-ecological theory, socio-cultural theory and the contextual developmental perspective in explaining adolescents' social processes and social interactions within peer relationships.
>
> - Identify adolescents in the Indian context and review their interpersonal processes within peer groups and peer relations.
>
> - Select any one of these cultural frameworks to explain the social processes and interactions within the selected framework.
>
> - Record any unique observations that emerge during the course of your investigation and explore reasons for the uniqueness of these observations.

Adolescents and social media

'Media' is a term that may range from traditional media such as television, radio and film that is generally unidirectional in nature, to digital media found on the internet that can facilitate bidirectional information exchange and engagement. Further, there is social media that allows the flow of messages in all directions through variety of paths. Social media platforms include communication via cell phones, laptops, tablets and social networking sites – Facebook, WhatsApp, You-Tube, Instagram, Twitter – and similar other sites and applications that allow speedy and easy communication, status updates and social networking among individuals.

Scan the QR code to view this video

The Positive Potential of Peer Pressure and Messing Around Online

Mimi Ito, Professor at the University of California, Irvine, examines the diversity of youth experience with new media and how it relates to questions of equity, access, and learning opportunities..

Highlights of this video:

- Teenagers have an idea of what a typical teenager looks like, very closely allied with the new media technologies that teens use.

- Adolescents' use of media is just as stratified as any other kind of activity that they engage in.
- The extreme dichotomies regarding the positive and negative effects of media use has a strongly technically determinist frame and also ignores the diversity of user experience.
- Who is getting access to the kinds of experiences that are productive and engaging, and who is not?' And what are the factors contributing to that?
- Media use that can be friendship-driven participation and interest-driven participation are quite distinct.
- There is a need to develop some alternative assessments and ways of thinking about dispositions, metacognitive capacities, preparation for future learning understanding the diverse outcomes of media use.
- New technology can really lower the barriers of access to connected learning experiences.

From the above highlights of the video by Mimi Ito, professor at the University of California, it is clear that adolescent's engagement with social media is diverse, distinct and has the potential to lower barriers to access, while providing for learning experiences. However, justifiably so, it is a matter of concern for most caregivers, parents and society at large.

Adolescents usually drift away from parents and struggle to explore their identity. At such times, they experience a feeling of loneliness, and a few of them start feeling depressed. They are more inclined to shift their attention to media as ways of coping with these kinds of emotions that arise during adolescence (Padilla-Walker, 2006). The use of social media for a variety of reasons has dramatically risen over the past few years, having both positive and negative implications on adolescents' development. According to Internet and Mobile Association of India's data, the number of internet user in India reached 478 million by June 2018 (Patil et al., 2019).

Adults often make their own assumptions regarding adolescents' use of social media without knowing exactly what the adolescent children are doing in their social networking spaces. This may be perceived as disobedience or non-compliance to parents and adults, whereas, adolescents may be trying to express their individuality and autonomy through the use of media platforms (Padilla-Walker, 2006). Teens may be texting, posting, tweeting or learning and communicating new ideas and information. Whether this is a futile exercise or a worthwhile one cannot be superficially decided. Vygotsky emphasized that human communication processes give rise to particular ways of thinking, and Wertsch furthered this idea, explaining that human action, which arises in cultural contexts, is tied to thought processes. This suggests that adolescents' digital practices shape their identity and influence their development as they shape their practices (Campbell, 2015).

Scan the QR code to view this video

Daniel Siegel: Why Teens Turn from Parents to Peers

Best-selling author and renowned neuropsychiatrist Daniel Siegel explains why adolescents turn to their peers and away from their parents for security, attachment, and approval.

Highlights of this video:

1. Attachment defined as the way a young child is dependent on an older individual to basically develop four S's- to be **S**een, to be **S**afe, to be **S**oothed and to be **S**ecure
2. Peer pressure
    - Kids moving into adolescent turn towards their peer – this is natural;
    - NEED to be a member of a peer group – this is evolution
    - Can sacrifice morality for membership (matter of life and death)
3. Social skills in adolescence is good for healthy adulthood
    - Supportive relationships essential for happiness, longevity, medical health and mental health
    - Adults need to honour this

Patterns of media use in adolescence

The amount of time spent in using social media depends on the social contexts in which it is consumed and also the motivational factors for using the media. Early adolescent children generally spend more time in media use as they are just exposed to media and they have enough time to spend with the media, whereas, as children enter middle school and further high school, their time of utilization of media may decrease due to lack of time as a result of more academic activities and their changing needs and interests. Adolescent media exposure varies with a number of background characteristics. It is generally observed that adolescent girls spend more time with certain forms of media than boys do; video games and computers are largely accessed by boys. Media exposure also depends on the socio-economic indicators of household. Here again, there are different aspects that may influence differently for different adolescent children. Affordability and accessibility to different social media platforms through various electronic devices, family structure, parenting styles and many other intervening factors from different contexts interplay in the lives of adolescent students and their use of media. Higher income households may be able to provide their children more access to media, but adolescents' use of media in these households depends on parents' control over their children. Lower income household may not be able to afford electronic devices due to which children from these homes may have limited access to media. Nevertheless, in today's times, almost every household has the minimum basic requirements of electronic devices, especially smart phones, which allow adolescents from these households to access social media sites. Adolescents' use of media here again depends on the family culture in terms of time spent with these children and attention given to them or lack of involvement of adults in children's life. Similarly, children from single-parent homes also spend more time with media due to lack of attention from their parents and also lack of resources to provide alternative sources of activities to engage with.

The context and quality of social media use by adolescents depends on their age, interests, family culture, peer influence and many more factors. In the initial years, adolescents' use of social media may be too general for purposes of entertainment and leisure. Gradually, as they grow into late adolescence, the whole context of social media use changes. Some adolescents may use social media exclusively for leisure, either by themselves or sharing with family; some may use it for education purposes too; a few may use social media for conforming to peer groups and being a part of the group; and others may use it to spend their time in solitude. By and large, most of the adolescents use social media to establish a sense of self by assuming potential roles and identities, building self-confidence, seeking moral guidance, social acceptance or status (Roberts, D.F., et al., Chapter 16)

The nature and characteristics of adolescents, as a consequence of their inherent traits and contextual influences, affect their interpretations of media content. Mostly, negative influences of media on adolescents are perceived, due to which the focus of attention is directed towards these effects rather than looking at adolescence per se. General perceptions of a global society or community in a wider social context about the influences of social media use on adolescents with regard to youth violence, sexual activity, substance use, and so on, question the role of media, thus instigating an investigation of social media content and its effects on adolescents' beliefs and behaviour in that direction. Thus, positive effects of media in promoting prosocial behaviours in adolescents are often bypassed.

There is a need to understand adolescent development in addition to the media processes and effects to enable an understanding of the effects of adolescent development on uses and responses to media and the effect of media on adolescent socialization and identity development.

Mass media and adolescence

Lenhart et al. affirms technology and online communication as a very important tool for socialization. Peer relationships and friendships are of salient importance to the psychosocial development of adolescents and their overall well-being. These relationships have been even more eased out through social media, which provides a means of constantly staying in touch with peers and friends. The frequent use of social media has resulted in the emergence of a new connotation of 'friendship' that is viewed as 'elastic', 'flexible' and 'changing over time' (Wood et al., 2016). This may also have implications for adolescents' behavioural outcomes, academic performances, decision-making, emotional health and well-being.

Media differs from other socializing agents like family, peer, school or community in terms of adolescents' control over their media choices as compared to other sources of socialization. In the resulting process of self-socialization, adolescents gain more control over their socialization and choose among a wide range of media materials and platforms to suit their preferences and personalities. As compared to other social contexts, adolescents gain more agency in co-constructing their own environment with their 'so-called friends' and socializing themselves without any scrutiny or authority of parents or adults.

Adolescents often make use of media for entertainment as a part of their leisure. Swidler asserts that media can provide materials towards the construction of adolescents' identity. Adolescents make use of media, especially for gender-role identity. They construct representations of man and woman and their physical and behavioural gender ideals as portrayed in images through music, movies, television, magazines, advertisements and the social networking sites. Both boys and girls use the information acquired from media to learn gender, sexuality, relationships for identity exploration and identity formation. Other than these, they also learn about occupational information contributing to their goals and aspirations. Use of media by adolescents is a common strategy to cope with such negative emotions as anger, anxiety or depression. Another important potential of media consumption is developing a sense of connectedness with a larger peer network sharing similar values and interests. Adolescents' use of media consumes a large amount of time in their life, leaving hardly any time to spend with their parents or family. The consequences of media use may be explicit in their rejection of authority of adults and discarding the values of adult world (Arnett, 1995).

It is very important to recognize the role of family, school, community and culture in influencing adolescents' choice of media and the interpretations they make in it. Their use of media may be influenced by the ideals and principles that that would have already learnt from the other contexts before being exposed to any media. Parents and schools often shoulder the responsibility of controlling adolescents' media use that may hamper their development. Adolescents very frequently receive contradicting messages from the media that are quite different from those that they receive from families and communities, and this creates confusion partly responsible for their alienation that we commonly see in today's generation of teens (Arnett, 1995).

> **Extended Activity:**
> **Contextual–developmental Perspective**
>
> **The Context**
>
> The contextual developmental perspective proposed by Chen and colleagues was used to explain the adolescents' socialization processes within peer relationships. This perspective introduced to the two fundamental dimensions that characterized children's specific behaviours as a consequence of varying societal values. The two dimensions were social initiative (the tendency to initiate and maintain social interactions, often indicated by children's reactions to challenging situations) and self-control (the regulatory ability to modulate behavioral and emotional reactivity).

Analyze the two characteristic dimensions of adolescents' behaviour influenced by different types of media.

Guiding questions-
- How does the role of media reflect the social initiative dimension in adolescents and how does it impact the developmental outcomes of adolescents?
- What role does culture play in determining the extent of social initiative and self-regulation in adolescents' use of media?
- How does media use influence adolescents with low levels of self-regulation? Is this influence unidirectional or bidirectional? Support your opinion with specific examples.

Social media use in Indian context

Socialization through media is quite different in Western cultures compared to non-Western cultures, though the invasion of Western media has opened up similar possibilities in non-Western cultures in contemporary times.

The wide use of social networking sites by Indian youth is to stay in touch with family and friends and with acquaintances. The excessive usage of social media results in their addictive behaviour facilitated by the egocentric construction of social networking sites. Elkind and Bowen, posit that adolescents often engage in what has been referred to as "imaginative audience behavior", which makes them pretend or behave in ways that can please others who they feel are constantly watching them. The strong feeling of being recognized and acknowledged on social media boosts their self-worth and self-esteem. They use social media platforms to boast about their huge network of friends and their illusionary beautiful lives they lead, to escape from reality. This leads to comparison of lifestyles among the youth and at times depression when they are likely to be drowned in those thoughts influenced by the online posts and comments. This does not actually result in true friendships, but just random names on friends' list. (Bharucha, 2018). The extravagant outburst of social media use, especially social networking sites, have refined interpersonal communication and restructured relationships. Majorly, those who lack self-presentation skills choose to communicate through online platforms rather than face-to-face communication, which leads to their compulsive use of the internet due to the absence of self-regulation and eventually results in sleepless nights, missing regular meals, low academic grades, lack of physical exercise, poor adaptation and social anxiety. Negative feedback on social media platforms have been usually observed to lower the self-esteem of adolescents leading to their low well-being (Wood et al., 2016). These sites have become an integral part of Indian youth today, who are considered as "digital natives" as against the ones who learnt digitalization and are technology immigrants. The previously mentioned problems of unrestrained usage of social media have been confirmed for Indian youth by research studies (Bharucha, 2018).

FIGURE 3.17 Adolescent's Feeling of Being Recognized and Acknowledged on Social Media, Boosting Her Self-worth

However, there are studies that have exhibited positive results of social media use. Wang et al. reported that social communication use is positively correlated with well-being and people who use social networking sites frequently have higher levels of well-being (Bharucha, 2018).

A survey conducted by the World Economic Forum and the Observer Research Foundation revealed that India's youth of today are quite ambitious and possess the ability to take independent decisions with respect to their career prospects. Their readiness to plunge into any kind of efforts in the form of additional training or skill development programmes with the changing and demanding times is very much evident. Lack of information asymmetries on jobs and skills plus a lack of guidance for setting realistic career goals and making professional choices are hindrances to their career opportunities. Media and internet sources serve as important sources of information among the youth of India, presenting an opportunity to expand their awareness about education pathways, employment opportunities, skill needs and available skill development programmes. However, the 'Future of Work, Education and Skills' Survey reveals that just 14% of surveyed firms reported using online recruitment channels (Kedia et al., 2018).

A study of teenagers' use of social networking sites in the city of Trivandrum, in Kerala, India, reveals that a very negligible portion of students use the internet for more than two hours, while many of them spend more than two hours for social networking, adding that girls spend more time than boys (Varghese, 2013). A study on teenagers in an urban city in Mangalore, India, reported that social networking sites were largely used for making friends and studies; the majority of them belonged to some group or the other, and they reported more positive experiences in teens than negative ones (Darshan, 2014).

The heavy use of social media by Indian youth is not restricted to urban India. Negative effects of social media use are reflected in rural adolescent children too. The use of social media is used predominantly for entertainment and communication rather than for the constructive purpose of education and personality development (Patil et al., 2019).

While social media has certainly changed the way we live for our betterment, not all changes in the Indian sphere are for the better. There is a strong need for timely intervention strategies to channellize the potential effects of media on adolescent children. The society needs to begin to address, for instance, cyber bullying and parental engagement with the virtual community.

Parents, teachers, schools and significant others need to recognize the wealth of the digital world for adolescents and value their practices in the social media sphere.

Teens and Social Media with Bethany Stolle

This will take you to a video that is a talk by Bethany Stolle giving insights about teens and social media

Scan the QR code to view this video

Social contexts in adolescence **163**

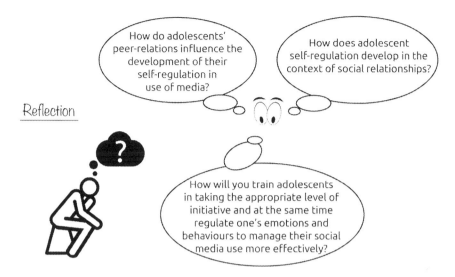

Summarizing this entire discussion on the relationship between peers and mass media in adolescent development through the framework of the three guises of 'self' as given by McAdams and Cox (2010), we see that the Author "I" is dormant for many years in waiting. It is not till adolescence and young adulthood that this capacity to reflect on life and the ability to put life in a meaningful narrative happens. From the various development theories, we see that it is from adolescence that the individual is able to go back and forth in the past, present and future to construct a narrative for oneself. In adolescence, individuals hone cognitive skills that enable them to construct causal sequences in life-narrative accounts and to derive overarching life themes. The adolescents' efforts to construct narrative identity may resemble the fantastical personal fables but this eventually evolves to realistic narratives based on psychosocial development.

However, we need to take note that this guise of self also builds on the strong foundation of the evolution of the actor-self and agent-self. This is evident in the development of appreciation of intentionality in the initial years, the emergence of self-awareness in the latter years of life and the development of theory of mind as important milestones that need to precede authorship.

Narrative studies of life transitions have also shown that (McAdams & Cox, 2010):

- Self-exploration and elaboration which are features of authorship are associated with higher levels of ego development;
- For positive authorship, the first step is making narrative sense of negative life events is exploring and elaborating on their nature and impact; step two is constructing a positive meaning or resolution;
- Finding positive meanings in negative events is what McAdams's conceptualizes as the redemptive self – a self where they see that there has been always

a positive impact of negative life events. This makes them more sensitive to others and committed to make the world a better place. Hence, these people are more generative;
- Generative people operating from the redemptive self construct accounts of difficult transitions, emphasizing learning, growth and positive personal transformation;
- Mills study found that coherent positive resolutions of difficult life events at age 51 predicted life satisfaction at age 61 and were associated with increasing ego resiliency between young adulthood and midlife. Therefore, what kind of meaning one gives to the authorship in adolescence has its bearing in the early adulthood and even in later stages of life;
- Deriving positive meanings from negative events is associated with life satisfaction and indicators of emotional well-being.

Conclusion

Against this backdrop we may wonder, what is the role of education in the life of adolescence with so many social agents that influence adolescence development? It is evident from the discourse that

1. All of us have the three guises (Actor, Agent and Author) from which the "I" operates'
2. We all are different in the way we operate from these guises;
3. There is a variation in the satisfaction and adjustment levels that we enjoy in our lives;
4. Having guises is important but not sufficient for an adjusted and joyful life;

We need to operate in narratives from the Author "I" aligned with the redemptive self-perspective.

We have seen various development perspectives. Using the cognitive development perspective and the Eriksonian identity perspective, the agent-self explores various life options with respect to ideology, occupation and relationships, chooses what kind of person to become – what to value, what work to do, whom to love, what dream to follow – in the future, reshaping the individual through commitment. Right through the development, we see that socio-emotional and cultural factors play a role in defining the individual. Culture intersects with the socio-emotional factors to be agents of identity, agency and authorship. Social agents also play a key pivotal role in the adolescence to be generative. Through this chapter we have discussed the various roles of family, school, peers and mass media as social agents in the development of the adolescence. It is hoped that through education, these influences would cultivate generalizable competencies, create opportunities for individuals to grow and express positive authorship, provide aidful resources and provide room for self-directedness and well-being of every individual.

> **Key terms:** adolescence, social contexts, family, school, peer, media, fortuity, social-cognitive theory, human agency, ecological theory, socialization, socio-cultural, contextual-development, social processes, multidisciplinary, redemptive self

Bibliography

Abbassi, N. (2016). Adolescent identity formation and the school environment. In K. Fisher (Ed.), *The translational design of schools: An evidence-based approach to aligning pedagogy and learning environments* (1st ed., pp. 83–103). Rotterdam, The Netherlands: Sense Publishers.

Agbenyega, J. S. (2005). *An investigation into the barriers and facilitators of inclusive education in Ghana: A policy reform study*. Clayton, Australia: Monash University.

Agbenyega, J. S. (2008). Developing the understanding of the influence of school place on students' identity, pedagogy and learning, visually. *International Journal of Whole Schooling, 4*(2), 52–66.

Ajrouch, K. J., Hakim-Larson, J., & Fakih, R. R. (2016). Youth development: An ecological approach to identity. In *Handbook of Arab American psychology* (pp. 91–102). Retrieved from https://scholar.uwindsor.ca/psychologypub/50

Albert, D., Chein, J., & Steinberg, L. (2013). The teenage brain: Peer influences on adolescent decision making. *Current Directions in Psychological Science, 22*(2), 114–120. doi:10.1177/0963721412471347

American Psychological Association. (2002). *Developing adolescents*. Retrieved from www.apa.org/pi/families/resources/develop.pdf

Anagurthi, C. (2017). *Applying an ecological model to predict adolescent academic achievement* (Wayne State University Dissertations). Retrieved from https://digitalcommons.wayne.edu/oa_dissertations/1684

Arnett, J. J. (1995). Adolescents' uses of media for self-socialization. Journal of Youth and Adolescence, *24*(5), 519–533.

Asbridge, D. J. (1984). *A process of identity formation in relation to peers and peer groups*. Paper presented at the Annual Convention of the Rocky Mountain Psychological Association. Retrieved from https://files.eric.ed.gov/fulltext/ED246379.pdf

Ashcroft, B. (2001). *Post-colonial transformation*. London, UK: Routledge.

Bahadur, A., & Dhawan, N. (2008). Social value of parents and children in joint and nuclear families. *Journal of the Indian Academy of Applied Psychology, 34*, 74–80.

Baltes, P. B., & Baltes, M. M. (1990). Psychological perspectives on successful aging: The model of selective optimization with compensation. In P. B. Baltes & M. M. Baltes (Eds.), *Successful aging: Perspectives from behavioral sciences* (pp. 1–34). Cambridge, UK: Cambridge University Press.

Bandura, A. (2006). Adolescent development from an agentic perspective. In F. Pajares & T. Urdan (Eds.), *Self-efficacy beliefs of adolescents* (pp. 1–43). Greenwich, CT: Information Age Publishing.

Baumeister, R. F., & Muraven, M. (1996). Identity as adaptation to social, cultural, and historical context. *Journal of Adolescence, 19*, 405–416.

Benson, J. E., & Johnson, M. K. (2009). Adolescent family context and adult identity formation. *Journal of Family Issues, 30*(9), 1265–1286. doi:10.1177/0192513X09332967

Bharat, S. (2008). Single-parent family in India: Issues and implications. *The Indian Journal of Social Work, 49*(3), 55–64.

Bhat, N. A. & Patil, R. R. (2019). Single parenthood families and their impact on children in India. *Delhi Psychiatry Journal, 22*(1), 161–165.

Bharucha, J. (2018). Social network use and youth well-being: A study in India. *Safer Communities, 17*(2), pp. 119–131. doi:10.1108/SC-07-2017-0029

Bi, X., Yang, Y., Li, H., Wang, M., Zhang, W., & Deater-Deckard, K. (2018). Parenting styles and parent–adolescent relationships: The mediating roles of behavioral autonomy and parental authority. *Frontiers in Psychology, 9*, 2187. https://doi.org/10.3389/fpsyg.2018.02187

Bronfenbrenner, U. (1979). *The ecology of human development: Experiments in nature and design.* Cambridge, MA: Harvard University Press.

Bronfenbrenner, U., & Morris, P. A. (2006). The bioecological model of human development. In W. Damon (Series Ed.) & R. M. Lerner (Vol. Ed.), *Handbook of child psychology: Vol 1. Theoretical models of human development* (pp. 793–828). New York, NY: Wiley.

Brown, B. B., & Larson, J. (2009). Peer relationships in adolescence. In R. M. Lerner & L. Steinberg (Eds.), *Handbook of adolescent psychology: Contextual influences on adolescent development* (pp. 74–103). Hoboken, NJ: John Wiley & Sons. https://doi.org/10.1002/9780470479193.adlpsy002004

Buchanan, C. M., Eccles, J. S., Flanagan, C., Midgley, C., Feldlaufer, H., & Harold, R. D. (1990). Parents' and teachers' beliefs about adolescents: Effects of sex and experience. *Journal of Youth and Adolescence, 19*(4), 363–394. https://doi.org/10.1007/BF01537078

Bukowski, W. M., Buhrmester, D., & Underwood, M. K. (2011). Peer relations as a developmental context. In M. K. Underwood & L. H. Rosen (Eds.), *Social development: Relationships in infancy, childhood, and adolescence* (pp. 153–179). New York, NY: Guilford Press.

Buss, D. M. (2008). Human nature and individual differences: Evolution of human personality. In O. P. John, R. W. Robins, & L. A. Pervin (Eds.), *Handbook of personality: Theory and research* (3rd ed., pp. 29–60). New York, NY: Guilford Press.

Campbell, T. M. (2015). *Filtered identities: A digitally active mid-adolescent's identity construction in social networking spaces.* Dissertation, Georgia State University. Retrieved from https://scholarworks.gsu.edu/mse_diss/10

Caspi, A. (2002). Social selection, social causation and developmental pathways: Empirical strategies for better understanding how individuals and environments are linked across the life course. In L. Pulkkinen & A. Caspi (Eds.), *Paths to successful development. Personality in the life course* (pp. 281–301). Cambridge, UK: Cambridge University Press.

Chaudhary, N., & Sharma, N. (2012). *Adolescent psychology around the world* (J. J. Arnett, Ed.). New York, NY: Psychology Press.

Chen, X. (2012). Culture, peer interaction, and socio-emotional development. *Child Development Perspectives, 6*, 27–34.

Chen, X., & French, D. C. (2008). Children's social competence in cultural context. *Annual Review of Psychology, 59*, 591–616.

Collins, W. A., & Steinberg, L. (2006). Adolescent Development in Interpersonal Context. In N. Eisenberg, W. Damon, & R. M. Lerner (Eds.), Handbook of child psychology: Social, emotional, and personality development (pp. 1003–1067). Hoboken, NJ: John Wiley & Sons.

Colyard, V. (1986). *Attitudes of early adolescents toward single-parent and stepparent families: implications for home economics curriculum.* Doctoral Thesis, Iowa State University. Retrieved from https://lib.dr.iastate.edu/cgi/viewcontent.cgi?article=9236&context=rtd&httpsredir=1&referer=

Corsaro, W. A., & Nelson, E. (2003). Children's collective activities and peer culture in early literacy in American and Italian preschools. *Sociology of Education, 76*, 209–227.

Crockett, L. J. (2002). Agency in the life course: Concepts and processes. In L. J. Crockett (Ed.), *Vol. 48 of the Nebraska symposium on motivation. Agency, motivation, and the life course* (pp. 1–29). Lincoln, NE: University of Nebraska Press.

Darshan, B. M. (2014). Teenagers and social media: A study in Mangalore City. *National Conference on Social Networking Media: Boon or Bane? 1*(1), 136–139.

D'Cruz, P., & Bharat, S. (2001). Beyond joint and nuclear: The Indian family revisited. *Journal of Comparative Family Studies, 32*, 167–194.

Deb, S., & Walsh, K. (2010). Anxiety among high school students in India: Comparisons across gender, school type, social strata and perceptions of quality time with parents. *Australian Journal of Educational & Developmental Psychology, 10*, 18–31.

Eccles, J. S. (2004). Schools, academic motivation, and stage-environment fit. In R. M. Lerner & L. Steinberg (Eds.), *Handbook of adolescent psychology* (pp. 125–154). Hoboken, NJ: John Wiley & Sons.

Eccles, J. S., & Roeser, R. W. (1999). School and community influences on human development. In M. Bornstein & M. Lamb (Eds.), *Developmental psychology: An advanced textbook* (4th ed., pp. 503–554). Mahwah, NJ: Lawrence Erlbaum.

Eccles, J. S., & Roeser, R. W. (2011). Schools as developmental contexts during adolescence. *Journal of Research on Adolescence, 21*(1), 225–241. doi:10.1111/j.1532-7795.2010.00725.x

Erentaitė, R., Vosylis, R., Gabrialavičiūtė, I., & Raižienė, S. (2018). How does school experience relate to adolescent identity formation over time? Cross-lagged associations between school engagement, school burnout and identity processing styles. *Journal of Youth and Adolescence, 47*, 760–774.

Erikson, E. H. (1959). *Identity and the life cycle*. New York, NY: International Universities Press.

Graf, S. C. (2003). *Cross-cultural study of adolescent identity formation and autonomy within the context of parent-adolescent relationships*. Doctoral Dissertation, Florida State University. Retrieved from http://purl.flvc.org/fsu/fd/FSU_migr_etd-407

Gray, S., Romaniuk, H., & Daraganova, G. (2018, November). *Adolescents' relationships with their peers*. LSAC Annual Statistical Report 2017 chapter Published by the Australian Institute of Family Studies.

Hagestadt, G. O., & Neugarten, B. L. (1985). Age and the life course. In R. H. Binstock & E. Shanas (Eds.), *Handbook of aging and the social sciences* (pp. 35–61). New York, NY: Van Nostrand Reinhold.

Hansen, D., Bretl, B. L., & Amini, B. (2019). *Adolescent development in context: Social, psychological, and neurological foundations*. Lawrence, KS: University of Kansas Libraries.

Harter, S. (1990). Self and identity development. In S. S. Feldman & G. R. Elliott (Eds.), *At the threshold: The developing adolescent* (pp. 388–413). Cambridge, MA: Harvard University Press.

Hinde, R. A. (1987). *Individuals, relationships and culture*. Cambridge, UK: Cambridge University Press.

Hitlin, S., & Johnson, M. K. (2015). Reconceptualizing agency within the life course: The power of looking ahead. *American Journal of Sociology, 120*, 1429–1472.

Hogan, R. (1982). A socioanalytic theory of personality. In M. Paige (Ed.), *Nebraska symposium on motivation: 1981* (pp. 55–89). Lincoln, NE: University of Nebraska Press.

Hoof, A. V. (1999). The identity status field re-reviewed: An update of unresolved and neglected issues with a view on some alternative approaches. *Developmental Review, 19*(4), 497–556. doi:10.1006/drev.1999.0484

Hoskins, D. H. (2014). Consequences of parenting on adolescent outcomes. *Societies, 4*, 506–531. doi:10.3390/soc4030506

Janardhana, N., & Manjula, B. (2018). Adolescents romantic relationship: Dynamics of parent-child relationship from India. In *Maternal and child health matters around the world*. doi:10.5772/intechopen.81634

Kapadia, S. (2008). Adolescent-parent relationships in Indian and Indian immigrant families in the US: Intersections and disparities. *Psychology and Developing Societies, 20*(2), 257–275. https://doi.org/10.1177/097133360802000207

Kedia, S., Gutta, S., Chapman, T., & Mishra, V. (2018). *Here's what young Indians really want from life*. Retrieved from www.weforum.org/agenda/2018/10/here-s-what-young-indians-really-want-from-life/

Khan, A., Jain, M., & Budhwani, C. (2015). An analytical cross-sectional study of peer pressure on adolescents. *International Journal of Reproduction, Contraception, Obstetrics and Gynecology, 4*(3), 606–610. doi:10.18203/2320-1770.ijrcog20150060

Kuhn, D., & Franklin, S. (2012). The second decade: What develops (and how)? In W. Damon, R. S. Siegler, R. M. Lerner, D. Kuhn, & N. Eisenberg (Eds.), *Child and adolescent development: An advanced course*. Hoboken, NJ: John Wiley & Sons.

Kuppens, S., & Ceulemans, E. (2019). Parenting styles: A closer look at a well-known concept. *Journal of Child and Family Studies, 28*, 168–181. https://doi.org/10.1007/s10826-018-1242-x

Kurup, V. S. K., Geetha, V. C., & Prasanth, P. (2016). Psychosocial adjustment and structure of family: A comparison between joint and nuclear families. *International Education and Research Journal, 2*(3). Retrieved from http://ierj.in/journal/index.php/ierj/article/view/175

Kuther, T. L. (2018). Socioemotional development in adolescence. In T. L. Kuther (Ed.), *Lifespan development: Lives in context*. Thousand Oaks, CA: SAGE Publications.

Laff, R., & Ruiz, W. (2019). A closer look at parenting. In A. Johnson (Ed.), *Child family and community*. College of the Canyons.

Laible, D. J., Carlo, G., & Roesch, S. C. (2004). Pathways to self-esteem in late adolescence: The role of parent and peer attachment, empathy, and social behaviors. *Faculty Publications, Department of Psychology, 315*. Retrieved from https://digitalcommons.unl.edu/psychfacpub/315

Lerner, R. (2009). *Handbook of adolescent psychology* (2nd ed. & R. M. Lerner & L. Steinberg, Eds.). Hoboken, NJ: John Wiley & Sons, Inc.

Llorca, A., Richaud, M. C., & Malonda, E. (2017). Parenting, peer relationships, academic self-efficacy, and academic achievement: Direct and mediating effects. *Frontiers in Psychology, 8*. doi:10.3389/fpsyg.2017.02120

Marin, P. F., & Brown, B. (2008). *The school environment and adolescent well-being: Beyond academics* (Child Trends Research Brief, 26). Retrieved from www.childtrends.org/wp-content/uploads/2013/04/child_trends-2008_11_14_rb_schoolenviron.pdf

McAdams, D. P. (1999). Personal narratives and the life story. In L. A. Perwin & O. P. John (Eds.), *Handbook of personality: Theory and research* (pp. 478–500). New York, NY: Guilford Press.

McAdams, D. P., & Cox, K. S. (2010). Self and identity across the life span. In M. E. Lamb, A. M. Freund, & R. M. Lerner (Eds.), *Handbook of lifespan development* (Vol. 2, pp. 158–207). New York, NY: Wiley.

McElhaney, K. B., Allen, J. P., Stephenson, J. C., & Hare, A. L. (2009). Attachment and Autonomy during Adolescence. In R. M. Lerner & L. Steinberg (Eds.), *Handbook of adolescent psychology: Individual bases of adolescent development* (pp. 358–403). Hoboken, NJ: John Wiley & Sons. doi:10.1002/9780470479193.adlpsy001012

Nurmi, J. (2004). Socialization and self-development. In R. M. Lerner & L. Steinberg (Eds.), Handbook of adolescent psychology (pp. 85–124). Hoboken, NJ: John Wiley & Sons.

Nyman, J., Parisod, H., Axelin, A., & Salanterä, S. (2019). Finnish adolescents' self-efficacy in peer interactions: A critical incident study. *Health Promotion International, 34*(5), 961–969. doi:10.1093/heapro/day048

Overstreet, L. (2020). *Social development.* Retrieved March 7, 2021, from https://socialsci.libretexts.org/@go/page/3043

Padilla-Walker, L. M. (2006). Developmental needs of adolescents and media. *Faculty Publications, Department of Psychology, 483.*

Patil, M. A., Bharti, H., Amte, A., Singh, B. K., & Desai, M. (2019). Profile of adolescent social media user in rural area. *Pediatric Review: International Journal of Pediatric Research, 6*(1), 22–28. doi:10.17511/ijpr.2019.i01.04

Pedditzi, M. L., & Marcello, P. (2018). School social context, students' self-efficacy and satisfaction in high school. *The Open Psychology Journal, 11,* 249–260.

Pellerone, M., Spinelloa, C., Sidoti, A., & Micciche, S. (2015). Identity, perception of parent-adolescent relation and adjustment in a group of university students. *Procedia – Social and Behavioral Sciences, 190,* 459–464.

Population Council & UNICEF. (2013). *Adolescents in India: A desk review of existing evidence and behaviours, programmes and policies.* New Delhi, India: Author.

Povedano-Diaz, A., Muñiz-Rivas, M., & Vera-Perea, M. (2020). Adolescents' life satisfaction: The role of classroom, family, self-concept and gender. *International Journal of Environmental Research and Public Health, 17*(1), 19.

Ragelienė, T. (2016). Links of adolescents identity development and relationship with peers: A systematic literature review. *Journal of the Canadian Academy of Child Adolescent Psychiatry, 25*(2), 97–105.

Rani, M., & Khajuria, J. (2017). Adjustment problems of adolescents of joint family and nuclear family. *International Journal of Advanced Educational Research, 2*(4), 97–101.

Rehman, R., & Singh, H. (2015). Family type and adjustment level of adolescents: A study. *International Journal of Dental and Medical Research, 1*(6), 22–25.

Robinson, J. (2014). *Adolescent peer group orientation, attachment/parenting styles and mental health.* Doctoral Thesis, Deakin University. Retrieved from https://dro.deakin.edu.au/eserv/DU:30066236/robinson-adolescentpeer-2014A.pdf

Rudo, P. W. (1996). *Structure and agency in youth transitions: student perspectives on vocational further education.* Doctoral Thesis, University of Surrey. Retrieved from https://www.proquest.com/openview/19163aee3ce34e16b84f6ad7ad2b61b6/1?pq-origsite=gscholar&cbl=51922&diss=y

Ryan, A. (2001). The peer group as a context for the development of young adolescent motivation and achievement. *Child Development, 72*(4), 1135–1150.

Sahni, S., Gupta, B., Nodiyal, K., & Pant, V. (2016). Attitude of Indian youth towards homosexuality. *The International Journal of Indian Psychology, 4*(1), 59–69.

Sandhu, D., Singh, B., Tung, S., & Kundra, N. (2012). Adolescent identity formation, psychological well-being, and parental attitudes. *Pakistan Journal of Psychological Research, 27*(1), 89–105.

Schunk, D. H., & Meece, J. L. (2006). Self-efficacy development in adolescence. In F. Pajares, & T. Urdan (Eds.), *Self-efficacy beliefs of adolescents* (pp. 71–96). Greenwich, CT: Information Age Publishing.

Sebastian, C., Burnett, S., & Blakemore, S. J. (2008). Development of the self-concept during adolescence. *Trends in Cognitive Sciences, 12*(11), 441–446. doi:10.1016/j.tics.2008.07.008

Simons-Morton, B. G., Crump, A. D., Haynie, D. L., & Saylor, K. E. (1999). Student-school bonding and adolescent problem behavior. *Health Education Research, 14*(1), 99–107. doi:10.1093/her/14.1.99

Singh, R., Pant, K., & Valentina, L. (2017). Impact analysis: Family structure on social and emotional maturity of adolescents. *Anthropologist, 17*(2), 359–365. doi:10.1080/09720073.2014.11891445

Smetana, J. G. (2017). Current research on parenting styles, dimensions, and beliefs. *Current Opinion in Psychology, 15*, 19–25.

Sondhi, R. (2017). Parenting adolescents in India: A cultural perspective. In *Child and adolescent mental health* (pp. 91–102). doi: 10.5772/66451

Stumpers, S. A., Breen, L. J., Pooley, J., Cohen, L., & Pike, L. (2005). A critical exploration of the school context for young adolescents completing primary education. *Community, Work & Family, 8*(3), 251–270.

Svodziwa, M., Kurete, F., & Ndlovu, L. (2016). Parental knowledge, attitudes and perceptions towards adolescent sexual reproductive health in Bulawayo. *International Journal of Humanities Social Sciences and Education, 3*(4), 62–71. http://dx.doi.org/10.20431/2349-0381.0304007

Tijani, A., & Ogunbanwo, B. (2009). Emergence of single parenthood in Nigeria and its implication to child rearing. *Continental Journal of Nursing Science, 1,* 9–12.

Tome, G., & Matos, M. G. (2012). How can peer group influence the behavior of adolescents: Explanatory model. *Global Journal of Health Science, 4*(2), 26–35.

Varghese, T., Nivedhitha, D., & Krishnatray, P. (2013). Teenagers' usage of social networking media in a south Indian state. *International Journal of Scientific & Engineering Research, 4*(12), 622–636.

Vygotsky, L. S. (1978). *Mind in society: The development of higher psychological processes.* Cambridge, MA: Harvard University Press.

Wood, M. A., Bukowski, W. M., & Lis, E. (2016). The digital self: How social media serves as a setting that shapes youth's emotional experiences. *Adolescent Research Review, 1,* 163–173. doi:10.1007/s40894-015-0014-8

Xiao, Z., Li, X., & Stanton, B. (2011). Perceptions of parent-adolescent communication within families: it is a matter of perspective. *Psychology, Health & Medicine, 16*(1), 53–65. doi:10.1080/13548506.2010.521563

Zimmerman, B. J., & Cleary, T. J. (2006). The role of self-efficacy beliefs and self-regulatory skill. In F. Pajares & T. Urdan (Eds.), *Self-efficacy beliefs of adolescents* (pp. 45–69). Charlotte, NC: Information Age Publishing.

4
ADOLESCENCE AND WELL-BEING

CHAPTER 4: Adolescence and Well-Being

Overview

After reading this chapter, you will be able to achieve the following objectives

- Understand the multi-dimensional concept of well-being in face of the emergence of multiple disconnected and uni-dimensional views of well-being emanating from various disciplines
- Able to take cognizance of the emotional, cognitive, and psychological dimensions of well-being as it resonates with contemporary times and at the same time recognize the participatory framework of well-being as rooted in culture, context, and identities of individuals at a specific point in time based on the 'Ecological Systems Theory' and 'Life Course Theory'
- Appreciate a strength based approach to positive well-Being using Seligman's PERMA model
- Capture the essence of well-being perspective through development of human potentialities in different areas and environmental resources rather than focusing on the presence or lack of diseases or disorders
- Revisit the psychological determinants of adolescents' well-being to underscore the importance of their impact on adolescent development
- Focus attention on specific aspects of well-being as influenced by social contexts
- Able to address adolescent well-being needs comprehensively in the educational arena by gaining insights into the evidence-based findings on adolescent well-being in the Indian context and the various initiatives taken by the Indian Government
- Expand the comprehension of the constantly emerging and adapting concept of well-being using the multidisciplinary framework as proposed by Soutter, A., et al
- Appreciate the implications of the complex and interrelated nature of well-being and envisage well-being as a necessary foundation of education rather than framing it as an outcome.

Well-being: a multidimensional concept

Different fields of study have attempted to understand the most 'desired' variable for human beings, i.e. 'well-being'. So, in an attempt to understand and make it a reality, studies on well-being have been done in multiple fields, including economics, sociology, psychology, the health sciences and education.

As is true for many of the constructs in social sciences, well-being's many definitions and applications reflect these varied approaches to studying and communicating findings about it. Economists, for example, have drawn from surveys, GDP and employment rates to explore the links between wealth and happiness. Health scientists, in turn, have examined data from their field, observed practitioners and interviewed patients and their families to consider how medical interventions affect health-related quality of life. Educationists inquire of what type of education contributes to well-being of their students. We have seen that state of health has moved from the conception of absence of disease to well-being conception. Such insights from various disciplines are rarely taken collectively; hence we have multiple unidimensional views of well-being.

There is one common question that underlines research in different disciplines – what makes life worth living? These answers have informed policy, programs and practice for different age groups, including adolescence.

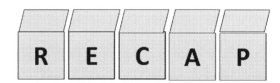

The period of adolescence, as we have seen in the previous chapter, has certain unique characteristics. Let's go over a few of these characteristics to be able to understand the concept of well-being covered in this chapter.

1. Adolescence is defined as the transitional period from childhood to adulthood, characterized by critical physical, psychological, emotional and social changes;
2. Moreover, adolescence is a period of risk-taking, and unhealthy behaviours often do not only affect health within this period but also later in life;
3. Adolescence is considered a period of contradictions; in fact, at the same time, it is the healthiest period of the entire life span (with respect to psychophysical parameters) and the time in which one-third of the total disease burden of adulthood is determined;
4. Adolescence is a dynamic and flexible period of knowledge and adaptation to target health interventions, so that adolescents can make positive lifestyle choices to enhance their well-being;
5. In this view, autonomy, agency, positive behaviours and social connection with family, school and community are recommended in order to limit the incidence of a health-jeopardizing conduct.

Activity: Adolescent Characteristics: Positive or Negative?

Directions: Complete the crossword by filling in a word that fits each clue given below for an assigned number and direction (Across/Down).

Adolescence and well-being

Across

2 I can tackle any situation easily without getting stressed
3 My friends tease me and humiliate me every day
5 Most of the times, I want to say "No" and end up saying "Yes"
7 I take charge of things without anyone's persuasion
11 I either make poor decisions or none at all
12 I sometimes don't understand who I am
14 My friends and family spend lot of time with me and support me at all times
18 I am an important member of my class
19 I am able to reflect, mobilize and regulate their actions to reach long term goals that they set for themselves
20 I deeply look into the matter before forming an opinion

Down

1. I broke up with my partner of my opposite sex because of lack of trust
4. I get angry immediately, when someone triggers me
6. I don't have any health problems related to my body
8. I take into consideration my group members' perspectives
9. I have access to all kinds of materials, books, good schooling etc.
10. I don't have any bad habits of smoking or drinking
13. I share a very close relationship with my teacher, with whom I share all my feelings
15. I cannot think out of the box, I always settle for conventional ideas
16. My parents allow me the freedom to make choices
17. I feel I do not have much to be proud of

Word Bank: Agency, Assertiveness, Autonomy, Bullying, Coping, Creativity, CriticalThinking, DecisionMaking, IdentityCrisis, SelfEsteem, InterpersonalRelationship, ManagingEmotions, OpenMindedness, PhysicalHealth, Resources, Responsible, RomanticRelationship, SelfConcept, SocialConnectedness, SubstanceAbuse

Think and Reflect:

- Identify the above characteritics as desirable or undesirable for an adolescent. Tabulate them under positive or negative characteristics and discuss with your peers as to why you consider them positive or negative.
- How are these characteritics essential for the positive well-being of an adolescent?
- Also list additional characteritics other than the ones listed above that you feel are essential for an adolescent's well-being.

From the previous chapters we have seen that the current approach to understanding adolescence has legitimized an optimistic view that interventions in ecological systems such as home, peers and other societal influences have the potential to alter the course of life for improved life outcomes. The concept of positive development to be promoted among adolescents is the focus of research endeavours. It also attested that the belief for understanding adolescent behaviour using the person-centred approach is necessary. This lays the foundations for a multidisciplinary and distinctive way of viewing the concept and need for well-being for adolescence.

Let us introduce you to an activity to start with.

Adolescence and well-being 175

Read through these examples carefully and reflect on these cases.

> Vaidehi was a 14 year old studying in the eighth grade. She resided with her parents. Her previous years' academic record showed predominantly A and B grades. She was talented and gifted. But suddenly she was absent from her school during her eighth grade. She was serious and feared going to school, being in crowds of people, leaving home, and demanded lot of attention. She started feeling nervous and things started depressing her.

> James was a ninth grader, who enjoyed history, art, and physical education. He hated doing homework. He had good grades in his previous years. He suddenly stopped answering in class and feared criticisms from teachers and peers. He started making excuses to avoid going to school. He somehow managed to finish his schooling and went to college. He stared performing well in college. His aspirations grew and he started working really hard to fulfil his aspirations.

> Abdul was a 17 year old boy studying in tenth grade. He liked school until he got in about sixth or seventh grade. He failed to make eye contact with anyone he spoke. He made the decision to drop out of school a few weeks prior to the end of his tenth-grade school year. He felt bored at school. One of the reasons he did not want to go to school was that his girlfriend broke with him and joined her ex-boyfriend. He contemplated suicide by thinking of different ways.

> Gurpreet was a 19 year old boy who was open about discussing his experiences and a jovial child. He was dressed neatly and maintained good eye contact while speaking. He enjoyed art and music classes and studied a musical instrument. He had high aspirations for himself. He scored well in academics and was liked by everyone around. He was quite good at managing his own problems and coping with stress.

Look at these cases and think about the adolescent phases of ups and downs.

- What does it tell or indicate?
- Is it normal or unusual according to you? Why do you think so?
- Scrutinize these cases in line with the different components of well-being like life-style habits, social skills, emotional status or mental skills, ponder on the questions given below and discuss it with your peers

Pick up any two of the above mentioned components and discuss each case in relation to these components
  ▸ What do you think about their psychological or mental states?
  ▸ Can the reasons for their mental states be the same or do you think they can be different?
  ▸ Why do you think is there a similarity/difference?
  ▸ Reflect back on the various aspects of adolescents discussed in the previous chapters.

Cues: gender, socio-economic status, context (urban/rural), caste, religion, etc.

Do you think it possible to help the adolescents cope with these vital phases? If so, suggest a few remedies that you think are possible to help these adolescents in coping with these phases.

There are many more questions that may arise looking at different kinds of ups and downs in lives of adolescents. In this chapter we will explore the different concepts of adolescents' well-being and the underlying reasons, consequences and ways of fostering adolescents' well-being.

The origin of psychology has often considered adolescence as a difficult stage in the process of development into adulthood. Yet, adolescence as a stage of opportunities and positive energy has been reiterated in the previous chapters. According to Offer and Schonert-Reichl, many adolescents successfully transit this stage without experiencing particular difficulties or traumas and report a level of relative well-being (Žukauskienė, 2014).

Understanding theoretical conceptions of well-being

Well-being in childhood and adolescence is a growing field of study and discussion, though the phenomenon has assumed a wide range of differing concepts. Well-being is a multidimensional phenomenon, integrating biological, psychological, social and spiritual dimensions. It refers to the emotional and cognitive dimensions of the subjective experience resulting from individual evaluation of various dimensions of an individual's life. Well-being can be understood from both hedonic and eudaimonic perspectives which are interrelated. Hedonic well-being refers to the emotional dimensions of the individuals' positive life-experiencing, including absence of negative emotions, presence of positive emotions, life satisfaction and social involvement. Eudaimonic well-being refers to the psychological well-being that focuses on harmony between the individuals' goals and values and life experiences and is associated to individuals' personal development (Moreira et al., 2015).

While hedonic perspectives typically represent well-being as a particular outcome (happiness or pleasure), the eudaimonic perspective considers well-being as a way of living (Soutter et al., 2011). With exceptions, contemporary well-being scholars recognize that both philosophical perspectives resonate with people today and that being conversant in each allows scholars and practitioners to reflect upon a wider range of values, needs and desires.

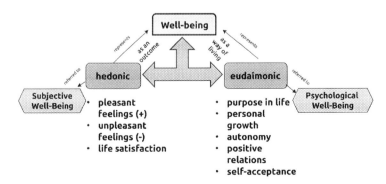

FIGURE 4.1 Eudemonic and Hedonic Perspectives of Well-Being

Andrews et al. referred to well-being as

> healthy and successful individual functioning (involving physiological, psychological and behavioural levels of organization), positive social relationships (with family members, peers, adult caregivers, and community and societal institutions, for instance, school and faith and civic organizations), and a social ecology that provides safety.
>
> (Žukauskiene, 2014).

This definition includes different dimensions of adolescent lives coherent with the conceptualization of the concept of adolescence with an integrated perspective. Another participatory framework of well-being, designed by researchers at the University of Wisconsin-Madison, is theoretically grounded in Bronfenbrenner's Ecological Systems Theory and Elder's Life Course Theory, influenced by the work of Carol D. Ryff and Connie Flanagan. This model recognizes that well-being is rooted in the culture, context and identities of participants at a specific point in time (Bintliff, 2020).

The theories and framework that formed the base of this participatory framework are briefly introduced in the following:

- You have already learnt in detail about **Bronfenbrenner's Ecological Systems Theory** in the previous chapter. The theory explains how the individuals and their environments interact to influence how they grow and develop. The model identifies five environmental systems with which an individual interacts (see Chapter 3).
- **Elder's Life Course theory** introduces five basic concepts – cohorts, transitions, trajectories, life events and turning points. The participatory framework applies this to understand the multidimensional aspects of adolescent well-being. Glen Elder identified four dominant and interrelated themes in the life course approach: interplay of human lives and historical time, timing of lives, linked or interdependent lives and human agency in making choices. These themes facilitate the understanding of adolescent well-being dimensions identified through the participatory framework (Hutchinson, 2018).
- John Flanagan, an American psychologist developed the Quality of Life Scale (QOLS) to evaluate global quality of life. It measured five conceptual domains of quality of life: material and physical well-being; relationships with other people; social, community and civic activities; personal development and fulfilment; and recreation (Dantas & Ciol, 2014).
- The **Ryff Scales of Psychological Well-Being** is a theoretically grounded instrument that specifically focuses on measuring multiple facets of psychological well-being. It measures six aspects of well-being and happiness: autonomy; environmental mastery; personal growth; positive relations with others; purpose in life; and self-acceptance. Ryff's six-factor model of psychological well-being potentially provides a comprehensive theoretical

178 Adolescence and well-being

framework for investigating positive functioning of adolescents (Gao & McLellan, 2018).

The participatory framework overall refers to the various dimensions of well-being and the spheres of influence that enable adolescents to identify people, systems and policies that hinder or promote well-being.

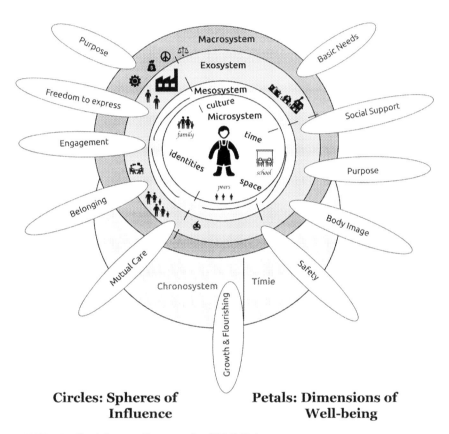

FIGURE 4.2 Participatory Framework of Well-Being

Adolescents' well-being is highly associated to several indicators of developmental trajectories, including engagement with school, academic achievement, optimism and coping strategies. It is a protective factor against negative indicators of health. Adolescents with high levels of well-being are more resilient, present lower delinquency behaviours and aggression, lower depressive and anxiety symptoms, higher self-esteem, self-efficacy and adaptation (Moreira etal., 2015).

Engagement with school
Academic achievement
Optimism
Coping strategies
Resilience
Delinquent behaviour
Aggression
Depressive symptoms
Anxiety
Self-esteem
Self-efficacy
Adaption
And
more......................

An approach to positive well-being: PERMA

Let us first understand well-being through the perspective of positive psychology, which is a scientific study of what makes life most worth living.

Positive Psychology

This video provides an overview of positive psychology and introduces to the applications of the tenets of positive psychology to make life worth

Scan the QR code to view the video

This school of thought believes that strengths of an individual is as important as the weaknesses; therefore building on strengths is important. Different psychologists who attempt to answer this question have identified different elements that contribute to the concept of well-being. Martin Seligman is one such psychologist who encourages us to channellize our energies based on our strengths to make life more fulfilling and meaningful.

In 2009, Seligman, Ernst, Gilham, Reivich and Linkins defined positive education as "education for both traditional skills and for happiness" (p. 293). Peterson believed that schools are the ideal places of such opportunities and emphasized the responsibility of schools to foster adolescents' character and well-being beyond academic learning. Seligman et al. considers positive education as an ideal remedy for adolescent depression and a source of increased life satisfaction, learning and creativity, increased social cohesion and civic citizenship for the adolescents. The results of positive education have been associated with academic achievement, better physical health and low-risk behaviours in adulthood (Kern et al., 2015).

Seligman introduced the PERMA model of flourishing, in which psychological well-being is defined in terms of five domains: positive emotions (P), engagement (E), relationships (R), meaning (M), and accomplishment (A). The dimensions included in this model were considered to be valued by youth and aligned to existing school structures and strategies (Kern et al., 2015).

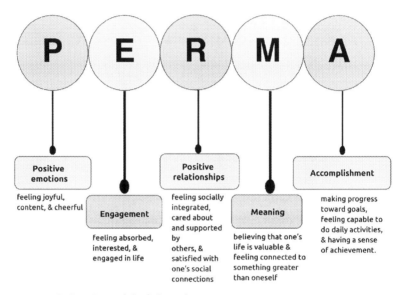

FIGURE 4.3 PERMA Model of Flourishing

Seligman advanced that these five pillars contribute to overall well-being, are important areas that people pursue for their own sake and can be defined and measured independently of one another.

An empirical investigation conducted to explore within the education setting whether the PERMA constructs could be measured as separate dimensions, using items from a well-being assessment conducted with a group of Australian adolescent students, exhibited the multidimensional aspect of well-being on both the positive and negative sides of the mental health continuum. All five constructs of the model were reflected in different items of the survey to which the adolescents responded. The study suggests the use of a multidimensional approach to well-being by schools to enable them to adapt systematic well-being approaches to the developmental needs of students (Kern et al., 2014).

The realm of potentialities and environmental resources for adolescent well-being

Studies in the recent years have portrayed adolescents as a valuable asset in the developmental process. The positive youth development (PYD) perspective points to the multiple changes that occur during adolescence as representing the plasticity inherent in the system of development, providing the potential for positive functioning of adolescents. This perspective encourages one to look at the development of human potentialities in different areas and environmental resources rather than focusing on the presence or lack of diseases or disorders. Well-being in adolescence seems to be unique to the adolescent stage due to the kind of multiple changes that make adolescence a plastic period of life, embedded in a wide range of social contexts that can be capable of promoting well-being and positive development (Viejo et al., 2018).

The large, rapid changes associated with adolescence such as rapid physical growth and significant physical and psychological changes may have major effects on the health of individuals, and conversely, variations in health may significantly affect the transitions of adolescence. Adolescents grow to become stronger and faster and achieve higher maturity, reasoning abilities, immune function and the capacity to withstand any kind of stressors as compared to childhood. Despite these normative characteristics, deaths and disabilities are prevalent in adolescence due to difficulties that arise with behavioural and emotional control. It is the high rate of accidents, suicide, homicide, depression, alcohol and substance abuse, violence, reckless behaviours, eating disorders and health problems related to risky sexual behaviours that are killing youth in different societies. The health of adolescents is integrally shaped by the daily contexts in which they grow and develop, thus displaying differences between developing and developed nations. WHO, records that a large portion of adolescents living in poor countries face the devastating daily living conditions that are primary threats to their health. Youth in the developing world continue to face serious threats to their immediate well-being, including starvation and infectious diseases such as malaria and tuberculosis. Dietz talks about such unique problems as obesity, eating disorders and sedentary lifestyles of adolescents in developed countries, which may affect their long-term health (Žukauskienė, 2014).

182 Adolescence and well-being

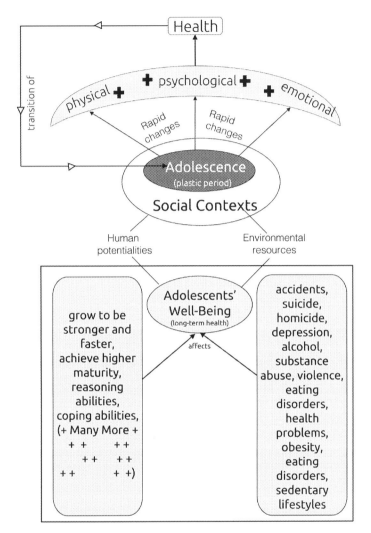

FIGURE 4.4 The Realm of Potentialities and Environmental Resources for Adolescent Well-Being

Essen and Martensson has asserted that it is practical to assume that the concept of health is comparable to the concept of well-being (Kaur, 2019). Around the world, 80% of adolescents do not have any physical activity, which results in obesity further and increasing the likelihood of mental health problems (which is also result of many other factors – social isolation, shame, guilt and poor body image). Adolescents who perceive their health challenges as nutritional deficiency and chronic health problems are at greater risk of mental health problems. Older adolescents are likely to encounter increased pressures of exams and future goal-setting, which also lead to mental stress (Long et al., 2017).

Thus, we see that this perspective encourages us to look at adolescence development and well-being taking into account not only the potentialities (e.g. coping abilities and maturity) of the adolescents but also considering the environmental resources that interact with the potentialities in the life of an adolescent. These environmental factors are nothing but the various relations that the adolescent has with the material and social world. We term these as the correlates of well-being of adolescents, which we explore in the next section.

Correlates of well-being

The beginning of this chapter introduced us to the participatory framework of well-being grounded in Bronfenbrenner's Ecological Systems Theory (1977). This asserts the influence of relationships of adolescents in different contexts on their well-being. This has been also summarized in Figure 4.2 which shows how the spheres of influence are related to the aspects of well-being shown as petals of well-being.

These spheres of influence are crucial because they have the potential to create positive and negative implications for the identity and agency aspects of adolescence development. In this chapter we will focus on specific aspects of well-being as influenced by social contexts.

Socio-economic status

Socio-economic status is also another factor that may influence adolescent health and well-being.

Socio-economic differences in health have been observed to be inconsistent in different ages and stages of life and also within the stage of adolescence. Class differences have also been observed in terms of psychological well-being in adolescence in some contexts. Economic stressors are found to affect adolescents' well-being through the mediating effects of disrupted family processes, parenting, spousal relationships and parent-adolescent relationships.

For example if we consider our Indian context, poverty in families may result in decreased resources for adolescents in terms of nutrition, educational access, and health facilities. Parent's lack of attention towards their adolescent children, frequent fights between spouses, father addicted to drinking, and many other factors may lead to adverse health outcomes in adolescent children. There may be other examples of affluent families which may be able to provide all kinds of resources, but may not be a conducive and nurturing family in itself. Adolescents from single parent-families may suffer mental health problems as compared to two-parent families. Call et al. asserts that the negative effects of family or home factors can be buffered by the effects of adolescents' other contexts like peers, school, community, romantic relationships, which can maintain the well-being of adolescents, though not all the time (Žukauskienė, 2014).

Self-concept

Individual and interpersonal processes play an important role in the identity development of adolescents. Self-concept can be described as the cognition and evaluation of specific aspects of self, the ideal self, and the overall self-regard including, gender identity, family status, personal goals, and self-esteem.

Adolescent self-concept has been found to vary with gender, age, and educational transition. Marsh asserts that self-concept becomes more organized and hierarchical through adolescence, and the level of the self-concept decreased during preadolescence and increased during late adolescence and adulthood. The process of individuation is often related to higher well-being during adolescence. Adolescents with a negative self-concept encounter problems in social functioning and are more likely to exhibit problem behaviours which in turn may lead to mental health problems hinder their well-being. O'Dea points out to the findings of empirical studies, which have shown associations between negative self-concept and aggressive behaviour, rule-breaking and delinquent behaviour, anxiety and depressive symptoms, and eating problems (Žukauskienė, 2014).

Self-esteem

Self-esteem is considered to be an individual's positive or negative attitude towards the self as a totality and as such has cognitive and affective components. Self-esteem is also considered to be an indicator of mental health in adolescents. Adolescent self-esteem has received a great deal of attention because, on average, it declines during adolescence, particularly for girls. However, it is believed that particularly, adolescents who conform to normative gender roles show increased self-esteem. Being insulted or humiliated by others can lead to lowering of self-esteem and increase the risk of poor mental health, anxiety, eating problems and depressive symptoms in adolescents. Low self-esteem has also been associated with anxiety and Winter states that self-esteem has been found to be the most important factor for retaining psychological and social health during adolescence (Žukauskienė, 2014). Mahajan and Sharma opine that adolescents are deeply concerned as to how others view them and are apt to display self-consciousness and are embarrassed on being criticized by others (Rais, 2011). Pathak et al. stresses the high prevalence of behavioural & emotional problems in Indian adolescents (Kaur, 2019). A study of Indian adolescents found boys reporting lower rates of peer acceptance and being more vulnerable as compared to girls, thus leading to more depressive symptoms in boys. Supportive family and community networks are found to be important protective factors for adolescent mental health by nurturing hope and protecting them from stress (Long et al., 2017).

Autonomy

Adolescents' autonomy is very important for making decisions and choices for their future career goals, within the school context and outside, and lack of autonomy in such times may result in increased participation in high-risk behaviours. Ryan and Deci (2000) emphasise the need and importance of academic autonomy in adolescents for their psychological well-being. Ryan and Connell hold that lack of academic autonomy or even low level of this kind of autonomy may result in higher levels of anxiety and negative coping strategies in school.

The significance of adolescents' construction of a sense of a personal self and the establishment of a healthy sense of independence has been reiterated in the previous chapters. This can be considered as a strong indicator of different types of well-being in adolescence. Empirical evidence shows associations between exploration and anxiety and depressive symptoms, suggesting that the process of exploration may assume the significance of a personal lack of self-confidence, ambiguity about one's personal identity, and, for these reasons, mediate the development of emotional problems during adolescence (Žukauskienė, 2014).

Body image

A very characteristic feature of adolescence in predicting self-esteem, eating disorders, and psychological adjustment is body image, which is referred to the adolescents' thoughts, feelings and perceptions about their physical appearance and image. As we have seen in chapter 1, both adolescent boys and girls are concerned about their image and appearance in order to fit into the groups with whom they identify with and at the same time maintain their own unique style and identity. These perceptions of adolescents are strongly related to their psychological well-being. Additionally, adapting to the characteristic bodily changes occurring at this age is related to their social adjustment, psychological well-being, and health behaviours. Studies have shown that adolescent girls' body dissatisfaction increases during early adolescence, whereas boys' body image and psychological well-being becomes more positive during adolescence compared with childhood. McCabe and Ricciardelli perceive that girls indicate a higher level of body dissatisfaction than adolescent boys irrespective of cultural differences due to the fact that the sociocultural ideal for the male body is probably very similar across a broad range of cultural settings. Smolak & Ge et al. are of the view that body dissatisfaction impedes adolescents' self-esteem, and psychological well-being through eating disorders, dieting behaviours, obesity and depression particularly for girls. Recent studies have demonstrated that body size as indicated by BMI has been positively related to body dissatisfaction among preadolescent and adolescent boys. McCreary and Sasse concede that adolescent boys who desire to develop muscularity tend to show higher levels of depression and lower self-esteem (Žukauskienė, 2014).

Parents and peers of adolescent boys and girls communicate messages that are bound by social and cultural norms regarding the ideal body to adolescents and pressure from these sources to lose or gain weight lead to negative consequences like low self-esteem, body dissatisfaction, or eating disorders. Media is another major source of negative body image development in adolescents. Magazines, television shows, films, social networking sites like Facebook, Instagram, Twitter, WhatsApp and many other applications communicate a stereotypic body image aesthetically appreciated in societies and this is quite religiously interpreted and followed by most of the adolescents.

Activity:

Create a story board using a visual organizer to illustrate how an adolescent with a previously low self-concept took positive steps to improve their perception of their body and increase their self-esteem.

- Share your story with the rest of the class.
- Discuss problems that could be encountered by the adolescent in this process.
- What consequences do you foresee for this adolescent in future, if s/he had not received help in time?

Timing of puberty

The timing of puberty also has its own influences on adolescents' development. We have already seen in chapter 1 that, puberty in adolescents usually begins at about ages 10 to 12 in girls and 12 to 14 in boys. Adolescents attaining puberty at an earlier age than their peers become part of a deviant group within their peer environment, and hence develop behaviour problems as compared to their so called normal peers. This affects the adolescent's social prestige, social adaptation, and self-concept. The changes associated with puberty are perceived to be more stressful when they occur early, with these stresses resulting in an increased risk for the development of behaviour problems including depression and anxiety, conduct disorders, and substance abuse. On the contrary, adolescent boys who mature earlier than their peers, are able to adjust well and are found to be high achievers with fewer attention and social problems than later-maturing boys, and early maturing boys appear more satisfied with their physical appearance (e.g. body image) than later-maturing boys. Having said that, studies have also found substance use and delinquency to be correlated with early maturation among boys and also suicide attempts and depression among these adolescent boys. late maturation is considered as a risk for poor adjustment and negative self-perception (Žukauskienė, 2014).

Reinforce your Learning

Directions: Look at each of the variable in the top boxes. In the bottom box of the corresponding number, write down a statement that indicates the influence of the respective variable on adolescent well-being.

Observe the interplay of these variables in influencing the well-being of adolescents. Discuss your reflections in the class with your peers and your facilitator.

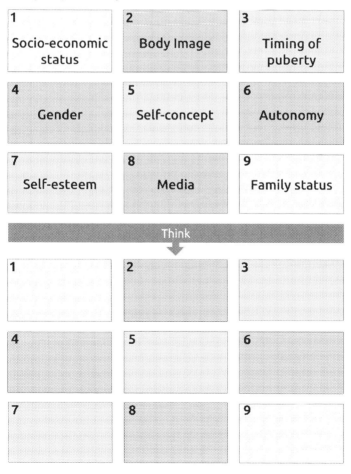

Well-being in social contexts

The beginning of this chapter introduced us to the participatory framework of well-being, grounded in Bronfenbrenner's Ecological Systems Theory (1977). This asserts the influence of relationships of adolescents in different contexts on their well-being.

We have seen in depth in the previous chapter, the positive and negative implications of the various social contexts on the identity development of adolescents. Here in this chapter, we will focus on specific aspects of well-being as influenced by social contexts.

Parent-adolescent relationships and well-being

Family contexts play a very important role in adolescents' psychosocial adaptation and in avoiding deviant and risky behaviour. The positive outcomes of close and satisfactory parent-adolescent relationships and peer relationships on adolescents' development have been reiterated time and again. Secure attachment relationships with attachment figures satisfy adolescents' basic psychological needs, enabling them to take agency of their life events and cope with adversities if needed. The quality of parent-adolescent relationships assists the adolescents in their social relationships, emotional regulation and coping with developmental issues and is highly correlated with an adolescent's overall life satisfaction. Adolescents in a longitudinal study by Noack and Puschner hailed from families with low connectedness They reported higher levels of aggressiveness and depressive mood.

Parental practices and styles also impacted adolescent well-being through levels of self-esteem. Perceived parental involvement influenced adolescents' personal self-worth, self-efficacy and self-esteem. It is essential to adolescents' psychological well-being. Baumrind suggests an authoritative/democratic parenting style for positive developmental outcomes, positive adolescent self-evaluations, higher levels of adolescent self-esteem and adjustment, along with higher levels of intrinsic motivation for learning. Parenting also enables adolescents' ability to adjust and cope with situations. Maccoby and Martin suggested that the authoritarian/autocratic type of parenting would result in negative child development, including lack of social competence, lack of spontaneity, external moral orientation, low motivation for intellectual performance, low self-esteem and external locus of control. Parental psychological control is found to predict adolescent delinquency and low self-esteem.

Conger et al. believes that high-quality parent-child relationships predict lower levels of adolescent depression and delinquent behaviours and also protect against antisocial behaviours for children in families experiencing marital conflict or disruption. Parental support can protect adolescents against depression and feelings of low self-worth by maintaining close relationships with their children, whereas parent-adolescent conflicts are found to influence negative life events for adolescents. Physical punishment meted to adolescents as disciplinary measures resulted in symptoms of depression, suicidal thoughts, ensued alcohol abuse, lower self-esteem, more feelings of loneliness and distress and more antisocial characteristics, especially in girls. A meta-analysis of 88 studies found relations between corporal punishment and aggression, lack of empathy, mental health problems and other maladaptive behaviours, leading to the conclusion that "although corporal punishment does secure immediate compliance it also increases the likelihood of eleven negative outcomes" (Žukauskienė, 2014).

Adolescents' relationships with non-parental figures and well-being

In their search for independence, adolescents form relationships with peers and other adults in their lives. Also with changes occurring in family structures as a result of social changes that have taken place globally, adolescents are living in differing structures: nuclear families with both parents employed, single-parent family households, step-families and so on. Lack of time to spend with parents at home make adolescents turn towards other social figures outside the family, for instance, peers, relatives, grandparents, uncles/aunts, teachers at school or their paid tutors. Significant others' support is found to be related to adolescents' academic functioning. including higher levels of positive academic attitudes, motivation, school attendance and academic achievement.

The role of non-parental adults in adolescents' lives has been well researched in distinct areas which can act as potential resources for adolescents' well-being. Research on resilience found protective effects of role models on externalizing and internalizing behaviours and compensatory effects on school outcomes. Yancey et al. (2002) found that adolescents with an identifiable role model received higher grades, had higher self-esteem and reported stronger ethnic identity than their counterparts who lacked role models. Studies found that having non-parental adult role models protected adolescents at a high risk due to poverty or low-income, negative behaviours and participation in violence and substance use. Exceptionally, studies have also displayed negative influences of non-parental adults on adolescents through modelling of unlawful and destructive behaviour (Hurd et al., 2009). Other individuals who are a few years older than the adolescents, e.g. seniors at school or their older friends or cousins, play the role of mentors in inspiring the adolescents and influencing their decisions. Zimmerman et al. (2002) found that adolescents who reported having a relationship with a natural mentor were unlikely to engage in violent delinquency than their other peers who may not have any mentor to guide them. And then there are these adults, the significant others, who have a strong influence on adolescents and on whom the adolescents believe and rely in times of distress. The significant others provide emotional and instrumental support and warmth to adolescents, resulting in adolescents' low involvement in misconduct regardless of the behaviour of close friends and family members.

The family system, including grandparents, can act as potential resources for adolescents' well-being. Ruiz and Silverstein (2007) in a study has asserted the association of closeness and informal involvement of grandparents and reduced adjustment difficulties among grandchildren, thus emphasizing the role of grandparent involvement and joint activities in creating emotionally close and supportive relationships with grandchildren and in affecting their well-being. This especially has been found more relatable in single-parent families and step-families, where involvement of the closest grandparent was more strongly associated with reduced total difficulties and specific adjustment difficulties. Various studies have identified grandparents as potential resources in moderating the negative influences of parental divorce, remarriage, parental separation and multiple family transitions on adolescent children (Žukauskienė, 2014).

Practice Exercise

You have already read about adolescents' social contexts and their influence in the previous chapters. The individual contexts and the interactions between the contexts hold significant importance for adolescent well-being and is again re-iterated here in this chapter.

Read these cases given here and analyze them with respect to the adolescent's well-being in that particular case.

- How will you visualize the well-being of adolescent in each of these case in the present times and beyond the adolescent stage?
- What are the various possibilities of either promoting or impeding the well-being of the adolescent in this particular case?
- What do you infer about the various contexts in which the case is situated?

> Sara's mother Jane is highly educated and working as a full-time professor. Jane had been divorced since the last five years. She had a very strained relationship with Sara, who lives with her and her husband. Sara is often found smoking and irregular in attending school.

> Natasha studies in the tenth class. She lives in a chawl system of houses. She does not have the necessary resources to lead a good life. She is well connected with her neighbours, with whom she shares close relationships. She also has many friends in her neighbourhood.

> Veera is a first generation learner. Her parents work as labourers. They have high aspirations for her. They enroll her in an English school and try to give her all the necessary things that she needs. Veera works very hard, though she has to spare a lot of time at home helping her parents too. She wants to grow up to be a doctor and make her parents proud.

> Mukhtar stays in a joint family. His parents, grandparents, aunt and uncle, siblings and cousins all stay together in one house. His parents are so busy in their work that they have almost no time for Mukhtar. His aunt is a graduate and she is capable of taking Mukhtar's studies. She accompanies him to the school for Parent-teachers meet. His grandparents are of a very loving and caring nature.

> Rohan has frequent arguments with his father over trivial matters. His mother doesn't share a cordial relationship with her husband and Rohan. Rohan keeps distance with his parents, however he connects well with his sister and experiences love and care from her. She too takes care of him whenever he is in distress or needs help.

School context and adolescent well-being

Another very important social context where adolescents spend most of their time is the school context. As an institution considered to play a major role in the life of adolescents, schools are looked upon at a higher pedestal in equipping adolescents with the necessary skills and dispositions they will need to live and learn in the 21st century. Dewey believed youth's well-being as an educational creed, even while educators undeniably have a future-focus for their students. The term 'well-being' has its existence in curriculum documents, policy documents and mission statements of educational associations worldwide. Yet, there still is a lack of clarity as to what extent and how do educational experiences relate to well-being of adolescents in the school milieu (Soutter et al., 2011).

Schools seek to affect student's health in a number of ways – teaching-learning, physical education, extracurricular activities (sports and cultural), nutrition, health and medical services and so on. Teaching-learning activities can affect students through instruction, teacher skills and competencies, class size, access to resources and overall school climate. To add to all these, academic pressures can be sources of stress for students and can have negative effects on the mental health of students (Marin & Brown, 2008).

School-related adolescent well-being has been strongly associated with perceived aggressive behaviours generally noticed in the school setting. Bullying is another feature often observed in school settings and has been associated with several subjective health complaints such as headache, backache, abdominal pain and dizziness, fatigue and sleep problems. It has been observed that social support as perceived by children act as protective factors against bullying and health complaints. Higher parental warmth and support is a probable precautionary factor for less involvement in bullying and other undesirable behaviours, while peers and friends also play a mixed role in controlling such behaviours. Thus, the school context comprising teachers and peers is a very essential part of the child's support network providing social support in different forms (Vaičiūnas & Šmigelskas, 2019).

School-based interventions possess a great potential in reducing the risk factors and increasing the protective factors to promote the mental health and well-being of children and adolescents. School connectedness has been shown to be related to later reduced violence, less risky sexual behaviour, less drug use and less dropping out. Families being part of the social ecology shoulder equal responsibility by partnering with schools to cultivate connectedness (McNeely et al., 2010).

Brewster and Bowen found teacher support during the middle-school years influence adolescents by decreasing their behaviour problems and improving academic outcomes. Teacher social support, e.g. emotional and instrumental support, is observed to raise the self-esteem of adolescents. Positive relationships with teachers and guidance counsellors who act as mentors to adolescents result in their increased physical health, self-esteem, life satisfaction, high school completion and decreased levels of smoking, depressive symptoms and suicide ideation, risk-taking, violence and gang membership (Žukauskienė, 2014).

Yet a UNICEF report published in 2018 reports the school environment as an unsafe space to study and grow for millions of students around the world. It is estimated that approximately 150 million students aged 13–15 experience peer-to-peer violence in and around school, with at least a third of students being bullied and a third involved in physical fights (Ameratunga et al., 2018). Brindis points out that schools cannot carry the burden alone. Beyond what goes on inside the school walls, schools must coordinate their practices with the rest of the community – health care providers, after-school programs and perhaps most importantly, students' families (Marin & Brown, 2008). When students, teachers, parents and communities collaborate, schools will be better equipped to address the students' negative experiences, which often have lifelong consequences. However, schools are often found to be hesitant in widening the scope of their resources from education to wider social influences, and experimental evidence linking such efforts with improved adolescent health is sparse (Ameratunga et al., 2018)

Weist and Murray assert the essentiality of training and involvement of a range of people to create a cultural shift in the educational context and bring about positive changes for promoting successful mental health promotion programmes in schools. Partnership between health and education sectors can lead to meaningful engagement and lasting changes.

A 'whole school approach' for promoting positive mental health recognizes the importance of working collaboratively with all parts of the school community – students, families and staff – while acknowledging the impact of local and government policies. Internationally, this has been implemented through schools adopting social and emotional programmes in the USA, Australia and the UK. Positive results in terms of not only positive mental health but also increased academic attainment has been achieved in places where this approach has been implemented (Reilly et al., 2018)

A study assessing the effectiveness and cost-effectiveness of a multicomponent whole-school health promotion intervention (SEHER) among grade 9 students of 74 government-run secondary schools in Bihar, reported substantial benefits and considerable reductions in bullying, violence, symptoms of depression and smoking. Also reported was improved sexual health knowledge and attitudes towards gender equity in groups where the intervention was delivered by counsellors as compared to groups in which teachers delivered the intervention. The effective interventions were seen with external facilitators and not teachers who had ample other responsibilities to shoulder and hence could not give the same importance to those interventions (Ameratunga et al., 2018).

It is thus very essential to understand factors associated with positive psychological experiences to provide a meaningful guide and plan appropriate interventions that can facilitate optimal functioning of adolescents and promote their well-being. The application of positive psychology in an educational context gave rise to a new paradigm, the positive education. Seligman defined this approach as "traditional education focused on academic skill development, complemented by approaches that nurture wellbeing and promote good mental health". This conceptualization underscores the importance of the relationship between school environment and student health and well-being. The fundamental goal of positive education is to promote flourishing or positive mental health within the school community. Seligman's PERMA (Positive emotion, Engagement, Relationships, Meaning, and Accomplishments) model of flourishing claims that these five characteristics are the keys to happiness and well-being (see Figure 4.3) (Lombardi et al., 2019)

In light of the need for school-based interventions for adolescent well-being, significant opportunities need to be made available to adolescents in order to feel empowered and learn life skills for health and well-being from an educational point of view.

Scan the QR code to access the EPOCH measure of Adolescent Well-being

The EPOCH Measure of Adolescent Well-being

The EPOCH Measure of Adolescent Well-being adapting the PERMA model for adolescents, capturing five positive characteristics that is believed to promote flourishing: engagement, perseverance, optimism, connectedness, and happiness. A paper describing the development and psychometrics of this measure was published in Psychological Assessment.

Credits: Margaret L. Kern, Lisbeth Benson, Elizabeth A. Steinberg, Laurence Steinberg

Note for Readers: You are welcome to use this measure for research, non-commercial or assessment purposes, giving credit as noted in the measure. There is no cost involved in using the measure for these purposes. For commercial purposes, please contact the University of Pennsylvania Center for Technology Transfer.

If you do choose to use this measure, first complete this form:
https://docs.google.com/forms/d/1eamBshwjtJyQDsWG72qum8Czi_J2IlZ3Q7r5FE5ojEA/viewform?usp=sen

Peer relationships and adolescent well-being

Peer relationships have been linked to both the current and future well-being of children. Peers play a significant role in adolescents' academic development, social functioning and psychological well-being. Evidence suggests not with strong certainty, that supportive relationships with both peers and parents in early adolescence are associated with positive psychological traits such as happiness and optimism. Negative aspects of peer relationships (bullying, peer victimization) and rejection or risky behaviours (alcohol use, substance abuse, sexual activity) all have long-term consequences (dropping out of school, mental illness and other behavioural problems for adolescents). Adolescents in difficult relationships with their peers are likely to experience such maladjustment as loneliness, depression, anxiety and low self-esteem.

Media use and adolescent well-being

The influence of social media on adolescents' well-being has been a prime concern. Studies of media like Facebook and Instagram report mixed findings, yielding either small negative, small positive or no effects of the time spent using social media on different indicators of well-being, such as life satisfaction and depressive symptoms. It has been observed that different social media platforms have differential effects on adolescents' well-being and indicates that the effect of social media use on well-being differs from adolescent to adolescent (Beyens et al., 2020)

Positive effects of social media use by young adolescents have been observed in terms of increased self-confidence, self-esteem, outgoing behaviour and reduced shyness and depression. At the same time, heavy media use has been associated with low life satisfaction, negative experiences, depression, anxiety, attention problems and stress in adolescents. The majority of adolescents today are exposed to social media in some form or the other for purposes of making friends, video chatting, texting, instant messaging to socialize, make plans or discuss academic work and so on (James et al., 2017).

Cara L. Booker opines that social media on one hand allows for social interaction between people, while on the other hand is a sedentary activity that can be done in a solitary environment. Irrespective of whether the use of social media is done in groups or in isolation, it may result in poor physical and mental health and other risk factors – increased obesity, decreased physical activity, low self esteem and social isolation. Whether done in isolation or with friends, there may be risks to using social media, which could lead to poorer physical and mental health in adulthood. Risk factors such as social isolation, low self-esteem, increased obesity and decreased physical activity may all contribute to later-life health issues.

Considering the age of digital technologies and social media, we must understand that multiple sites, apps, devices and other media use are an integral part of the adolescents' life and woven into the fabric of their culture, thus making it their way of life. Adolescents turn to media for everything, and they believe it is their right to do so and also necessary for their well-being.

Personal, social and cultural factors play important roles in increasing adolescents' vulnerability and/or resilience to social media material. These young teens need to be continuously protected from the harmful effects associated with their engagement with social media. It thrusts strong responsibility on adults and others who are responsible for adolescents' well-being to become sufficiently digitally literate to be able to facilitate adolescents' safe use of social media and generate positive health outcomes (Goodyear et al., 2018).

Although there are many evidences of the positive effects of the roles of significant others or non-parental figures, the characteristics of these personalities and the contexts within which their support is provided may interact to yield inconsistent outcomes for adolescents.

Theory and research highlight the differential effects of social support in terms of the source of support and also in terms of gender, as determined by the characteristics of the provider and the recipient. Adolescent girls have been found to receive more support from peers than boys, whereas boys have been seen to receive more support from family sources than girls do (Colarossi & Eccles, 2003).

196 Adolescence and well-being

> After completing Chapter 4, return to this activity.
>
> Refer to the figure 4.6
>
> The figure indicates a number of well-being indicators corresponding to the Asset, Appraisal and Action categories proposed by the Anne K. Soutter, Alison Gilmore and Billy O'Steen framework.
>
> Select any one context from School, Peers, or Media.
>
> Write a descriptive essay on how the selected context shoulders the responsibility of fostering the well-being of adolescent children. Identify instances in which the context fails to promote adolescent well-being. Provide suggestions for the facilitating well-being of adolescents in such instances. Substantiate your points with appropriate examples.

Adolescents' well-being in Indian context: research-based evidences

Though it has been observed that societies frequently witness diverse psychosocial disorders such as antisocial behaviour, drug use, depression and eating disorders during adolescence, adolescents from other societies like India are not an exception.

India is home to almost 20% of the world's total adolescent population. Large numbers of adolescents in India face challenges: poverty, lack of access to health care facilities, unsafe environments and so on. An estimated 20% of adolescents experience major depression (Kaur, 2019). A large number of studies of Indian adolescents reports a prevalence of mental health disorders among 6.5 % of adolescents at the community level and 23.3% in the school setting, suggesting the role of the pressure to succeed in an increasingly competitive academic environment. Suicide among adolescents is considered to be a leading cause of death in India and is seen to be on the rise. Various studies record a higher rate of mental challenges in adolescent females as compared to males coinciding with the statement of United Nations Global Strategy for Women's Children's and Adolescent's Health 2016–2030, which said that girls aged 10–19 are more affected than boys for all mental and substance use issues. The gender differences are attributed to factors such as varying access to education, exposure to child labour and sexual abuse (Long et al., 2017).

Many serious diseases in adulthood have their roots in adolescence. A review article (Sivagurunathan et al., 2015) discusses the magnitude of adolescent health problems, existing adolescent health programmes, their services and the challenges in achieving universal coverage of wholesome adolescent health in India. The various health problems among Indian adolescents include diverse sexual and reproductive health problems attributed to societal and cultural factors such as early marriage, early pregnancy due to social pressure, lack of awareness and so on.

Nutritional health also was another concern in adolescents. Eating disorders, e.g. anorexia nervosa or binge eating due to body dissatisfaction and depression was quite prevalent among adolescents. Mass media has a very important role to play in influencing adolescents' lifestyle patterns. Children of this age group are generally inspired by celebrities and model them in various aspects of image building. In India suicide among adolescents is found to be higher than any other age groups. The group 15–29 years of age accounts for 40% of suicide deaths in men and 56% of suicide deaths in women in. A considerable proportion of adolescents are known to have mental health problems. Substance abuse is yet another serious issue due to adolescents' ignorance of its consequences. National Family Health Survey III data shows in the age group 15–19, about 11% of adolescent boys and 1% of adolescent girls consumed alcohol, in that 3% consume it daily; about 29% boys and 4% girls use some kind of tobacco. Parental substance abuse and lack of parental supervision are seen to lead to adolescent substance abuse.

A study on the prevalence of lifestyle-related concerns among school adolescents highlights sociocultural pressures and environmental changes as influencing adolescent living. Availability of ready-made edibles in appealing shapes and flavours, advertisements and acculturation seem to lure the adolescents not only among urban and metro but also among rural adolescents into habits of eating unhealthy food like fast food items, bakery items and cold sugared drinks. Economic and technological advances have transformed traditional and healthy sleeping habits, use of leisure time and engagement in physical activity by irregular sleeping, inactivity and sedentary activities (computer games, surfing the internet, use of mobile phones for social networking and so on). This results in various conduct problems (increased aggression, malnutrition, premarital sex in adolescents leading to adjustment problems, low academic performance, juvenile delinquency and even adult criminality and psychopathology, (Singh & Misra, 2012).

Another study examined gender differences in multiple aspects of an adolescent's lifestyle (dietary habits, food consumption, sleep, sports, games, physical activity, sedentary and leisure patterns). The study revealed that adolescent girls, especially in their late adolescence, lacked opportunities to participate in sports, outdoor activities or any community activities as compared to boys. Girls were found to be more inclined to stereotypical leisure activities such as dancing and religious activities. Adolescent girls from rural areas were found to be deprived of healthy food items and limited engagement in sports or games while male school-going adolescents fared less favourably in cultural activities. Rangnathan et al. point to the role of multiple eco-cultural factors, including socialization, opportunities, resources and discrimination resulting in variation of lifestyles between male and female school adolescents. Gender-discriminatory practices of socialization in Indian society resulted in increased autonomy for adolescent boys and imposed many restrictions for adolescent females, leading to low self-regulation and increased health risks in females as compared to males. Another distinct feature can be discerned about the urban setting, which is characterized by low family engagement, increased peer contacts, multiple socialization processes, growing mall culture, exposure to media and availability of financial resources that can pave way for increased leisure choices in such settings and may lead to unhealthy sedentary activities. While on one hand, findings of a study show rural adolescent girls being deprived of healthy food and positive leisure resulting in their malnourishment and mental-health related difficulties, another study shows urban female adolescents' lives threatened by lack of privacy and a decrease in familial and social support due to a relatively greater engagement with media-related activities. The traditional healthy lifestyle habits (eating to just satisfy hunger, milk intake, regular sleep habits, rising early in the morning, yoga practices) are ignored and overlooked largely by today's adolescents, which may pose increasing health risks and lower the well-being of this group of children (Singh & Misra, 2016).

A study assessing the prevalence and pattern of substance use among male adolescents in New Delhi city underlines the distressing state of substance use in adolescents and attributes this to the changing cultural values, increasing economic stress and dwindling supportive bonds. Substance use in adolescence is commonly associated with unsafe sexual behaviour, school and social misbehaviour and poor academic performance, resulting in high crime rates, 'eve-teasing' (sexual harassment and assault) and impulsive murders. Factors that were inclined towards these results were identified as nuclear family, less members in the family, parental abuse status, low educational status, friends and illiteracy/school-drop out (Daniel et al., 2017).

A nationwide study of the pattern and profile of children using substances in India revealed many insights. Substance use was seen prevalent in almost all regions, cities and smaller towns across all states and not confined to metropolitan areas as generally perceived. The pattern of substance use was more similar across various settings, though with an earlier onset and more dysfunction among out-of-school and street children. The majority of victims of substance abuse were school dropouts and from the lower socio-economic status. Substance use was found to be present among girl children too (Dhawan et al., 2017).

Though adolescents residing in urban areas may have ample opportunities for economic and social well-being, there is evidence of health disparities in adolescents of urban India. The rearing of children in urban settings may increase the risk of mental health, substance use, obesity and physical inactivity. Substance abuse, media exposure, peer influences all lead to undesirable habits in adolescents, giving rise to health problems (Ramadass et al., 2017).

India witnesses one of the highest suicide rates among those aged 15 to 29, academic stress accounting as one of the major reasons for suicides among both female and male students in India. Caste-based discrimination is another major factor that lies at the root of student suicides in India, reporting on the lack of institutional support and infrastructure for students from lower-class backgrounds. In India, job security is seen as a very important benefit of a good education, creating immense pressure on students. Dr Harish Shetty, a psychiatrist, points out the inability of young students to cope with small frustrations, failure and loss, often coupled with social alienation in creating such critical situations for them. The survey by the

Centre for the Study of Developing Societies, records about 4 in 10 students in India experiencing bouts of depression, indicating the impact of social expectations and academic rigor on students' suicidal behaviours and decisions.

Depressive disorders are identified by the World Health Organization (WHO) as a priority mental health disorder of adolescence because of its high prevalence, recurrence, ability to cause significant complications and impairment. Depression in adolescents often results in suicide, school dropout, pregnancy, antisocial behaviour and substance abuse. Community and school studies in India have also shown depression as the most common psychiatric disorder among adolescents. Usually, depression in adolescents is barely recognized as a severe mental health problem since it is not explicitly expressed as a result of embarrassment in seeking psychiatric help. Biological changes occurring in this period in addition to social factors play their roles in the development of depression (Malik et al., 2015)

Youth with depression are considered at high risk of mental disorders such as antisocial behaviour and substance abuse disorders. The majority of studies conducted on Indian adolescents found 50% of school-going adolescents with depression. Results have been showing associations of depression with gender, religion and birth order of individuals. Females are found to report more signs of depression than males, which are also attributed to their hormonal changes in puberty. There are also others who have reported a higher prevalence of depression among males than females, attributed to diverse culture points and other variables. A few factors such as feelings of guilt, pessimism, sadness, failure and inability to cope with academics result in feelings of depression in 10th and 12th grade students. Other factors such as parental fighting, punishment at home or school, teasing at school, loss of parents and substance abuse have effects, though trivial. The magnitude of these problems in adolescents and their associated factors are quite obvious, yet it is also known that these problems do not receive attention or treatment at the right time. Parents, teachers and others shoulder the responsibility of identifying these problems, creating awareness and counselling students to cope with their problems and alleviate the factors responsible for depression (Jha et al., 2017).

Government initiatives for adolescents

The Government of India has come up with many programmes and interventions to address the well-being of adolescents. However, there has been very scarce evidence of policy response to the mental health needs of adolescents and their well-being. A policy review and stakeholder analysis on India's response to adolescent mental health was undertaken to assess the policy environment for addressing adolescent mental health in India in 2018. The review recommends the need to focus on the different phases of adolescence, especially the marked developmental differences that exist in various stages of adolescence. The policies and programmes reviewed identify stress, anxiety and depression as common mental health problems in adolescents and points to the associations between bullying/cyber bullying and adolescent suicide. The policies also recognize tobacco use, alcohol and other intoxicants as very common among both urban and rural youth. These documents explicitly point to the social and educational determinants operating at individual, family and community levels affecting adolescent well-being and daily stress, parental pressure, peer pressure, academic pressures resulting in mental health issues for adolescents (Roy et al., 2018).

The policies referred to by the reviewers were the National Youth Policy (NYP), 2014; National Mental Health Policy (NMHP), 2014; National Mental Healthcare Act (MHA), 2017; Rashtriya Kishor Swasthya Karyakram (RKSK; National Adolescent Health Programme, 2014); Sarva Shiksha Abhiyan (SSA), 2014 concerned with education; and Yuva Spandana (YS), 2015 concerned with adolescent welfare in the state of Karnataka

The recent initiatives by the government were the:

- The Rashtriya Kishor Swasthya Karyakram (RKSK) launched in 2014 by the Ministry of Health and Family Welfare (MOHFW), for adolescents in the age group of 10–19 years, to target their nutrition, reproductive health and substance abuse
- The Mental Health Care Act 2017 passed on 7 April 2017 to effectively decriminalize attempted suicide, which was punishable under Section 309 of the Indian Penal Code and has additionally vouched to tackle the stigma of mental illness.

The review of these policies and programmes revealed mixed findings. It was found that different policies addressed different aspects of well-being and health to different extents. Though the documents have taken cognizance of the social and educational level determinants operating at the individual, family and community level, other social determinants such as social norms and parental conflicts have been ignored.

The concerns that were shown in the scope and delivery of the proposed mental health interventions are worth contemplation. They reflected a lack of clarity on mental health as a public health issue; insufficient information was available on the issues faced by the adolescents. Several major challenges in implementation of these polices were identified. Fragmented governance, lack of inter-sectoral collaboration, budget constraints, scanty human resources and very little engagement of young people in the development of these policies or in their implementation were a few of these challenges.

Though there have been quite a number of achievements on child mortality, e.g. a social development indicator such as the delayed age of marriage benefitting adolescent health, the review identifies the need to address the specific determinants of adolescent ill-health and their consequences. A broader, life-course approach is recommended in the design and delivery of the interventions and the coordinated involvement of diverse sectors and platforms for prevention and treatment. Equity as a guiding principle throughout is suggested and contextual realities and specific subgroup vulnerabilities to be considered in framing and implementing policies. The study suggests integration of these treatment interventions in routine health care through school-based delivery of counselling interventions. The national adolescent health policy (the RKSK) was identified as the potentially the most appropriate policy for such a coordinated and integrated approach but needs to work closely with the education and mental health policies.

Notwithstanding all these evidence-based findings on adolescent well-being, policies and interventions, it is quite evident as to why adolescent well-being needs to be addressed comprehensively in the educational arena. Teachers and educators need to be well aware of the problems and issues faced by adolescents in specific contexts and have clarity on the meaning of mental health, physical health, well-being and other correlates of well-being in order to be able to deal with arising situations in their school contexts to promote children's well-being. Schools also need to be aware of the potential benefits of the whole-school approach recognizing the social, political, economic and demographic contexts within which schools operate to increase engagement with the school community and work holistically to promote student health and well-being.

Task: In light of the various initiatives and efforts taken by the government, how do you visualize adolescents' life and well-being in future?

Encapsulating the concept of well-being

To conclude, we can say that well-being may be conceived as a complex system, one that is emergent, adaptive, growth-minded, often surprising and irreducible to its many parts as posited by Johnson. We would summarize all the discussions

202 Adolescence and well-being

revolving well-being using the multidisciplinary framework that is relevant to and resonates with school community as proposed by Soutter et al. (2011). The framework suggests seven domains organized under three mutually interacting categories: Assets, Appraisals and Actions.

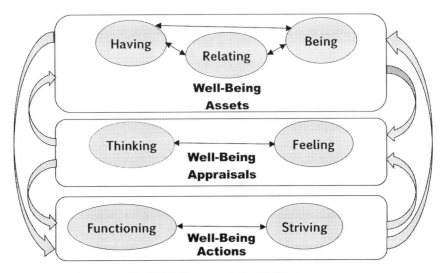

FIGURE 4.5 Soutter et al.'s (2011) Framework for Well-being

- **Assets** include external, intrapersonal and interpersonal variables, conditions and circumstances associated with well-being. These are summarized within the domains *Having, Being and Relating*.
- **Appraisals** include the affective and cognitive processes, indicators and outcomes discussed within Feeling and Thinking.
- **Actions** involve the use and pursuit of those assets or the *Functioning and Striving* that motivates and directs one's involvements and engagements.

In this framework, well-being is constantly emerging and adapting to the prevailing contexts, and in concert with the interactions of the various parts. These interacting categories of Assets, Appraisals and Action with their domains have been discussed in the previous chapters. An attempt to hold these various variables together in the context of adolescents' well-being is given in Figure 4.6.

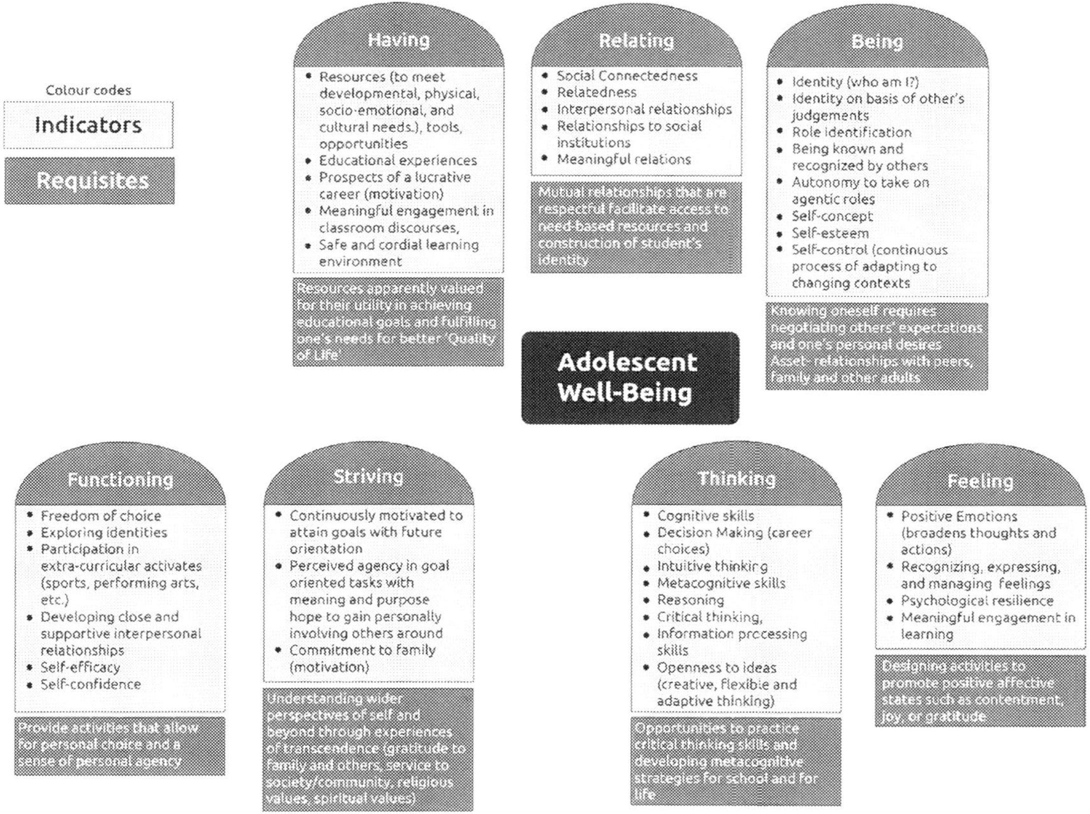

Adolescence and well-being 203

Being
- Identity (who am I?)
- Identity on basis of other's judgements
- Role identification
- Being known and recognized by others
- Autonomy to take on agentic roles
- Self-concept
- Self-esteem
- Self-control (continuous process of adapting to changing contexts

Knowing oneself requires negotiating others' expectations and one's personal desires. Asset-relationships with peers, family and other adults

Relating
- Social Connectedness
- Relatedness
- Interpersonal relationships
- Relationships to social institutions
- Meaningful relations

Mutual relationships that are respectful facilitate access to need-based resources and construction of student's identity

Having
- Resources (to meet developmental, physical, socio-emotional, and cultural needs), tools, opportunities
- Educational experiences
- Prospects of a lucrative career (motivation)
- Meaningful engagement in classroom discourses,
- Safe and cordial learning environment

Resources apparently valued for their utility in achieving educational goals and fulfilling one's needs for better 'Quality of Life'

Feeling
- Positive Emotions (broadens thoughts and actions)
- Recognizing, expressing, and managing feelings
- Psychological resilience
- Meaningful engagement in learning

Designing activities to promote positive affective states such as contentment, joy, or gratitude

Thinking
- Cognitive skills
- Decision Making (career choices)
- Intuitive thinking
- Metacognitive skills
- Reasoning
- Critical thinking,
- Information processing skills
- Openness to ideas (creative, flexible and adaptive thinking)

Opportunities to practice critical thinking skills, and developing metacognitive strategies for school and for life

Striving
- Continuously motivated to attain goals with future orientation
- Perceived agency in goal oriented tasks with meaning and purpose
- hope to gain personally involving others around
- Commitment to family (motivation)

Understanding wider perspectives of self and beyond through experiences of transcendence (gratitude to family and others, service to society/community, religious values, spiritual values)

Functioning
- Freedom of choice
- Exploring identities
- Participation in extra-curricular activates (sports, performing arts, etc.)
- Developing close and supportive interpersonal relationships
- Self-efficacy
- Self-confidence

Provide activities that allow for personal choice and a sense of personal agency

Adolescent Well-Being

Colour codes

Indicators

Requisites

FIGURE 4.6 Adolescents' Well-being Using Soutter et al.'s (2010) Framework for Well-being

An important notion that emerges from this framework is that assets are not limited to material in terms of physical resources and immaterial possessions, but extends to intrapersonal traits and characteristic plus supportive relationships that gain value through cognitive and affective appraisals by individuals and by societies. Appraisals contribute to what is considered as 'valuable' or 'wealth' through a social interaction with social agencies. Actions are not only for 'self-engagement' and 'achievement' but "to develop a deep and meaningful appreciation of what they engage with, collaboration with peers to find creative solutions to modern problems, and to effectively enhance the well-being of individuals, their communities, and the environment." is what constitutes actions related to well-being. Literature shows that the common understanding too has challenged the notion that money relates to well-being. However, even economists argue that GDP, which has been relied upon to measure national well-being for more than 100 years, falls short of accurately representing it (Soutter et al., 2011).

Essence of well-being in education

In education settings we see that economic terminology is frequently used (Soutter, 2013).

- Academic scores, performances and academic credits are often framed as currency to be exchanged for future employment, and the marks they have are perceived to be the benefits that one ascribes with education beyond the classroom.
- Students are valued as resources to be developed and, through their efforts, contribute to the growing human capital.
- Students refer to the value of education and more specifically schools in instrumental terms, reflecting a utilitarian philosophy that is pervasive in economic policy.
- Students explain that they are motivated to complete their assignments in order to get the qualifications/scores/appreciation and approval. Notably, as indicators of school performance, both test scores and educational qualifications share similar characteristics with income. Each is considered an objective, relatively "value free" indicator of well-being.

When we in education pay greater attention to having these outcomes of education as a focus of education, rather than the processes undertaken to achieving them, this reflects a hedonistic, rather than eudaimonic perspective. The process of education is nothing but the 'Being' aspect of education related to its reflection in the actions of an individual. These are not limited to self, but to the society with whom the individuals relates.

Looking at the application of the frame as given by Soutter et al. (2011), let us try and look at its implication for teaching and learning in higher education.

While teaching and learning the subject of psychology, it is not only relevant to youth in terms of the subject content (utility value). This also has application for their day-to-day life. In the process of teaching and learning, both teacher and student alike through their interactions should be able to appreciate the value of the role of constructs of self, social agencies and interactions and social dynamics not only for their own well-being, but also for the broader social and political well-being of the spaces in which they operate. With the knowledge about psychological theories of self and relatedness, along with the many cognitive and affective errors and misjudgments people make on a daily basis in their relationships, youth may be better prepared to use their assets, to function as it were, and to strive towards appropriate and meaningful goals. If, however, psychology is presented as a skill set or knowledge base to retain solely in order to reflect back on a summative assessment for qualifications, then the value of academic credit acquisition may drive their efforts. As a result, the asset potential of that knowledge for use, in ways that enhance and sustain well-being, is diminished.

Thus, what one has is an asset only if it is valued as such, and, arguably, if it can be used wisely, thoughtfully and meaningfully in ways that have beneficial outcomes that extend beyond the self. Those contributions may, in turn, be utilized by other people, collectives or institutions as assets to enhance and sustain well-being at a personal, societal and environmental level.

These perspectives have important implications for educators, many of whom are expected to transmit 'bodies of knowledge' in ways that imply knowledge is static and bounded. Consideration of learning, knowing and meaning-making as an ongoing process of relating, or a dynamic and evolving web of associations that both frame and guide behaviour, presents an interesting alternative to current schooling structures, which are often fragmented both in content and in delivery.

'Education' and 'well-being' share a relationship that is complex and interrelated. Education provides knowledge that supports future well-being. The classroom is a fluid and complex environment requiring both 'persistent' and 'in depth' observation in order to capture youths' educational experiences as they unfold (Soutter et al., 2011). The constant change and complex cultures of the classroom environment necessitates methodologies that apprehend the surge of zeal, essence and emotions of the typical classroom, both at an individual and at a collective level. On the other hand, we see that well-being research has much to offer to the evolution of education policy and research. Theoretical and empirical research has significantly clarified a fundamentally ambiguous construct over the course of the last decade, yet the term 'well-being' continues to be used without a clear contextual meaning. Understandings in this domain can be further enhanced through collaborative efforts between researchers and teachers, along with the students themselves, whose voices are conspicuously peripheral in much of the existing base of well-being scholarship.

An interesting thought experiment would be to consider how education might be experienced if well-being was not framed as the outcome, but as the necessary foundation supporting students as they work towards curricular aims and learning goals.

> **Key terms:** adolescence, well-being, emotional, psychological, hedonic, eudaimonic, participatory framework, positive well-being, positive education, PERMA, positive youth development, correlates of well-being, social contexts, assets, appraisal, and actions.

Bibliography

Ameratunga, S., Clark, T., & Banati, P. (2018). Changing school climates to promote adolescent wellbeing: Two trials with one goal. *Lancet, 392*(10163), 2416–2418. doi:10.1016/S0140-6736(18)32280-3

Beyens, I., Pouwels, J. L., van Driel, I. I., Keijsers, L., & Valkenburg, P. M. (2020). The effect of social media on well-being differs from adolescent to adolescent. *Scientific Reports, 10*(1), 10763. doi:10.1038/s41598-020-67727-7

Bintliff, A. V. (2020). *Multidimensional aspects of adolescent well-being*. Retrieved from www.psychologytoday.com/intl/blog/multidimensional-aspects-adolescent-well-being/202005/multidimensional-aspects-adolescent-well

Colarossi, L. G., & Eccles, J. S. (2003). Differential effects of support providers on adolescents' mental health. *Social Work Research, 27*(1), 19–30.

Daniel, L. T., Krishnan, G., & Gupta, S. (2017). A study to assess the prevalence and pattern of substance use among male adolescents in suburban area of Delhi. *Indian Journal of Social Psychiatry, 33*, 208–212.

Dantas, R. A. S., & Ciol, M. A. (2014). Flanagan quality of life scale. In A. C. Michalos (Eds.), *Encyclopedia of quality of life and well-being research*. Dordrecht, The Netherlands: Springer. doi:10.1007/978-94-007-0753-5_1057

Dhawan, A., Pattanayak, R. D., Chopra, A., Tikoo, V. K., & Kumar, R. (2017). Pattern and profile of children using substances in India: Insights and recommendations. *The National Medical Journal of India, 30*, 224–229.

Gao, J., & McLellan, R. (2018). Using Ryff's scales of psychological well-being in adolescents in mainland China. *BMC Psychology, 6*, Article 17. doi:10.1186/s40359-018-0231-6

Goodyear, V. A., Armour, K. M., & Wood, H. (2018). *The impact of social media on young people's health and wellbeing: Evidence, guidelines and actions*. Birmingham, UK: University of Birmingham.

Hurd, N. M., Zimmerman, M. A., & Xue, Y. (2009). Negative adult influences and the protective effects of role models: A study with urban adolescents. *Journal of Youth and Adolescence, 38*, 777–789.

Hutchinson, E. D. (2018). A life course perspective. In *Dimensions of human behavior: The changing life course*. Thousand Oaks, CA: SAGE Publications.

James, C., Davis, K., Charmaraman, L., Konrath, S., Slovak, P., Weinstein, E., & Yarosh, L. (2017). Digital life and youth well-being, social connectedness, empathy, and narcissism. *Pediatrics, 140*, S71–S75. doi:10.1542/peds.2016-1758F

Jha, K. K., Singh, S. K., Nirala, S. K., Kumar, C., Kumar, P., & Aggrawal, N. (2017). Prevalence of depression among school-going adolescents in an urban area of Bihar, India. *Indian Journal of Psychological Medicine, 39*, 287–292.

Kais, S. (2011). *Impact of family climate and parental encouragement on academic achievement among adolescents* (14–17 Years). Doctoral Dissertation, Aligarh Muslim University.

Kaur, M. (2019). Analysis on the level of well-being among Indian secondary school adolescents. *Bioscience Biotechnology Research Communications, 12*(3), 676–681.

Kern, M. L., Waters, L. E., Adler, A., & White, M. A. (2015). A multidimensional approach to measuring well-being in students: Application of the PERMA framework. *The Journal of Positive Psychology, 10*(3), 262–271. doi:10.1080/17439760.2014.936962

Lombardi, E., Traficante, D., Bettoni, R., Offredi, I., Giorgetti, M., & Vernice, M. (2019). The impact of school climate on well-being experience and school engagement: A study with high-school students. *Frontiers in Psychology, 10*, 2482. doi:10.3389/fpsyg.2019.02482

Long, K., Gren, L., Long, P., Jaggi, R., Banik, S., & Mihalopoulos, N. (2017). A picture of Indian adolescent mental health: an analysis from three urban secondary schools. *International Journal of Adolescent Medicine and Health, 31*(4), 20170035. doi:10.1515/ijamh-2017-0035.

Malik, M., Khanna, P., Rohilla, R., Mehta, B., & Goyal, A. P. (2015). Prevalence of depression among school going adolescents in an urban area of Haryana, India. *International Journal of Community Medicine and Public Health, 2*, 624–626.

Marin, P., & Brown, B. (2008). *The school environment and adolescent well-being: Beyond academics* (Child Trends Research Brief). Washington, DC: Child Trends.

McNeely, C., Whitlock, J., & Libbey, H. (2010). School connectedness and adolescent well-being. In S. L. Christenson & A. L. Reschly (Eds.), *Handbook of school-family partnerships* (pp. 266–286). New York, NY: Taylor & Francis.

Moreira, P. A., Cloninger, C. R., Dinis, L., Sá, L., Oliveira, J. T., Dias, A., & Oliveira, J. (2015). Personality and well-being in adolescents. *Frontiers in Psychology, 5*, 1494. doi:10.3389/fpsyg.2014.01494

O'Reilly, M., Svirydzenka, N., Adams, S., & Dogra, N. (2018). Review of mental health promotion interventions in schools. *Social Psychiatry and Psychiatric Epidemiology, 53*(7), 647–662. doi:10.1007/s00127-018-1530-1

Ramadass, S., Gupta, S. K., & Nongkynrih, B. (2017). Adolescent health in urban India. *Journal of Family Medicine and Primary Care, 6*, 468–476.

Roy, K., Shinde, S. Y., Sarkar, B. K., Malik, K., Parikh, R., & Patel, V. (2018). India's response to adolescent mental health: A policy review and stakeholder analysis. *Social Psychiatry and Psychiatric Epidemiology, 54*, 405–414.

Ruiz, S. M., & Silverstein, M. (2007). Relationships with grandparents and the emotional well-being of late adolescent and young adult grandchildren. *Journal of Social Issues, 63*, 793–808.

Seifert, C. A. (2005). *The Ryff scales of psychological well-being*. Retrieved from https://centerofinquiry.org/uncategorized/ryff-scales-of-psychological-well-being/

Singh, A. P., & Misra, G. (2012). Adolescent lifestyle in India: Prevalence of risk and promotive factors of health. *Psychology and Developing Societies, 24*(2), 145–160.

Singh, A. P., & Misra, G. (2016). Gender differences in lifestyle: Results of a survey among Indian school-going adolescents. *Social Change, 46*(3), 428–443. doi:10.1177/0049085716654816

Sivagurunathan, C., Umadevi, R., Rama, R., & Gopalakrishnan, S. (2015). Adolescent health: Present status and its related programmes in India. Are we in the right direction? *Journal of Clinical and Diagnostic Research, 9*(3), LE01–LE06.

Social media use diminishes well-being of teenage girls. (n.d.). Retrieved from www.healio.com/news/pediatrics/20180403/social-media-use-diminishes-wellbeing-of-teenage-girls

Soutter, A. K. (2013). *What does it mean to be well in school? An exploration of multiple perspectives on student wellbeing*. Doctoral Dissertation, University of Canterbury. Retrieved from https://ir.canterbury.ac.nz/bitstream/handle/10092/7774/thesis_fulltext.pdf;sequence=1

Soutter, A. K., Gilmore, A., & O'Steen, B. (2011). How do high school youths' educational experiences relate to well-being? Towards a trans-disciplinary conceptualization. *Journal of Happiness Studies: An Interdisciplinary Forum on Subjective Well-Being, 12*(4), 591–631. doi:10.1007/s10902-010-9219-5

Sterrett, E. M., Jones, D. J., McKee, L. G., & Kincaid, C. Y. (2011). Supportive non-parental adults and adolescent psychosocial functioning: Using social support as a theoretical framework. *American Journal of Community Psychology, 48*, 284–295.

Vaičiūnas, T., & Šmigelskas, K. (2019). The role of school-related well-being for adolescent subjective health complaints. *International Journal of Environmental Research and Public Health, 16*(9), 1577.

Viejo, C., Gómez-López, M., & Ortega-Ruiz, R. (2018). Adolescents' psychological well-being: A multidimensional measure. *International Journal of Environmental Research and Public Health, 15*, 2325.

Yancey, A. K., Siegel, J. M., & McDaniel, K. L. (2002). Role models, ethnic identity, and health-risk behaviors in urban adolescents. *Archives of Pediatrics & Adolescent Medicine, 156*(1), 55–61. https://doi.org/10.1001/archpedi.156.1.55

Zimmerman, M. A., Bingenheimer, J. B., & Notaro, P. C. (2002). Natural mentors and adolescent resiliency: A study with urban youth. *American Journal of Community Psychology, 30*(2), 221–243. doi:10.1023/A:1014632911622

Žukauskienė, R. (2014). Adolescence and well-being. In A. Ben-Arieh, F. Casas, I. Frønes, & J. Korbin (Eds.), *Handbook of child well-being*. Dordrecht, The Netherlands: Springer.

5
THE ADOLESCENT IN THE CLASSROOM

CHAPTER 5: Adolescent in the Classroom

Overview

After reading this chapter, you will be able to achieve the following objectives

- Understand classrooms as complex systems to view them as one dynamic system nested in a hierarchy of systems at different levels of scale, spatially and temporally situated
- Perceive the relationally organized nature of classrooms and the role of individuals and their agency within the classroom contexts in shaping the social structure of classrooms
- Able to view classroom contexts applying Bronfenbrenner's ecological theory and through the sociological perspective
- Get insights into classroom processes that occur between individuals and within groups situated in the classroom context.
- Get an idea of classroom in the context of teaching-learning practices
- Recognize the need to engage the adolescent learner in the classroom and reinforce the features of adolescents with main focus on adolescent classroom characteristics
- Able to conceptualize and assess classroom processes using the Teaching Through Interactions (TTI) framework by Hamre and Pianta's (2007)
- Apprehend the implications of classroom group processes and instructional practices for better psychosocial functioning of adolescents
- Able to appreciate the need to have life skills education for adolescents and gain knowledge about the developmental foundations of life skills approach and the conceptual approaches.
- Recognize the challenges in implementation of life skills in Indian context and understand the relevance of the UNICEF's Global Framework in the Indian context.
- Become aware of life skills in the twenty-first century and the key elements of life skills programs
- Comprehend life skills as evolving and contextual based on the discourse on life skills and acknowledge the shift in emphasis in the discourses on life skills from creating "ideal classrooms" to providing a realization of the "need" for equipping and strengthening certain skills and agency in adolescents within themselves for their well-being

Classroom ecology

Chapter 3 explored schools as contexts in which development takes place. The school is a social system that prepares students to occupy important roles in the society. Classrooms within the schools are complex systems including multiple components – student-teacher interactions, student-peer interactions, agency of both students and the teacher accompanied by their thoughts, actions, emotions, behaviours, dispositions, identities, social capital and also the properties of the physical and temporal environment as well. The classroom ecology can be viewed as one dynamic system nested in a hierarchy of such systems at different levels of scale, spatially and temporally situated. Mercer states that teacher and learner

DOI: 10.4324/9781003054351-5

agency has been often seen to emerge from the interaction between resources and contexts and the teachers' and learners' perception and use of them. The role of environmental influencers, including the social, emotional and psychological factors and their interplay across different interconnected levels and the resultant actions based on how the agents (teachers and learners) perceive them, are very crucial in determining the activities and environment of a classroom with respect to development of students (Larsen–Freeman, 2016)

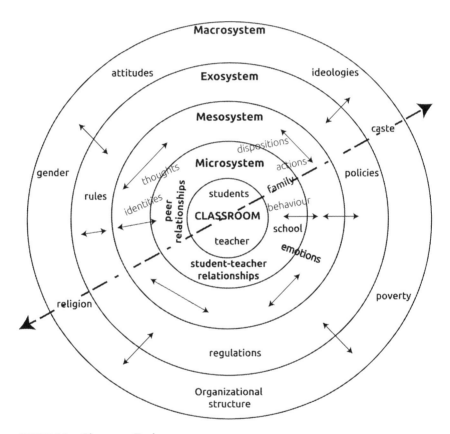

FIGURE 5.1 Classroom Ecology

Note: The dotted line indicates a possibility of a bidirectional non-linear relationship between the factors within the systems, where experiences in one system can impact another system without taking the linear path. The focus is more on the processes than the context. For example, experiences in the microsystem may directly impact the experiences in the exosystem without navigating through the mesosystem and vice versa.

Slavson and Schiffer have noted: children [and teachers] spend more time in schools than anywhere else except the home. For better or for worse, the school represents a large part of their daily lives. The school is not only advantageously situated with respect to the identification of developmental [and relational] problems, but also has the potential for carrying on preventive programs. The children [and teachers] are in a position to experience the effects of corrective measures in the very same setting which, in most cases, was instrumental in exposing their difficulties (Slavin, 2002).

Educational methodology needs to be looked at more critically in terms of both emotional and intellectual development. A teacher needs to be able to bring a balance among the multiple facets of students' minds, be it exploration, creativity, fantasizing or any other facet to foster appropriate behaviour and maturation to take place in students. Slavin (2002) believes that these views need to be considered within a group dynamic model, which would help teachers to better understand their complex roles as well as those of their students. Slavin states that classroom climates facilitating greater academic success essentially entails involvement of both teachers and students in conjunction with each other (Slavin, 2002).

Introduction to classroom dynamics

In general, when we refer to group dynamics, we refer to the description of group processes tending to ignore the role of individuals in shaping the group dynamics and the dynamics of the individual that plays in the group processes. The study of the dynamics of individual adjustment and the dynamics of the group process converge at a point where we look at the relationships of individuals with each other and also reactions of individuals to each other. This complex bidirectional relationship is an indispensable part of group processes and is crucial to the understanding of group dynamics. The dynamics of group processes is based on individual interpersonal relationships and extends further to a dynamics of the group process (Symonds, 1951). Group Dynamics is thus concerned with the formation of groups, their structure and processes and the way they affect individual members, other groups and the context. It refers to a system of behaviours and psychological processes occurring within a social group or between social groups.

Classrooms are social contexts or settings, where interactions take place between student and teacher, student and student, a group of students and teacher, and groups of students among themselves. These interactions are embedded in complex processes that affect and are affected by relationships between the components of the classroom. The social-psychological view of a classroom as group processes sees the students of a class as a miniature society with peers and teacher in which they experience interdependence, interaction, common striving for goals and structure. The classroom group as a whole and the interdependent relationships within the classroom setting are influenced by and influence the subgroups within the classroom context. These interactions include both formal and informal interactions, wherein formal interactions are invisible and not taken into consideration at times.

Classroom dynamics thus encompasses all these interactions and relationships including behaviours, actions, thoughts, emotions, beliefs, perceptions, instructional processes among others. The practices and processes as a result of classroom dynamics lead to the creation of a classroom culture which in turn affects this dynamic.

212 The adolescent in the classroom

Classroom dynamics generally follows an approach limiting itself to look at teacher-student relationships and interactions and focusing on teachers' agency in shaping classroom practices. However, we fail to see that the individual teacher and the individual learner are equally responsible for shaping classroom processes and practices. We need to acknowledge that there is more to the nature of classroom dynamics than merely the relations between two individuals and their reaction to each other. An individual may react to another individual, a group, status of the group, norms and regulations of the group, the environment and emotions of the group at a specific time, processes of the group, composition of the group, decisions of the group and so on. This reaction can be also a result of the beliefs and ideologies of the individual, the culture and context to which the individual belongs to, personal characteristics of the individual, group ideologies and processes among many other factors. In agreement with Giddens, we can assert that the agents (teachers and students) are shaped by and shape broader social forces that influence their beliefs and actions. Others have continuously pointed to the influence of social structures and individual agency on social institutions (Kennedy, 2009).

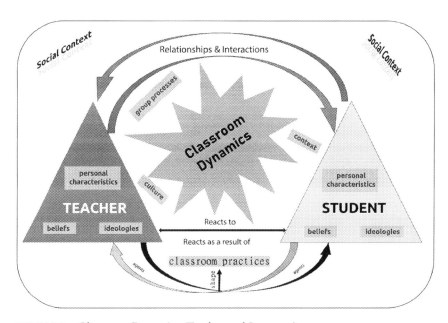

FIGURE 5.2 Classroom Dynamics: Teacher and Learner Agency

The previous discussion leads us to focus our attention on several dynamics occurring within classroom settings. It is very essential for one to know the causes of these dynamics and the responsiveness of the dynamics and ways to realign these in order to improve emotional and academic functioning of pupils within the classroom settings. The classroom contexts are comprised of various interactions and relationships between individuals. These individuals with their social contexts exercise their agency in shaping the social structure of the classrooms. However, these structures lead to a complex network of relationships. In this regard, we need to study the relational nature of classroom contexts.

Organization of classroom contexts

It is very crucial for an understanding of classroom group dynamics to moderate the inter- and intragroup activities, managing the hierarchical social structures in the classroom. Teachers can affect classroom dynamics at different levels. They can have direct impact on the peer groups by virtue of their own behaviour. The peer group dynamics are influenced by the nature of relationships and interactions teachers develop with students individually and collectively. Teachers can also impact peer groups by the kind of grouping strategies, seating arrangements, disciplinary practices, instructional methods or other methods that they adopt with the classroom group, which may impact the nature of opportunities the individuals avail in the classroom. Considering the relationally organized nature of classroom contexts, which constitute processes and structures that affect and in turn are affected by social interactions among individuals in groups, one cannot think of a unidirectional linear path to a specific outcome. A systems perspective of classroom dynamics and functioning, focusing on the role and interplay of various factors – classroom social structure, teachers' behaviour and management of classroom ecology, group affiliations, group norms and culture, and inclusion and exclusion practices – is essential in promoting classroom contexts that are supportive and responsive to students' positive development (Farmer et al., 2018).

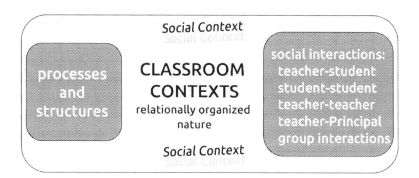

FIGURE 5.3 The Relationally Organized Nature of Classroom Contexts

Classroom context nested in a hierarchy of systems

Let us recapitulate the conceptualization of Bronfenbrenner's (1979) ecological theory from Chapter 3. The theory emphasizes culture as a context and a part of the socio-ecological environment. Social interactions and relationships are shaped by cultural beliefs, values and practices reflected in social norms and perceptions. Here, we will use this lens to understand the classroom context as the microsystem and all other interacting and interconnected systems influencing the classroom context.

Relationships do not exist in a vacuum. The nature of these relationships are influenced by many contextual factors. Bronfenbrenner' identifies four networks of interrelated factors that are simultaneously in motion and affecting learners. He calls them the micro-, meso-, exo-, and macrosystems. The microsystem contains the learner in a particular setting, such as a classroom; the mesosystem contains the relationships between the various settings that contain the learner; the exosystem includes the social structures and policies that guide mesosystem relationships; and the macrosystem describes broad institutions and forces that affect all of society and saturate all other systems. Examining the classrooms as microsystems, one needs to look at the interaction between contextual factors and classroom dynamics to understand classroom processes in context with respect to the roles of structure, agency and culture.

Classroom context: microsystem factors in the levels of meso-, exo-, and macrosystems

Let us understand the classroom as a context to describe factors in the meso-, exo-, and macro-systems that influence classroom life.

The macro-system context of the classroom constitutes largely social forces like gender, poverty, caste, religion, and other organizational structures in a particular society that affect schooling by regulating students' behaviour. The exo-system context of the classroom may include the rules, regulations, policies in the classroom and the school as a whole. The meso-system context of the classroom will encompass the wider state and school vision and policies and the enactment of these by stakeholders at the school/classroom level. Culture also penetrates these levels of systems. Macro-system cultural factors refers to social values and ideologies embedded within the expectations of the school. Meso and exo-system cultural factors can be viewed in students' and teachers' own cultural perspectives and beliefs within the school culture. The classroom context and the culture may be either mutually reinforcing or contradicting each other. More importantly we look at the micro-system cultural factors manifested in the behavioural patterns and interactions between students and teachers. Recognizing classroom as a dynamic system nested in a hierarchy of multiple systems at different levels, the term 'agency' derived from a sociological point of view can be used to describe the collective actions of students and teachers in creating classroom dynamics through their mutual relationships. All the same, students and teachers individually exercise their agency and play their roles in shaping the classroom (micro-system) dynamics as well as meso-, exo-, and macro-system social forces (Kennedy, 2009).

Classroom context: structure, culture and agency

Using the sociological lens, let us unpack the classroom context comprising the structure, culture and agency.

Social structure is observed to consist of interconnected elements: systems of social relations and systems of meaning. Social relations consist of patterns of roles, relationships, and power dynamics giving rise to hierarchy in status on the basis of class, gender, caste, socio-economic status, education, position or roles of individuals in different contexts at different times. Systems of meaning often referred to as culture, including not only the beliefs and values of social but also their language, and forms of knowledge, as well as the products, interactional practices, rituals, and ways of life established by these.

The term 'social structure' highlights the patterns of processes and interactions within a classroom context and is not just confined to influencing individual teachers or students but also strong enough to withstand the actions and reactions of these individuals who may be responsible to change these structures. Thus, structure undergoes dynamics that contribute to its reproduction over time.

When the beliefs and ideologies (culture) reflected in classroom processes (structure) transcends teachers or students (individuals), it determines the thoughts and actions of individuals in the context. Referring to the pattern of social structure will also entail the specific interests and activities of individuals within the context, where individuals are not considered to be static entities conforming to the existing structure. Thus, the structure i.e. classroom processes cannot be devoid of individuals' (teachers' and students') participation, be it willing or unwilling, conscious or unconscious. This indicates both the enabling and constraining nature of the classroom patterns and processes (structure) in creating a classroom environment. Structures lend to rules which in turn lends to an individual's agency. Hereby, we bring in the concept of agency which refers to the actions taken by teachers and students, individually and collectively, in the creation, recreation, and transformation of classroom processes and practices (social structures). This agency is possible due to the enabling nature of the structure or limited due to the constraints of structure and the capacity of agents is again determined by accessibility, power, resources and other dimensions of society (structure) in question. Reiterating here, classroom processes and practices (structures) are both the source and the consequence of human action, i.e. teachers' and students' behaviours and actions.

Culture (beliefs and ideologies) is a social and a layered pattern of cognitive and normative systems represented in the behaviour and actions of individuals (agents) and reflected in the interactions and relationships between individuals (students and teachers) and internalized in personalities (teachers and students) and institutions (classroom/school). Thus, culture is both the product of human interaction and producer of certain forms of human interaction. Culture is both constraining and enabling like the structure.

216 The adolescent in the classroom

Check your understanding

List down all the possible elements and components of your classroom context. Classify these elements or components into structure, culture and agency as per your understanding. Create a diagrammatic representation exhibiting the relationships between the three- structure, culture and agency.

Reflect on the following questions-

- What are your observations from your diagram?
- Do you see any overlaps?
- What kind of relationship networks do you see, simple or complex?
- Interpret these relationships as relevant to your classroom context?
- What are the implications of these relationships on student learning or outcomes?
- In what way will you as an educator exercise your agency to attain positive outcomes in your classroom context?

Structure, culture and agency: interwoven factors

Further, we can explain the reciprocal relationships between culture, structure and agency by seeing through the lens of Hubbard's model of social reproduction and Datnow's theory of teacher agency (Kennedy, 2009).

Hubbard's model of social reproduction and Datnow's theory of teacher agency place classroom interactions within a broader context, influenced by structural factors as well as the cultures and subcultures to which they belong.

Hubbard's model of social reproduction places emphasis on factors promoting and hindering student agency. Students' agency consists of actions, aspirations, motivations, attitudes, ideology, and instrumental strategies available for action. These components interact with social structure and practices and culture at large, which also interact with each other. All these factors of culture, structure and agency in classroom contexts affect the development of student-teacher relationships which in turn affect these factors. This student agency can be viewed both as a transformative potential and structural limitation in shaping student-teacher interactions and relationships.

Datnow's theory of teacher agency focuses on the equally important aspect of teacher agency. According to this theory, structure, culture and agency are reflexive concepts. We consider them as reflexive due to their reciprocity and interconnectedness. The teacher in the classroom brings with him/her certain beliefs and ideologies to the classroom. The teacher interaction in the classroom context based on these beliefs and ideologies builds a certain culture within that context. This culture and structure share a reciprocity of interconnectedness, whereby the teacher's actions retain the existing structure or changes the structure.

Extending from Gidden's theory, Datnow considers culture as a very important influential entity by itself. She notes that teachers' agency reflects the subcultures to which they belonged. She illustrates the dialectical nature of agency and structure, and agency and culture. She explains how teachers' action or behaviour (agency) can retain or change the existing situation/system (structure) and teachers' action or behaviour (agency) can be subject to embracing or avoiding certain beliefs and ideologies (culture).

Classroom dynamics and the roles of structure, agency, and culture within classroom processes can be understood by looking into Datnow's theory of teacher agency and Hubbard's theory of student agency and social reproduction. While students and teachers all have individual agency, how they use that agency will largely be influenced by structural factors as well as the cultures and subcultures to which they belong (Kennedy, 2009).

Classroom factors: within and beyond

Classrooms as contexts are subject to tensions and conflicts between social structure and human agency. Relationships and interactions between teachers and students need to dwell on mutually shared ideologies and structural factors in order to influence positive development.

There are a varied number of factors within and beyond the classroom that influence classroom interactions between students and teachers.

Students many a time feel pressured or coerced into undesirable behaviours or acts by their classmates or peers and such kind of pressures have been shown to correlate with the broader social impacts. Gender, poverty, caste and religion, among others, may be considered the kind of social impacts in a diverse country like India. Bowlby and Kobak consider family lives and early childhood experiences of students affecting classroom dynamics. Delpit, notes that teachers' cultural backgrounds influence their expectations of student behaviour and performance and there is often a mismatch between teachers' expectations and students' own expectations and experiences. These conflicting expectations result in unfavourable behaviours of teachers through their interactions with students which sometimes result in demeaning students. Notwithstanding these negative effects of emerging conflicts, Giroux claims that student-teacher relationships can also act as enablers in shaping the social structures thus empowering students within the structure. Kelly suggests that teachers should act as developmentalists using their own dispositions to overcome the inconsistencies that emerge out of rules, norms, notions and conventions. Giddens posits that teachers and students are shaped by, and shape these broader social forces that influence ideological perspectives and theories of action (Kennedy, 2009).

Below we present an overview of studies in India and abroad, highlighting the most common variables related to adolescents alongside the factors resulting in adolescent problems, thus affecting adolescents.

218 The adolescent in the classroom

SOCIAL GROUP (Family, Friends, Peer, Society & Culture)		AFFECTS ADOLESCENTS'
STUDIES	**FACTORS**	
Selection, Deselection, and Socialization Processes of Happiness in Adolescent Friendship Networks Workum, N.V., et al (2013)	HAPPINESS OF FRIENDS	EMOTIONS
Adolescent Friendships, BMI, and Physical Activity: Untangling Selection and Influence Through Longitudinal Social Network Analysis Simpkins, S. D., et al (2013)	• ENDOGENOUS SOCIAL NETWORK • PROCESSES & PROPINQUITY • GENDER • POPULARITY • RECIPROCITY.	RELATIONSHIPS HEALTH & BEHAVIOUR
Paradoxical Inequalities Adolescent Peer Relations in Indian Secondary Schools Jr, Murray. (2013).	• STATUS RELATIONS • DISTINCTIVE CULTURES	RELATIONSHIPS CLASSROOM CLIMATE
When Parents and Adolescents Disagree About Disagreeing: Observed Parent–Adolescent Communication Predicts Informant Discrepancies About Conflict Ehrlich, K. B., et al (2016)	• STRESS IN THE PARENT-ADOLESCENT RELATIONSHIP • LACK OF OPEN COMMUNICATION	RELATIONSHIPS HEALTH & BEHAVIOUR
Patterns of Adolescent Regulatory Responses During Family Conflict and Mental Health Trajectories Koss, K. J., et al (2017)	• LESS OUVERT • SUBJECTIVE DISTRESS • PEER PROBLEMS	RELATIONSHIPS HEALTH & BEHAVIOUR
Parent–Adolescent Socialization of Social Class in Low-Income White Families: Theory, Research, and Future Directions Jones, D. J., et al (2018).	SOCIALIZATION THROUGH COLOR, CLASS AND SES	RELATIONSHIPS SOCIETY & CULTURE
Parenting and Adolescent Identity: A Study of Indian Families in New Delhi and Geneva Sapru S. (2006).	ANCESTRAL & ACCULTURATED VALUES	ADOLESCENT IDENTITY
Adolescents Romantic Relationship: Dynamics of Parent-Child Relationship from India Janardhana, N., (2018)	• ROMANTIC RELATIONS • LOWER SES • CHOICE OF EITHER PARENTS OR PARTNER	RELATIONSHIPS ADOLESCENT IDENTITY
Influence of Peer Relationships on the Happiness of Early Adolescents S, S. S., et al (2018).	PEER RELATIONSHIPS	RELATIONSHIPS

Credits: Farrah Kerawalla

FIGURE 5.4A Studies Highlighting 'Social Group' as the Variable Related to Adolescents and the Factors Resulting in Adolescent Problems

The adolescent in the classroom 219

HEALTH AND BEHAVIOUR		AFFECTS ADOLESCENTS'
STUDIES	FACTORS	
Depressive Symptoms in Early Adolescence. Their relations with classroom problem behaviour & peer status Kiesner, J., et al (2003)	• PEER STATUS • DEPRESSIVE SYMPTOMS	HEALTH & BEHAVIOUR ACADEMICS
Violence in the Transition to Adulthood: Adolescent Victimization, Education, & Socioeconomic Attainment in Later Life Macmillan, R., et al (2004)	ADOLESCENT VICTIMIZATION	EMOTIONS SOCIETY & CULTURE
A Cross-Cultural Study of Adolescent Procrastination Klassen, R. M., et al (2009)	PROCRASTINATION	ACADEMICS SELF REGULATION
The Trajectories of Adolescents' Perceptions of School Climate, Deviant Peer Affiliation, and Behavioral Problems During the Middle School Years. Wang MT, Dishion TJ. (2012).	PEER AFFILIATIONS	CLASSROOM CLIMATE HEALTH & BEHAVIOUR
The use of psychoactive substances and adolescents' school performance Pestana, L., et al (2016)	PSYCHOACTIVE SUBSTANCES	ACADEMICS
Does one Size Fit All? —Linking Parenting with Adolescent Substance Use and Adolescent Temperament Kapetanovic, S., (2019)	• ADOLESCENTS' TEMPARAMENT • PSYCHOACTIVE SUBSTANCE	RELATIONSHIPS HEALTH & BEHAVIOUR
BEHAVIOURAL AND EMOTIONAL PROBLEMS IN SCHOOL GOING ADOLESCENTS Pathak, R., et al (2011)	• SOCIOENVIRONMENTAL STRESSORS • MALADAPTIVE OUTCOMES	HEALTH & BEHAVIOUR
Psychosocial Determinants of Tobacco Use among School Going Adolescents in Delhi, India Kumar, V., (2014)	• LOWER GENERAL SELF-EFFICACY • MALADJUSTMENT WITH PEERS, TEACHERS & SCHOOL	ACADEMICS RELATIONSHIPS HEALTH & BEHAVIOUR
PROBLEMS AMONG ADOLESCENTS IN NORTHERN KERALA NECESSITATES ADOLESCENCE EDUCATION Mumthas, D. N., & E, S. (2016).	• CONSTANT QUARRELS AMONG PARENTS • LACK OF CARE FOR CHILDREN • CYBER ADDICTION • DRUG ABUSE • SEXUAL ABUSE • STEALING	ACADEMICS SOCIETY & CULTURE HEALTH & BEHAVIOUR
Pubertal development and problem behaviours in Indian adolescents. Kanwar, P. (2020)	PUBERTAL TIMING	EMOTIONS

Credits: Farrah Kerawalla

FIGURE 5.4B Studies Highlighting 'Health and Behaviour' as the Variable Related to Adolescents and the Factors Resulting in Adolescent Problems

GENDER ROLES AND DIFFERENCES		AFFECTS ADOLESCENTS'
STUDIES	FACTORS	
Adolescents' Academic Achievement & Life satisfaction: the role of parents' education Crede, J., et al. (2015)	MOTHERS EDUCATIONAL ATTAINMENT	ACADEMICS
Adolescents Antisocial Behavior and Their Academic Performance: The Case of High Schools in Jimma Town Girma, H., Hassen, A., (2019)	GENDER DIFFERENCE IN ANTISOCIAL BEHAVIOUR	ACADEMICS
Challenges faced by Adolescent Girl in the Indian Context. Kuruvilla, D. M., (2015)	• GIRL DOMINANT ISSUES • GENDER DISCRIMINATION • USAGE OF ICT	ACADEMICS ADOLESCENT IDENTITY HEALTH & BEHAVIOUR
Education, poverty and "purity" in the context of adolescent girls' secondary school retention and dropout: A qualitative study from Karnataka, southern India Ramanaik S, et al (2018)	• GENDER-RELATED NORMS • POVERTY	ACADEMICS ADOLESCENT IDENTITY

Credits: Farrah Kerawalla

FIGURE 5.4C Studies Highlighting 'Gender Role and Differences' as the Variable Related to Adolescents and the Factors Resulting in Adolescent Problems

220 The adolescent in the classroom

ADJUSTMENT		AFFECTS ADOLESCENTS'
STUDIES	**FACTORS**	
Fitting in high school: how adolescent belonging is influenced by locus of control beliefs
Schall, J., et al (2016)	LOCUS OF CONTROL BELIEFS	RELATIONSHIPS
ADOLESCENT IDENTITY
Impact of Socio-Emotional Adjustment on Academic achievement of Adolescent Girls in Jammu and Kashmir
Gul, S. B. (2015)	URBAN-RURAL CONTEXT	ACADEMICS
EMOTIONS
Effect of Academic-related Factors on Adjustment Problems in Adolescents
Rajkumar G, et al (2016)	• INCREASING AGE
• TYPE OF SCHOOL
• MEDIUM OF INSTRUCTION
• TYPE OF ACCOMMODATION	ACADEMICS
HEALTH & BEHAVIOUR
Depression and Behavioral Problems Among Adolescent Girls and Young Women Employees of the Textile Industry in India
Gnanaselvam, N. A., (2018)	• FAMILY DEBT
• HISTORY OF ABUSE	HEALTH & BEHAVIOUR

Credits: Farrah Kerawalla

FIGURE 5.4D Studies Highlighting 'Adjustment' as the Variable Related to Adolescents and the Factors Resulting in Adolescent Problems

ACADEMICS AND CLASSROOM		AFFECTS ADOLESCENTS'
STUDIES	**FACTORS**	
The Impact of Adolescents' Classroom & Neighbourhood Ethnic Diversity on Same & Cross-Ethnic Friendships Within Classrooms
Munniksma, A., et al (2016)	SAME ETHNIC FRIENDSHIPS	CLASSROOM CLIMATE
Attentional Bias for Academic Stressors and Classroom Climate Predict Adolescents' Grades and Socioemotional Functioning
Scrimin, S., et al (2017)	• ACADEMIC STRESSORS
• CLASSROOM CLIMATE	ACADEMICS
EMOTIONS
Academic Achievement of Adolescents in Relation to Study Habits
Arora, M. R. (2016).	STUDYING HABITS	ACADEMICS

Credits: Farrah Kerawalla

FIGURE 5.4E Studies Highlighting 'Academics and Classroom' as the Variable Related to Adolescents and the Factors Resulting in Adolescent Problems

TECHNOLOGY		AFFECTS ADOLESCENTS'
STUDIES	**FACTORS**	
Adolescent Internet Gaming Disorder: A Narrative Review Field T. (2019)	INTERNET GAMING ADDICTION	ACADEMICS
Association Between Screen Media Use and Academic Performance Among Children and Adolescents: A Systematic Review and Meta-analysis Renau A., et al (2019)	• ACADEMIC STRESSORS • CLASSROOM CLIMATE	ACADEMICS

Credits: Farrah Kerawalla

FIGURE 5.4F Studies Highlighting 'Technology' as the Variable Related to Adolescents and the Factors resulting in Adolescent Problems

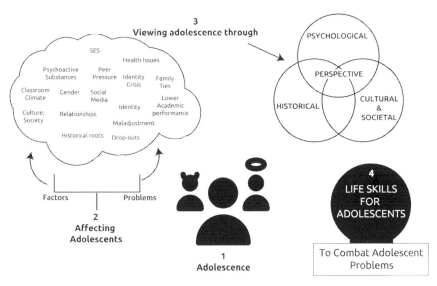

FIGURE 5.5 Factors Affecting Adolescents and Need for Life Skills to Combat Adolescent Problems

The following box article is an attempt to bring out the various forces that are at play in the life of an adolescent.

> **Box Article 1: Synthesis of Adolescence Studies: A Reflection   By Farrah Z .Kerawalia**
>
> Adolescence is a period of turmoil of thoughts, emotions, body language, expressions and identity. A lot of studies in India and abroad have emphasized, on different factors contributing to adolescent problems. These factors include peer relations, relationship strains, family and societal pressure, classroom climate, technology and social in use of psychoactive substances, own beliefs, defining one's, identity, physicality, gender, puberty, procrastination, socio-economic status, parents' education and qualification, victimization and bullying, psychological factors, networking, conflicts and temperament. These factors add to the storm and stress affecting adolescents causing depression, anxiety, adjustm.ent problems, academic problems, aggression and conflicts, loss of identity in a social structure, dropout from schools and at times massive steps such as suicide. A lot of recent studies suggest that adolescents commence to face these an in their early teens and tend to find their space of identity by succumbing to peer pressure, social status, use of hazardous substances and prioritizing partners or friends over family.
>
> Though adolescents all over the world are challenged during this phase, there lies a distinction is. factors that affect the adolescents in India and abroad. For instance, in Indian studies gender plays a critical role among adolescents which may not be an eminent factor in studies conducted abroad. In India during adolescence, the identity of a girl is challenged within as well as from the outside and this differential behaviour has compelled the girls to drop-out from schools, early marriage or to engage in workforce especially in. rural areas. On the other hand, studies conducted abroad, highlighted anti-social behaviour as a crucial element among adolescents which did not manifest to a large extent in Indian studies.
>
> A deepened understanding of this distinction navigates us to the conception of adolescence throwing light on the minuscule literature on the historical, cultural and social perspectives on adolescence. The need to universalize and naturalize adolescence as totality and being conscious of every adolescent's subjectivity inclines the researchers to focus on the evolving period of adolescence, their psychological determinants and the processes they undergo, aligned with the historical process deep-rooted in their culture and society that produce them.
>
> This transition from childhood to adulthood suggested by Margaret Mead proposes adolescence to be a function of certain cultural determinant. Therefore, the home and classroom space needs to withheld the psychological needs of the adolescents and parallelly be cognizant of their historical, cultural and societal factors. Adolescents in their quest of identity formation amid their upsurge of passions, internal revolutions, social change, lassitude, plurality of alternatives and in hunt of gregariousness need to be assisted in these spaces and this assistance can be amalgamated through "Life Skills". Life skills,in simple language refers to the skills needed in life to face the demands and challenges life has in store. Adolescents therefore, need to be embedded with life skills that allow them to cope up with stress and emotions, societal requisites,. resolve identity questions, indulge in critical thinking thus, making optimum decisions keeping their moral codes intact, communicating effectively and developing a strong gregariousness with empathy and being self-a'vare and expressing their true self to themselves and others.

Classroom factors: group processes

As we take a glance in the classroom within the four walls, we would agree that these forces that are at play in adolescence are not confined to individuals alone, but also have its bearing on classrooms which are constituted of a number of groups of adolescents. In addition to students experiencing social, emotional, physical, psychological adjustment problems, classroom dynamics can be referred to a greater understanding of group behaviours and interactions within the classrooms.

It is observed that small cohesive groups within the classroom often impacted the beliefs and behaviour of students, who generally tend to conform to certain groups as per the demands of these groups. Students generally try to follow a specific pattern of interaction and relationship to conform to a peer group and this in turn allows the formation of a distinct peer group. Peer groups exhibit vast similarities in their way of socialization, academic achievements, engagement in bullying, aggression, popularity, etc. This is an indication of how the extent of cohesiveness of the group determines its influence on the individual members of the group. There may be a few of them who behave in a way that complements the behaviour of others in the group. This usually occurs when they possess different levels of status and forms of behaviours, but behaviour of one may be necessary for the other's behaviour. Common examples of these can be mentor-mentee, bully-victim, leader-follower, and so on. This may result in social structures that may be egalitarian or hierarchical in nature. Classroom dynamics with a hierarchical social structure may lead to a coercive climate that supports bullying, social exclusion, decreased instructional engagement depending on dominant student characteristics (Farmer et al., 2018).

In a formal classroom setting, a set of rules and regulations, and expectations for classroom behaviour is already created by the teacher who is considered higher in status than the students. In spite of this, students tend to co-create their own shared rules, beliefs, and values as a part of the group processes of the groups they belong to and, these norms may hinder or promote healthy classroom culture. These group processes, norms, and structures contribute to the overall opportunities and experiences of students.

As it is widely known that students are taught in groups varying in numbers, the need to recognise group dynamics is strongly emphasized by Passow and Mackenzie. They believed that classroom difficulties like discipline problems and other issues like classroom climate, classroom management, and the use of peer groups could arise from a failure to understand group processes in the classroom. The classroom processes constitute many underlying processes and patterns that may not facilitate the understanding of individual personalities or interpersonal relationships. Individual members of groups may represent the behaviour of a collective group, which may impel the teacher to believe a certain aspect about the individual rather than focusing on the group needs and concerns, which actually drive the individual to do so, if the teacher does not possess knowledge of the group-as-a-whole phenomenon (Slavin, 2002).

Classroom in the context of teaching-learning practices

Although the peer group is an important aspect of classroom context, the classroom is also an intersection of the peer group taken collectively, the teacher, the individual students, and the academic activities, curricular and non-curricular activities, teaching practices, task characteristics and so on. Teaching and learning are complementary acts which comprise interpersonal processes. The process of teaching-learning is also a complicated process impacted by student-student relationships and the teacher-student relationships. Classrooms have been found to be places of either fostering or inhibiting the learning process as a result of peer relationships or student-teacher relationships. Classroom is a diverse context bringing with it a special, unique set of characteristics, as a result of being exposed to a variety of social influences surrounding it. These influences can range from the larger school values and ideologies in which the classroom is situated to the different sociological environments of class, caste, gender, socio-economic status and rural-urban differences that constitute the classroom. Thus, the classroom environment represents a unique developmental context involving instructional, social, and organizational interactions. Interactions between teachers and students, provides the resources and opportunities for developing students' competencies in the academic, socio-emotional and behavioural aspects. Jones et al. proposed that both classroom teaching practices and teacher-student relationships contribute to the quality of the classroom's instructional and emotional climates, which in turn impact children's outcomes (Wang et al., 2020).

A typical classroom interaction includes general instructions, teachers interacting with students in large groups and most of these interactions are perfunctory or compliance directed. Moreover, these interactions are largely focused towards fixated results in terms of basic skills and knowledge acquisition excluding the analysis, reasoning and problem-solving skills around meaningful challenges that an adolescent learner distinctly looks forward to. If we look at these interactions from a relational point of view, they quite often are lacking the personal, emotional and motivational properties that would be essential to engage the adolescent learner in the classroom.

Adolescent classroom characteristics

We have already learnt in the previous chapters about adolescent's cognitive development which is characteristic of meaningful, challenging and interesting school experiences that requires supportive relationships and competence-building opportunities. It is observed that, most of the time, this energetic group of students fail to engage or connect with their teachers or the learning material in the classroom with a sharp decline in energy levels within the classroom.

Adolescents' striving for autonomy and self-expression is generally assumed by secondary school teachers as negative forces to be tackled rather than positive energy to be harnessed and this misconception is often promoted in teacher education programmes and reinforced by school policies. This reflects in classroom practices in the form of highly controlled and punitive classroom strategies and teacher-driven instruction devoid of opportunities of exploration and curiosity. On the other hand, classroom practices also reflect under-involvement of the teachers who adopt a constructivist philosophy around learning and development leaving the learner to engage with challenges viewed as "older" or adult like but which require appropriate scaffolding and support. The nature of these classroom practices and student-teacher interactions are not aligned to the developmental tendencies of students and this mismatch results in narrowing rather than expanding the space of zone of proximal development and deprives the learners a sense of control, autonomy, choice, and mastery.

Adolescents are in continuous efforts of making meaning in their lives. They evaluate adult's or others' experiences and choices against their own choices which they feel are relevant or meaningful within their contexts. In this regard, it is a question whether high school curriculum offers teachers opportunities to address the relevance of what occurs within the classroom to the larger world in engaging the restless young minds. It has been observed that, involving students in significant, real-world, voluntary community service and then discussing it within the classroom in an ongoing way has reduced disruptive behaviour by 50% (Pianta et al., 2012). Classroom interactions need to be made more relevant by establishing connections between curricular material and real-world applications, perceived as meaningful by the learner and engaging relational processes that scaffold participation in learning. The essence of these connections can be either through close emotional connections with teachers for some students or through provision of challenges by teachers for others. The central role of teacher-student interactions and relationships in fostering student engagement forms the basis for analysing classroom processes that impact student outcomes.

Teaching Through Interactions (TTI) framework

A theoretically driven and empirically supported framework has been adopted to inform conceptualization and assessment of classroom processes. Hamre and Pianta's Teaching Through Interactions (TTI) framework conceptualizes, organizes, and measures classroom interactions between teachers and students under three major domains – emotional support, classroom organization, and instructional support. It recognizes that the starting point for understanding contextual influences on development is to recognize that development occurs through interactions between the capacities and skills of the person and the resources available to them in various settings, and that this process is very dynamic (Pianta et al., 2012).

Emotional support

As validated by attachment theory and self-determination theory, students who are more emotionally connected to teachers and peers throughout schooling, demonstrate positive trajectories of development in both social and academic domains. Positive teacher-student and student-student interactions enable teachers to support students' social and emotional functioning in the classroom.

Teacher sensitivity is another important feature of interaction in relation to engagement. Teachers need to be highly sensitive towards students' needs and problems and be able to attend to and be responsive to a whole lot of happenings in the classroom. A sensitive teacher will know her students well enough to respond in ways that can help reduce their problems.

Another element of emotional support refers to the degree to which classrooms and interactions are structured around the interests and motivations of both teacher and students. Students, especially adolescents are highly motivated and engaged in learning, when they are confronted with learner-focused tasks that promote their autonomy. Adolescent students are energetic with ideas and thoughts and their agentic nature enables them to take on multiple roles if provided with opportunities to interact in the classroom with peers and in large groups (Pianta et al., 2012).

Classroom organization

Classroom organization domain of the TTI framework refers to student-teacher interactions through which teachers organise behaviour, time, and attention. When teachers use effective behaviour management strategies and have organized routine management structures, students are likely to be more engaged in learning and hence are unlikely to exhibit undesirable behaviour. Behaviour management domain of the TTI framework refers to interactions in the classroom that approach towards positive behaviour and avoidance of misbehaviour in the classroom. Time management by teachers assists teachers in engaging students more productively which in turn promotes student learning (Pianta et al., 2012).

Instructional support

A very important dimension of classroom interaction is the instructional learning format which focuses on learning activities, instruction, projects and materials used in the classroom. Consistent with constructivist theories as well as information-processing views of learning and cognition, instructional formats should allow active participation of students not only in behavioural outcomes but also through cognitive engagement in learning. The quality of teachers' use of instruction and materials in engaging students in the classroom determines the quality of instruction and not the type of instruction or number of instructional materials.

Within a broad cognitively focused definition of instruction, three aspects of teachers' interactions with students that not only promote engagement but student learning outcomes, have been identified (Pianta et al., 2012). The aspect of concept development through instructional behaviours, conversations, and activities of the teacher depends on the teaching and learning practices associated with the development of cognitive skills as laid down in Bloom's Taxonomy

Opportunities for students' cognitive engagement can widely range from mere understanding to a higher order skill of evaluating and creating. These opportunities depend on whether teachers plan activities to take students towards deeper thinking or whether interactions between teachers and students focus on remembering facts, or simple tasks of recall and recognition. To avail the maximum benefits from these instructional opportunities, the aspect of feedback to students is very crucial. The TTI framework emphasises feedback that provides students with specific information not only about the content of learning but also about the process of learning leading to deeper understanding of the concept. To be able to navigate the instructional and social opportunities in classrooms, the aspect of language skills is a key determinant. Classes dominated by teacher talks are generally devoid of opportunities for promotion of language skills in students. A blend of teacher and student talk facilitating peer interactions and language related interactions foster exchanges of ideas, concepts, and perspectives enabling the development of specific language skills.

> **Task for the Learner**
>
> Note: The TTI framework is suggestive for conceptualizing classroom processes.
>
> Do you want to check your understanding of the Teaching Through Interactions (TTI) Framework?
>
> A. Attempt the following activity.
>   Maintain a reflective journal to reflect on your own classroom experiences of teaching adolescents. Browse through your notes and review the processes, aligned with the various dimensions and factors discussed through the TTI framework.
>
> B. Identify any other existing framework that can be adopted in conceptualizing and assessing classroom processes, relevant to the context that you have considered. Or Design a framework appropriate to your context to conceptualize and assess classroom practices

Classroom group processes and instructional practices: implications

The above discussion of classroom group practices and instructional practices show how diverse classroom environments can be associated with variations in educational and psychosocial outcomes for youth as demonstrated by research. Overall classroom experiences impact children's development through their interactions with curriculum, teachers, peers, and classroom organizational structures on an everyday basis. These interactions also provide opportunities for children to engage in not only different learning activities, but also develop relations with teachers and peers and improve their academic and socio-emotional skills. The quality of these interactions largely determine the children's likeliness or unlikeliness to demonstrate socio-emotional distress and to have adaptive psychological adjustment. Through the classroom experiences, students co-construct their identities by developing a sense of their competencies and skills, relationships between teachers and peers, and ability to self-regulate their own learning. These varied experiences build up to influence academic, behavioural, and socio-emotional development among adolescent students according to. This extends to the classroom components like the quality of teacher-student and peer relationships for better psychosocial functioning of adolescents (Wang et al., 2020).

Introduction to life skills

Psychosocial competence is a person's ability to deal effectively with the demands and challenges of everyday life. It enables an individual to maintain a state of mental well-being and to demonstrate this in adaptive and positive behaviour while interacting with others, his/her culture and environment. Psychosocial competence has huge implications for physical, mental and social well-being of individuals

(Manjunatha & Saddichha, 2011). Promoting psychosocial competence in students requires fostering such skills that enable them to cope with situations and enhance their social and personal competencies.

Skill development has been defined as an ability and capacity to effectively and adaptively carryout complex activities involving ideas (cognitive skills), things (technical skills), and/or people (interpersonal skills) and can be acquired through deliberate, systematic, and sustained efforts. A skill set is the knowledge, abilities, and experience needed to perform a job. Life skills is a term used to describe a set of basic skills acquired through learning and/or direct life experience that enable individuals and groups to effectively handle issues and problems. Life skills have been defined as "the abilities for adaptive and positive behaviour that enable individuals to deal effectively with the demands and challenges of everyday life" (WHO). Life skills include psychosocial competencies and interpersonal skills that help people make informed decisions, solve problems, think critically and creatively, communicate effectively, build healthy relationships, empathise with others, and cope with managing their lives in a healthy and productive manner. Acquisition of basic life skills can facilitate individuals to cope with emotional conflicts, strained relationships, peer pressures and many other psychosocial outcomes like depression, anxiety, adjustment, quality of life and so on. Thus, life-skill interventions can empower individuals to act responsibly, take initiative and control.

Need for life skills for adolescents

The adolescent period, as we reiterate, is a developmental period characterized by a heightened risk for developing depression and anxiety. Addressing adolescents' mood disorders, anxiety, depression symptoms make conducive classroom environments very crucial for their overall mental health (Wang et al., 2020). At the same time, we also acknowledge that adolescents are the most productive force with unlimited energy, vitality and idealism, and a strong desire to explore, experiment and create a better world. Adolescents' transition from childhood to adulthood needs to be smooth and effortless, however, many of them are unable to navigate this transition in a smooth way. They end up getting involved in activities that are undesirable and unproductive and are at high risk due to lack of proper guidance and motivation.

In this regard, effective and appropriate programmes beneficial to young adolescents for better psychosocial adjustment and functioning are necessary to be assimilated in the school curriculum in order to create awareness and provide the right direction to them. These programmes or interventions to enable adolescents' coping skills, decision-making skills, and enhance their personal and social competencies, need to be a part of classroom-based processes appropriated from the school-based programmes for children and adolescents and need to take the form of teaching of life skills in a supportive learning environment.

Developmental foundations of life skills approach

Referring back to Chapter 1, we recognise the health implications of adolescent development throughout life and the need of the education system to be responsive to the changes and developments happening around to promote adolescents' future lives and consequently wider societal gains in support of the 2030 Agenda for Sustainable Development.

Recalling the developmental changes occurring during the transition from childhood to adolescence and further to adulthood, one can obviously recognise the role of skills acquisition at every stage of development. Adolescent girls and boys undergo varied biological changes at different points of time making them vulnerable to these changes and taking immature decisions. Navigating from experiences of understanding oneself to the ability to understand and respond to other's feelings requires adolescents to develop a sense of empathy and understand others perspectives. Development of these skills may not be easy for every adolescent. The responsibility of fostering these skills in adolescents and enabling them navigate through the experiences of transition lie with the stakeholders in the milieu of adolescents. Knowing the adolescents as a group and as individuals, interacting with them individually and collectively, encouraging peer relationships, are some of the strategies that need to be adopted by the members in the social environment in which the adolescent is situated. Thus, it is equally essential for teachers, educators, family, peers and significant others to nurture and develop a sense of empathy and understand others perspectives.

As we have seen in the earlier part of this chapter, adolescents encounter varied experiences in classrooms as a result of group dynamics that exist. The pressure of conforming to groups, competing with others in groups, being accepted by group and so on results in their self-evaluation, which also determines their self-efficacy. At such times, skills such as coping with vulnerable situations, regulating one's emotions and negotiating and making decisions become quite difficult for some adolescents. Bandura pointed to self-efficacy as important to learning and maintaining behaviours, especially in the face of social pressure to behave differently. Thus, skills development is not just confined to outward behaviour, but also extends to internal qualities that support those behaviours.

Both intrapersonal and interpersonal levels of interactions as posited by Piaget and Vygotsky, take place at various stages of development emphasizing the strong influence of social interactions on adolescents' thinking and cognitive skills. Hansen et al. and Csikszentmihalyi and Schneider posit that early adolescents either learn to be competent or to feel inferior, resulting in long-lasting social, intellectual and emotional consequences.

The continuous interactions with self, other people and the environment is referred to as a collaborative process in a child's cognitive development. According to constructivist psychology, the adolescents individually are not the centre of knowledge-making but they themselves co-create the content through the interaction of information with their particular cultural environment. Their higher mental functions, rooted in social sources, include the actual development of the adolescents at the individual level, which is referred to as problem solving and the potential development that occurs in interaction with peers and more knowledgeable others, as propounded through Vygotsky's idea of the zone of proximal development (ZPD). This problem solving capacity applied to social or interpersonal situations is a very crucial skill for adolescents. Shure and Spivack state that children who are not able to attain their goals immediately, learn to cope with such situations, learn patience and tolerance and to regulate their emotions by learning to consider more solutions and consequences through their problem solving skills (Mangrulkar et al., 2001).

Altogether, the physical changes as a result of biological transformations, the psychological changes, changing relationships with peers, family and the social environment, and the growing ability of adolescents to think creatively, solve problems addressing varied perspectives, reflect and act according to situations and other developments are crucial points of their overall development. These rapid changes are accompanied by both positive and negative outcomes, thus underscoring the role of families, schools, teachers, and other stakeholders of education in creating the right opportunities and instilling the requisite skills in adolescents for better growth and development.

Various theories of human development like socio-cognitive theory, constructivist theory, social learning theory, which have been referred to in the previous chapters in the context of adolescent development, have huge implications for life skills education. The focus of these theories differ in terms of determining whether skills development is a way to behavioural development, or acquisition of skills as the goal itself or life skills as a way of empowering the agency of adolescents. Thus, skills development enables empowerment of adolescents by teaching to them, ways of thinking, decision-making, emotional management and regulation through their engagement and participation.

> **Box Article 2: Life Skills as Tools for Transformation   By Dr. Gauri Hardikar**
>
> Life Skills are the abilities which help an individual to adapt to the challenges of everyday life. These skills have been recognised as the critical factors for individual as well as social development. The term life skills' was coined to denote skills to tackle challenging issues like drug addiction and AIDS. In a United Nations interagency meeting convened by WHO in 1999, to reach a common understanding about the concept of life skills, life skills were defined as abilities which are psychosocial in nature (as opposed to skills, which are generally understood to be psychomotor). Life skills are transferable and can be used across coniexts. At the same time, since life stills refer to the abilities to a fulfilling life, they are inherently contextual in nature.
>
> WHO (1997) defined life skills as abilities for adaptive and positive behaviour which enable individuals to deal effectively with the demands and challenges of life. WHO identified 10 core life skills which can he considered for skill based initiatives for promotion of health and wellbeing of children and adolescents. The approach of life skills education advocated was preventive in nature, with focus on enhancing knowledge, attitudes and skills resulting in positive behaviours targeted at prevention of health problems.
>
> In an era of increasing complexity and rapid pace of change, this concept of life skills has evolved. The Organisation of Economic Co-operation and Development (OECD) has identified that the main challenges of the present times are in the environmental, economic and social spheres (OECD, 2018). The OECD Learning Framework 2030 proposes that individuals can navigate these challenges through translation of knowledge, skills, attitudes and values into competencies for action. In a world where the future is uncertain, unpredictable and complex, it is not enough to develop skills to survive. In the new age, individuals need to be empowered with the competencies to bring about transformative change, in oneself and in the environment. Hence, OECD defines life skills in terms of generic competencies. In addition to the key competencies outlined in its earlier report (OECD,2005), OECD Education 2030 project identities three further categories of competencies, termed as transformative competencies required to meet the complex demands of the present times. These competencies are the competencies of creating new value, of reconciling tensions and dilemmas and of taking responsibility.
>
> UNICEF adopts a rights-based and transformative approach in its conceptualisation of life sins. in its comprehensive life skills framework, life skills are defined as a set of abiliiies, attitudes and socio-emotional competencies that enable individuals to learn, make informed decisions and exercise rights to lead a healthy and productive life and subsequently become agents of change. Thus, life skills are conceptualised as cross cutting, interconnected and overlapping application of knowledge, values, attitudes and skills which are integral to quality education and are universally applicable and contextual. UNICEF advocates education for life skills as quality education which is humanistic and rights based, holistic through catering to the needs of the cognitive and social needs of the learner, utilising multiple pathways and systems approach and stressing, on life long learning, as life skills acquisition continues throughout the life span.
>
> Thus, in addition to being viewed as abilities to adapt to change, life skills are increasingly viewed as transformative competencies, which reflect what an individual can actually do, not only to adapt to the changing environment but also to transform the environment for positive outcomes for self and society. Thus, the focus of life skills development has expanded from enabling individuals to respond to change to making individuals proactive agents in creating positive change.

Life skills: conceptual approaches

Life skills encompass a wide-ranging and often unstructured set of skills and attitudes that is difficult to rigidly define. Different organizations term life skills as applicable to their own programmatic focuses and strategies. Thus, this concept has many connotations driven by varied interventions and multiple activities undertaken by organizations under the name of life skills. The multiple conceptual approaches to describing life skills, and the different terminologies associated with it lead to an ambiguity in understanding and articulating the exact nature of these skills and competencies. Bapna et al. (2017) claim that these ambiguities have resulted in challenges in areas of cross collaborative discussions, development of methods to measure life skills and in the design of interventions to develop those skills.

- The most widespread and commonly adopted definition of life skills is that of the WHO; they define life skills as "abilities for adaptive and positive behaviour that enable individuals to deal effectively with the demands and challenges of everyday life" Bapna et al. (2017). WHO has identified the following skills, namely, decision-making, problem-solving, creative thinking, critical thinking, communication, interpersonal skills, self-awareness, empathy, coping with emotions, and coping with stress.
- UNICEF defines life skills as a set of abilities, attitudes and socio-emotional competencies that foster decision-making and agentic abilities in the youth to bring about positive change.
- The Collaborative for Academic, Social and Emotional Learning (CASEL 5) framework addresses five broad and interrelated areas of competence and highlights illustrative examples for each: self-awareness, self-management, social awareness, relationship skills, and responsible decision-making.
- The comprehensive Hilton Pellegrino framework has categorized 21st century competencies into three domains, cognitive competencies, intrapersonal competencies and inter-personal competencies as essential for youth to be successful in education, the workplace, in health and in civic participation.
- The 21st century skills framework are grouped into learning and innovation skills, digital literacy skills and career and life skills

A close examination of these varied conceptual approaches gives us descriptions of overlapping competencies clustered differently, as stated by Bapna et al. (2017). Additionally, the terminology of life skills is also associated with or synonymously referred to as non-cognitive skills, non-academic skills, social skills, 21st century skills, soft skills, social and emotional learning (SEL), and vocational and/or employability skills, among others. This has often led to ambiguity in understanding and articulating the exact nature of these skills and competencies, leading to challenges in areas of discussions on life skills and in the design of interventions to develop those skills (Bapna et al., 2017).

Challenges in implementation of life skills in Indian context

Many challenges have been faced in the implementation of life skills education in the Indian context. These challenges are traced back to factors like challenges with funding, lack of trainers, and/or institutional access to life skills learning, and the perceived importance given to cognitive skills and academic outcomes in education as compared to non-cognitive skills. Goswami, identified infrastructure and capacity issues and the approach to education itself as challenges in achieving employability targets in India. With these challenges faced, a need for fundamental rethinking on approach to education is argued in view of developing countries to approach the target of education levels achieved in developed countries. Intel in an education brief recommends a focus on high quality education that encompasses life skills education that equips a person with the new nature of skills required in India's new economy. The Organization for Economic Co-operation and Development (OECD) report on Indian education policy stresses on the need for a coherent approach in designing and implementing policies with a focus on improving the quality of education and its learning outcomes to meet the needs of an innovation-driven economy. Suggestions by reports and studies indicate life skills education as a recommended method to address the problem of unemployability which has been found to be a result of poor quality education in India (Talreja et al., 2018).

UNICEF identifies the impact of primary interdependent issues like inequality, fragile knowledge society and depleting human capital in the Indian context. Adolescent girls and boys are subject to innumerable vulnerabilities based on sex, age, caste, socio-economic status and geography, wherein adolescent girls face bigger challenges in this transition. Caste, religion and geography multiply these gender deprivations. In India, children and adolescents are found to have low levels of understanding and conceptual clarity around learning, analytical skills and knowledge of human rights, including gender equality. Results about poor learning levels of children have been consistently reported by National Achievement Survey (NAS), State Learning Achievement Surveys (SLAS), Annual Status of Education Report (ASER) and Programme for International Student Assessment (PISA). Inequities and exclusion of young children incapacitate them from creating, accumulating and using knowledge, resulting in a fragile knowledge society. Lack of psychosocial competencies and interpersonal skills resulting from a fragile knowledge society drives inequalities in health, education and life chances, thus depleting human capital at large (UNICEF, 2019).

UNICEF's global framework relevant to Indian context

In light of these core issues faced by India, UNICEF's Global Framework came up with a theory of change for systematic development of a breadth of skills, at scale, across the life course of the learner as applicable to the Indian context. It aimed to empower adolescents by increasing their agency and assets, equipping them with the ability to make strategic life choices and take action towards personal and social transformation, which in turn can lead to fostering equitable and knowledge-based societies and building stronger human capital.

The framework broadly mentions effective pedagogical strategies, enabling environments, a multiple pathways approach and a systems approach.

- Effective pedagogical strategies learner centred approaches depending largely on the enabling role of teachers and facilitators and the use of age appropriate learning materials to support the pedagogies.

- Enabling environments to ensure learners' engagement and participation and safety of learners in physical, social and emotional aspects.
- A multiple pathways approach with a focus on equity and inclusion through delivery of both formal education, and non-formal and informal education channels
- A systems approach addressing the inclusion of skills in national policies and plans, curricula frameworks, coordination and partnership frameworks, budgeting and financing, human resources and capacity development, monitoring & evaluation and certification frameworks.

The framework envisages tangible outcomes of the development of skills in four areas, namely, achievement of a knowledge society through improved education outcomes (Learning to Learn), realization of economic development through improved employment and entrepreneurship (Learning to Do), attainment of enhanced social cohesion through improved civic engagement (Learning to Live Together), and empowerment of each individual through life skills (Learning to Be).

In the context of rethinking education and learning in a rapidly changing landscape, the Delors Commission created a report (The Delor's Report) in 1996 emphasizing the importance of a humanistic approach to education and established "the four pillars" of education, namely: learning to be, learning to know, learning to do, and learning to live together, The report forms the basis for learning throughout life which is considered as one of the important keys to the 21st century. The skills outlined by the UNICEF framework were aligned with the four pillars of education as emphasized by the Delors Report (UNICEF 2019).

A cluster of 10 core skills were identified within four interdependent and overlapping dimensions:

1 Empowerment: Self-Awareness, Communication, Resilience
2 Citizenship: Empathy, Participation
3 Learning: Critical thinking, Creativity, Problem Solving
4 Employability: Negotiation, Decision-making

For example, negotiation and decision-making skills under the employability dimension can also be considered relevant under empowerment dimension in terms of agency in decision-making or negotiating with others. Citizenship skills that involve understanding and practicing citizenship concepts like democracy, rights, responsibilities, equal opportunities, identity, etc. demand critical thinking; that which involve participation skills like monitoring the government, managing conflict speaking before public bodies demand the ability of decision-making, negotiating and skills of communication. Citizenship skills include specific skills from all the four dimensions: communication, empathy, participation, critical thinking, problem solving, negotiation and decision-making.

Considering the fact that all skills can be developed throughout the life course in a progressive manner and across different contexts, a progression compatible with the national curricular framework is necessary while embedding these skills in curricula. Learning, self-awareness and interpersonal skills are considered skills to be emphasized in early years of a child but do not lose its importance in adolescence, a stage of identity formation when attitudes towards socialization, gender equality and human rights begin to consolidate. Need for communication and participation skills start to gain prominence in the 6 to 14 years age group and continue developing through late adolescence and adulthood. Resilience and employability skills are found to build upon the skills developed through childhood and become prominent from 14 to 19 years and onwards. But it is very important to understand that life skills need to be integrated with other foundational skills like reading and mathematics and not focused in isolation. Employability and productive citizenship gain prominence in adolescence (11–19 years). Children who miss out on developing foundational skills need these as the foundation for life skills and technical skills. Brain science acknowledges that "although foundational cognitive skills become less malleable after age, these, in addition to social, negotiation and resilience skills may be the most effective way to improve adolescents' transition into employability". Life skills and foundational skills are equally important and complementary to each other. These skills need to be developed concurrently in an integrated manner. Nurturing life skills in children enable them to navigate smoothly through their learning processes in every stage of their development. Education with life skills as its integral component, will facilitate more opportunities and improved options for adolescents, provided these life skills are able to address the evolving and dynamic challenges and needs of the 21st century.

Life skills in the 21st century

The advent of technology has drastically changed the way we interact and work with people. Demands of workplaces also have changed in terms of hiring people who can adapt to the changing needs of the 21st century. The 21st-century skills comprise skills, abilities and learning dispositions that have been identified as being required for success in 21st century society and workplaces by educators, business leaders, academics, and governmental agencies. Educationists have termed "21st century skills" involving a cluster of skills and one example of which is the P21 framework, that is intended to replace the 20th century curriculum that Dede terms the "legacy curriculum". A P21 framework for 21st-century learning is designed to combine these set of skills for preparing students for today's innovation focussed workforce and also support teachers in teaching those skills. This framework uses core academic subjects as a vehicle for

- teaching life and career skills;
- learning and innovation skills; and
- information and media skills.

The problem of employability is a major concern in India besides other countries. Some countries like the US, China and Singapore have been responsive to the changes and been able to address these concerns to certain extent. However, India still needs to address the issues of employability Gupta, R., 2018).

Though, in the latter part of the chapter, we will be looking at the various models and approaches of teaching life skills, here we focus on the ways of teaching life skills in school in India within the formal education system, as reported by UNESCO. Life skills are being taught either as a specific subject or as a part of extracurricular activities in school or integrated in the school subjects. Though the desired way of teaching life skills is by imparting life skills through all the subjects taught in school, P21 curricular framework view life skills as a separate component that includes flexibility and adaptability, initiative and self-direction, social and cross-cultural skills, productivity and accountability, and leadership and responsibility.

P21 recommends that instruction in school subjects incorporate opportunities for students to also gain additional competencies critical for success in the 21st century:

- Learning and Innovation Skills (the so-called 4Cs) are Creative Thinking, Collaboration, Communication, and Critical Thinking and Problem Solving.
- Information, Media, and Technology Skills are the tools that students will learn to master both digital and non-digital media.
- Life and Career Skills are the habits and mindsets that students should develop when they learn from this framework. These skills include accepting feedback, working in teams, and adapting to change.

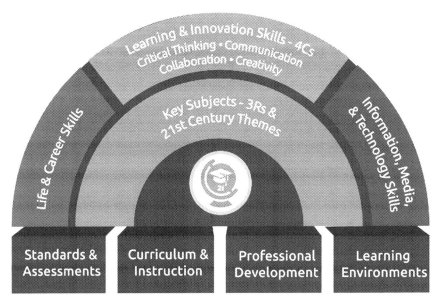

Source: https://www.battelleforkids.org/networks/p21

FIGURE 5.6 P21 Framework for 21st-Century Learning

Sternberg and Subotnik (2006) suggest fostering learners' capabilities in three areas:

- Reasoning (analytical, critical thinking and problem-solving skills),
- Resilience (life skills such as flexibility, adaptability and self-reliance) and
- Responsibility (wisdom or the application of intelligence, creativity and knowledge for a common good).

Scott's (2015) review of this model points to three components common to curriculum models, namely, inquiry, design and collaborative learning. Teaching life skills in the school curriculum by incorporating and emphasising inquiry skills and student collaboration calls for a shift from teaching content to making students work in groups to explore and understand concepts.

Considering the types of pedagogy and learning strategies essential to developing life skills, the specifics of a life skills programming needs to be understood in order to be able to handle the selection and development of the right programmes relevant to a particular setting. Thus, we move further to address the key elements of life skills programs (Gupta, 2018).

Key elements of life skills programs

If we consider the individual subskills with a specific focus, these skills can be placed under three key elements as proposed by Mangrulkar et al. (2001). The three key elements are

- skills development;
- information/content addressing relevant social and developmental tasks; and
- interactive methods of teaching and learning.

1. Under skills development element, one can focus on the following skills categories

    a) Social Skills

    - Communication skills
    - Negotiation/refusal skills
    - Assertiveness skills
    - Interpersonal skills (for developing healthy relationships)
    - Cooperation skills
    - Empathy and perspective taking

    b) Cognitive Skills

    - Decision-making/problem solving skills
    - Critical thinking skills

c) Emotional Coping Skills

- Managing stress
- Managing feelings, including anger
- Skills for increasing internal locus of control (self-management, self-monitoring)

The three skill categories overlap and complement each other.

2. Under information/content element, one can focus on the application of life skills in specific content areas like-

   a) Violence Prevention/Conflict Resolution
   b) Alcohol, Tobacco and other Substance Use
   c) Interpersonal Relationships
   d) Sexual and Reproductive Health
   e) Physical Fitness/Nutrition

Accurate and developmentally appropriate content of relevance to young people provides a context for learning skills. The specific content of a life-skills programme needs to be determined contextually, through dialogue and participation of those under consideration and based on the local health risks and competencies of young people.

3. Under interactive methods of teaching and learning element, some of the following methods can be outlined as methods for skill acquisition-

   a) cooperative learning
   b) peer support
   c) continual opportunities for rehearsal
   d) accurate feedback and constructive criticism
   e) modelling of skills by other peers and adults

These interactive teaching methods are effective in developing skills through interaction, role playing, open discussions, small group activities and other techniques. Bandura's social learning theory, posits that, people learn through observation and imitation and their behaviours are reinforced by their consequences, positive or negative. This is a strong premise that explains the success of interactive teaching techniques. Vygotsky's ideas of social interaction and active engagement for the child to develop problem solving and construct cultural practices and social norms also aligns with the interactive teaching methods element.

Activities over the life course take place in a variety of contexts or domains of human existence. It is thus essential for one to consider the context of different life situations in which these life skills need to be adapted and defined.

> **Activity:**
>
> Select an adolescent classroom context for which you want to offer a life skill program. Design a 'Life-Skill Framework' for the life skills program customizing it to your selected context.
>
> Review the following questions while designing the life skills program.
>
> ✓ What are your core beliefs and perceptions about the capacities of adolescents in the selected context?
> ✓ What are the changes that you would like to see in the development of adolescents in your context in their future?
> ✓ What are the issues or challenges that you foresee in addressing these changes for the healthy development of these adolescents?
> ✓ Which theory/ies or approach/es do you find as the best fit with your vision of change in addressing these issues and bringing about the desirable changes?

Life skills: evolving and contextual

Life skills are not static, but constantly evolving within the individual's personal, economic, social and cultural contexts. The diversity of contexts and the inherent abilities enable individuals to attain some life skills, while a few other life skills may not be attained. Thus, Goody encourages development of alternative skills for such individuals and promotes diversity rather than uniformity (Singh, 2003). Life skills also depend on the family contexts and gender differences. Gilligan argues that boys are always trying out ways to connect with others during times of crisis, whereas girls try to find their own voice at such times. These differences may have different implications for individuals in terms of development of skills. The strategies and activities for development of skills should take into consideration the disparities in social background, gender, cultural variations and so on. Thus, it is very crucial to lay emphasis on the contextuality of life skills, so that they can be adapted to specific contexts (Mangrulkar et al., 2001).

> **Box Article 3: Analysis of Life Skills Education activities conducted around the world**
>
> Life skills education activities conducted around the world reflect the priorities and areas of concern of the respective countries. For example, the USA, Canada, UK, Germany and Greece have many well-planned, tailor-made life skills education programmes that aim to promote positive behaviours around smoking, alcohol,, drug abuse, HIV, AIDS, contraception, perception about sexual activities and condom use through refusal slas, attitude change and personal goal setting (Botivin et al., 2001; Goudas, Dermitzaki, Leondari, & Danish, 2006; Goudas & Giannoudis, 2008; Holt, Tink, Mandigo, & Fox, 2008; Lillehoj et al, 2004; Menrath et al, 2012; O'Ficarn & Gatz, 1999; Smith et al., 2004; Teyhan et al, 2016; Thompson, Auslander, & Alonzo, 2012; Tuttle et al., 2006; Vicary et al, 2004; Weichold & Blumenthal, 2016; Wenzel et at., 2009). These programs address cognitive, affective, and behavioral competencies to develop self-efficacy, for positive social and personal behavior.
>
> Life skills education programs in developing countries such as India, South Africa,, Cambodia, Iran and Mexico often emphasize the development of communication skills, assertive skills, decision-making, building self-esteem, self-efficacy, reducing learning difficulties, decrease aggressive behavior, anger control,, and changing attitudes towards engaging in sexual behavior (James et al., 2006; Jegannathan, Dahlblom,, & Kullgren, 2014; Maryam et al.. 2011; Naseri & abakhani, 2014; Pari,athy & Pillai, 2015; Pick, Givaudan, Sirkin, & Ortega, 2007; Vatankhab, Daryabari, Ghadami,& KhanjanShoeibi, 2014;Yadav & Iqbal, 2009).
>
> Source: A narrative systematic review of life skills education: effectiveness. research gaps uid priorities (2019)

Life skills policies and programmes in India

A desk review on adolescents in India by the UNICEF reports that adolescent girls in India have limited agency compared to boys, whereas young boys themselves have limited agency and decision-making ability on important matters affecting their lives. Several programmes have been implemented that aim specifically to facilitate safe transitions into adulthood, especially for young girls. Among the programmes being implemented by the government, the Adolescence Education Programme (AEP), developed by the Ministry of Human Resource Development, Department of Education, and the National AIDS Control Organisation (NACO) for school-going adolescent boys and girls in Classes 9–11 seek to build adolescents' skills in making important life decisions; improve interpersonal communication; foster egalitarian gender role attitudes; and raise awareness about growing up matters, as well as about HIV. The Kishori Shakti Yojana aims at training adolescent girls in vocational skills as a means of empowerment and building their self-esteem. Programmes being implemented through Mahila Shikshana Kendras under the auspices of the Mahila Samakhya programme provides girls with non-formal education and leadership training. The Rajiv Gandhi National Institute of Youth Development has, likewise, implemented life-skills programmes which aim to instil leadership qualities and broaden the personality of young female and male participants.

Programmes implemented by NGOs focus largely on life-skills building and include those developed and implemented by NGOs like the Centre for Development and Population Activities (CEDPA), New Delhi; the Centre for Health Education, Training, and Nutrition Awareness, Ahmedabad (CHETNA); MAMTA, New Delhi; Sahayog, Mumbai; and Pathfinder International, New Delhi to name a few. The Self-Employed Women's Association (SEWA) in Gujarat and the International Council for Research on Women (ICRW) in New Delhi, Maharashtra, Bihar, and Jharkhand have also implemented programmes that could be used as demonstrating models (Acharya et al., 2009).

Life skills facets

There are different aspects that can steer effective life skills approach. These aspects can be

- Programme content: Developing relevant information, attitudes, and skills
- Mechanisms: Implementing participatory teaching practices, modelling of skills and reinforcement
- Teacher training: Building teacher's belief the potential of life skills education and their capacity to impart such skills
- Commitment: Advocating for the integration of life skills education in school curriculum

The various educational programmes and policies in India have approached life skills in different capacities including varied aspects. The National Curriculum

Framework (NCF) 2005 has emphasized on constructive learning experiences, and on the development of an inquiry-based approach, work-related knowledge and broader life skills. Central Board of Secondary Education (CBSE), in 2005, introduced life skills education as an integral part of the curricula through Continuous and Comprehensive Evaluation (CCE) for classes 6 to 10 and has developed life skills manuals for teachers teaching classes 6, 7 and 8. These manuals provide teachers broad guidelines for each of the ten core life skills identified by WHO. Sarva Shiksha Abhiyan (SSA) also has, under its agenda, life skills training focusing on upper primary girls.

Most of these efforts have largely ignored the context under consideration taking a general approach to life skills. There has been very minimal focus on curriculum integration and teacher development in this regard. Lack of systemic reforms have resulted in the difficulties in the successful integration of life skills in Indian school education. A few of these difficulties are reflected in the practices and processes within the system (Singh & Menon, 2015).

- Life skills have been very peripherally imparted through extracurricular or as passive 'values education' due to its existence in isolation from the main school processes.
- Pedagogy is more inclined towards rote learning and exam-based and result oriented assessment, thus deviating from learner-centric pedagogy
- A school culture devoid of life-skills-based education
- Paucity of teachers with the capacity and motivation to develop and integrate such life skills into classroom practices

Life skills education in India has to be conceived within the context of broader education system reforms. Life skills need to be age-specific and incorporated in an inclusive manner with trained educators who will be able to make use of participatory and experiential teaching practices for effective implementation of life skills.

The status of life skills in India as per the World Bank's SABER and UNICEF reporting indicates that

- policies, curriculum and funding allocated for life skills purposes, are, at least emerging, approaching towards minimum standards, whereas,
- mechanisms ensuring quality of life skills delivery, evidence of the impact of life skills interventions in Indian context and pre-service and in-service teacher training have hardly progressed or are completely absent

Life skill-specific interventions in India

In India and globally, many approaches to deliver life skills education have also been incorporated within other skill development activities.

Some of these include:

- Life skills and employment, that aims to equip children with technical knowledge as well as the soft skills required to succeed in the workplace, thereby directly translating their education into a source of livelihood. Examples in India include InOpen (life skills education as part of computer literacy programmes), IGNIS Careers (English language learning), Medha (soft skills for the workplace), and Lend A Hand India (vocational education).
- Life skills and values education, that tends to focus on inculcating such skills through values-based education. However, most of the times, these approaches are not effective due to its prescriptive nature and it add-on characteristic to the existing syllabi. Examples of schools that have integrated holistic development as part of their pedagogy include the Don Bosco school network.
- Early childhood education interventions that explicitly target a wide range of cognitive, language, emotional and social skills, from communication, self-regulation, conflict resolution skills, etc. Examples include Sesame Workshop India and Bodh.
- Life skills and child rights programs, address target mindsets and abilities such as self-awareness, leadership, and social influence, through their broader goals of tackling gender disparity, violence, health, etc. Examples in India include Educate Girls, Sanlaap, Ibtada and Shaishav.
- Higher order thinking skills programmes, catering to imparting 21st century skills, have attempted to bring in a shift from rote learning to support inquiry-based learning by building critical thinking and creative problem solving skills. Examples in India include Creya and THOTS Labs.

Life skills intervention models

Life skills programmes for children have also adopted different intervention models that move from an out-of-school approach to an approach integrated into whole-school practice, though this path may not be linear.

- Out-of-school programmes
  - Out-of-school programmes can be either informal or school linked programmes and distinct from school learning. Out of school platforms include community-based adolescent groups, sports, cultural activities and civic action. The Bridgespan Group, a nonprofit advisor and resource for mission-driven organizations and philanthropists, laid stress on aligning such out-of-school efforts with in-school initiatives to achieve effective learning at greater scale. Though out-of-school programmes do carry the potential of fostering life skills in learners, such programmes may fall

back in terms of certain factors like- absence of connect in learning and a lack of reinforcement, high rate of attrition, challenges of scaling up due to its intensive nature of being hands-on and resourceful.
- Informal and School linked programmes
  There are other informal life skills models that adopt a variety of mechanisms and are implemented by NGOs and there are school-linked programmes which may be not directly implemented by schools but may be facilitated by other trained personnel through the extracurricular life skills activities organized by the schools.

For example, India Khel Planet is an out-of-school programme focusing on life skills through play, i.e. through contextualized. This programme targets six core life skills namely emotional skills, leadership skills, collaboration skills, creativity skills, cognitive skills, and social and civic engagement skills

- Formal In-school Models
  The formal model of teaching life skills is a school-based programme implemented through an explicit curriculum delivered either as a stand-alone subject or integrated into core subjects.

- Stand-alone subject model
  The stand-alone subject model has been widely used in India. According to the requirements of this model, a specific time is designated in the time-table schedule for 'life skills' education and it goes unassessed most of the times. Though this model is relevant due to its systematic and transparent approach and the likeliness of having trained teachers focussed on the issues, there are a few lacunae in this model.
  - There seems to be more focus on moral education rather than the development of actual skills and abilities and it is highly prescriptive.
  - Teachers may not realize the importance of life skill as a subject due to more emphasis on exam oriented content.
  - The delivery of this subject will demand additional time other than the time available for the already overloaded curriculum.
- For example, 'India Going To School' programme partners with state governments to train government school teachers in delivering their content besides the existing curriculum in class 9. Teachers conduct a two hour session every Saturday. These sessions include storytelling, playing games or reading books on skills, which is followed-up by an online monitoring system through grading of community-based skills action project created by children.
- Curriculum-Integrated model
  The integrated approach is aligned with the incorporation of the specific life skills in the academic subjects such as science, civics, physical education, geography and others, enabling children to practically apply

knowledge and develop abilities necessary for life. This model too has its own constraints in terms of design and delivery, especially, with limited resources and dearth of professional capacity of teachers and school leaders. According to UNICEF data, this model has been implemented years back and yet teachers are not using life skills manuals in the classroom because of its complexity for use.

This model has the privilege of using the already existing school structures and is likely to involve maximum number of teachers. Though this model adopts a whole-school approach with a promise of building student abilities, it is accompanied with a few constraints.

- Teachers may not see the relevance of the issue to their subjects and some may not be competent to integrate life skills into their subject lesson plans.
- This kind of model is too resource – intensive and can be highly time consuming.
  - In India, Report Bee in collaboration with Character Lab piloted the Character Growth Card in some schools in Chennai. The Character Growth Card can be used by teachers to help students reflect on their own strengths and areas for growth, and to have a formative, rather than summative, conversation with the student about areas they can focus on. This Character Growth card was an initiative by the Character Lab aiming to help teachers systematically integrate character development practices into their lesson plans and daily interactions with students. Report Bee is now working in many schools across India.
  - The Akanksha Foundation, India aims to ensure the integration of life skills including self-esteem, sense of agency, aspirations into core curriculum subjects by supporting teachers and school leaders across schools in Mumbai and Pune. Akanksha has also initiated a Service Learning Programme (SLP) to empower students to develop leadership skills and understand how they can contribute to the community they live in.

Policy vision in the domain of education

The policy focus on life skills in India is broadly in the domains of education which encompasses life skills education for students and training for teachers and skilling towards employment. The position papers related to the NCERT give an overview of life skills education envisioned through policy (Talreja et al., 2018).

- The Education for Peace position paper has placed emphasis on factors such as peace and well-being and considers the role of the teacher in the context of mentorship. It stresses on teacher as a role model of values such as the art of listening, the humility to acknowledge and correct one's mistakes, assuming

responsibility for one's actions, sharing concerns, and helping each other to solve problems transcending differences.
- The Health and Physical Education position paper highlights a health and physical education curriculum for life skills building for both teachers and students. The life skills for students being (a) critical thinking (b) interpersonal communications skills and (c) negotiation skills while for teachers (a) communication skills (b) skills for being non-judgmental and (c) skills for having empathy. The paper provides suggestions to study NGOs as case studies to assimilate the learnings from them into the national curricula.
- The Ministry of Human Resource Development (MHRD), in a joint effort with NCERT and United Nations Population Fund, and guided by the principles of NCF 2005, have come up with the Adolescence Education Programme (AEP) with an aim of empowering adolescents with age appropriate and culturally relevant skills to respond to real life situations in positive and responsible ways. It also includes materials for training of teachers to facilitate the programme.

There are also Government-Sponsored Teacher Training Programs with a focus on life skills teacher training programs. A few of them are listed below-

- YUVA School Life Skills Programme empowering teachers, by affirming and validating them through primarily human resources inputs and the provision of enabling resources and a caring environment
- Public-Private Teacher Training to do mini-teacher training programs covering variety of topics including life skills
- Toolkits focused on teacher training emphasizing the importance of life skills in the classroom and suggestions for activities

The Dream and Dream report (Talreja et al., 2018) while reiterating the emphasis of skills in India's policy vision, highlights the facet of the policy in developing awareness and skills for vocations from high school onwards, and its tilt towards employability with the focus of the policy vision and funding on skilling the youth towards taking advantage of its demographic dividend. Thus, more attention is paid to developing vocational skills among high school students than developing life skills from a younger age towards life readiness. This strongly calls for attention to understand the adversities of youth in our country not just as a problem of unemployment but much beyond that in terms of promoting preparedness for modern times and facilitate facing 21st century life's possibilities and challenges with a focus on a holistic form of education.

The national programme for youth and adolescent development scheme guidelines recommend adoption of holistic approach to life skills development in policies and programs. It demands a specific situational analysis of each group of adolescents for designing the programme. It clearly points that life skills programming should be viewed as a response to adolescent's basic human rights where they are not looked upon as problems but as active participants in development. It suggests development of core values, attitudes, knowledge and skills through these programs (NPYAD Scheme Guidelines, 2014–2015).

Teacher development for life skills education (Singh & Menon, 2015)

The effectiveness of any life skill intervention for adolescent students places the onus on teachers or educators implementing the programmes, which essentially requires teachers to be capable of and to nurture positive attitudes towards life skills implementation. Thus, adequate training of teachers and educators is fundamental to the effectiveness of life skills education. Capacity building of teachers in this regard, should be inclusive of

- opportunities for self-assessment of their own attitudes, values, and life skills proficiency
- opportunities to practice and internalize these skills, and
- training to build confidence to enable them to practice these skills with comfort and build healthy relationships with students

Capacity building of teachers can be done through the development of life skills courses or modules in pre-service teacher training ongoing and sustained block- or district-level in-service support systems, and teacher self-assessment tools.

India Dream a Dream's Teacher Development Programme aims to train a wide range of teachers and community workers to facilitate the development of life skills among children in their own schools through a series of four life skills facilitation workshops spread over half a year, and using experiential methods and play to develop various skills in teachers, such as expanding their own creativity, listening and validation skills, and learning tools to meaningfully engage children.

Conclusion

Through this chapter, we have had a glimpse of the various sociocultural issues, discourses, patterns and modes of reasoning that have highlighted the importance of how complex, discussions and deliberations are in the area of life skill education and classroom dynamics. We have seen how contextual factors in the classrooms as well as the structural features of how events in a classroom are enacted and designed have a significant influence on what occurs. Discourses have moved emphasis from how to create "ideal classrooms" and "interactions" to providing a realization of the "need" for equipping and strengthening certain skills and agency in adolescents within themselves for their well-being. From the standpoint of the educator, it is important to realize that the dynamics of classroom mirror and reflect the desires, identities, social and linguistic capital that students bring with them into secondary classrooms along their ability and/or inclination for developing meaningful relationships.

Students' backgrounds and their social capital, will always determine their development through life-course and hence there is a dire need to develop or design a relevant intervention programme that is uniquely responsive to the needs of adolescents. Literature depicts a wide range of skills from social, cognitive, emotional among many others, which ultimately help adolescents to live a life that has the capacity for the desired transformation.

The emphasis on life skills is not only limited to developing the required capacities for better performance of adolescents, but also extends to life skills for transformation. Transformation for self and transformation for society is the higher objective of life skills education. We will now draw a parallel between the higher objectives of life skills education with the two terms performance and performativity given by Butler. Performance is an articulation of what already exists and is already established whereas, performativity, on the other hand, is an act of becoming, of creating oneself in the process of becoming. Put otherwise, performativity allows one to be transformed through one's actions, whereas performance simply displays what was already there (Nentwich et al., 2018).

Using the application of Butler's thinking in the context of life skills and our analysis of classroom dynamics in adolescents' classrooms, we would like to stress on the need to move from life skills for capacity development and betterment of performance of an individual to the performativity perspective, whereby, the individual grows and learns from the experience and shifts their ideas as a result of their experiences. It is only when the individual experiences such a transformation, that the individual is able to play a transformative role in society.

Going forward, this would be helpful for educators to explore classroom contexts and structures, and provide nurturing experiences through meaningful opportunities to advance the goal of life skills education.

> **Key terms:** adolescent classroom, classroom dynamics, micro, meso, exo, macro system, structure, culture, agency, group processes, Teaching Through Interactions (TTI) framework, group processes, psychosocial competence, life skills, UNICEF Global framework, , P21 framework for twenty-first century learning, evolving and contextual, life skills education, life skill interventions, teacher development for life skills education, performance , performativity

Bibliography

Acharya, R., Kalyanwala, S., Jejeebhoy, S. J., et al. (2009). *Broadening girls' horizons: Effects of a life skills education programme in rural Uttar Pradesh.* New Delhi: Population Council.

Adolescents in India: A desk review of existing evidence and behaviours, programmes and policies. (2013). New Delhi, India: Population Council & UNICEF.

Aishath, N., Haslinda, B. A., Steven, E. K., & Nobaya, B. A. (2019). A narrative systematic review of life skills education: Effectiveness, research gaps and priorities, *International Journal of Adolescence and Youth, 24*(3), 362–379. doi:10.1080/02673843.2018.1479278

Bapna, A., et al. (2017). *Handbook on measuring 21st century skills.* Retrieved from https://doi.org/10.13140/RG.2.2.10020.99203

Bronfenbrenner, U. (1979). *The ecology of human development: Experiments in nature and design.* Cambridge, MA: Harvard University Press.

Farmer, T. W., Dawes, M., Hamm, J. V., Lee, D., Mehtaji, M., Hoffman, A. S., & Brooks, D. S. (2018). Classroom social dynamics management: Why the invisible hand of the teacher matters for special education. *Remedial and Special Education, 39*(3), 177–192. doi:10.1177/0741932517718359

Gupta, R. (2018). *Skilling India: The role of pedagogy in developing life skills.* Working Paper, National Council of Applied Economic Research.

Hendrickx, M. H. G., Mainhard, M. T., Boor-Klip, H. J., Cillessen, A. H. M., & Brekelmans, M. (2016). Social dynamics in the classroom: Teacher support and conflict and the peer ecology. *Teaching and Teacher Education, 53*, 30–40.

Kennedy, B. L. (2015). Enacting competing ideologies: How classroom dynamics influence the education of disaffected early adolescents at a community day school [Data set]. University of Southern California Digital Library (USC.DL). doi:10.25549/USCTHESES-M2501

Larsen–Freeman, D. (2016). Classroom-oriented research from a complex systems perspective. *Studies in Second Language Learning and Teaching, 6*, 377–393. doi:10.14746/SSLLT.2016.6.3.2

Life Skills Education. (n.d.). Retrieved from https://cbse.nic.in/cce/life_skills_cce.pdf

Maithreyi, R. (2015). *A critical analysis of ideas around childhood, 'risks', and 'success'.* Doctoral Dissertation, National Institute of Advanced Studies, Bangalore.

Mangrulkar, L., Whitman, C. V., & Posner, M. (2001) *Life skills approach to child and adolescent healthy human development.* Washington, DC: Pan American Health Organization.

Manjunatha, N., & Saddichha, S. (2011). Universal mental health program: An extension of life skills education to promote child mental health. *Indian Journal of Psychiatry, 53*(1), 77–78. doi:10.4103/0019-5545.75548

National Programme for Youth and Adolescent Development (NPYAD). (n.d.). Retrieved from https://yas.nic.in/sites/default/files/NPYAD%20Scheme%20Guidelines%202014-15.pdf

Nentwich, J. C., & Morison, T. (2018). Performing the self: Performativity and discursive psychology. In C. B. Travis, J. W. White, A. Rutherford, W. S. Williams, S. L. Cook, & K. F. Wyche (Eds.), *APA handbook of the psychology of women: History, theory, and battlegrounds* (pp. 209–228). American Psychological Association. https://doi.org/10.1037/0000059-011

Pianta, R. C., Hamre, B. K., & Allen, J. P. (2012). Teacher-student relationships and engagement: Conceptualizing, measuring, and improving the capacity of classroom interactions. In S. L. Christenson, A. L. Reschly, & C. Wylie (Eds.), *Handbook of research on student engagement* (pp. 365–386). Springer Science + Business Media. doi:10.1007/978-1-4614-2018-7_17

Singh, D. B., & Menon, R. (2016). *Life skills in India: An overview of evidence and current practices in our education system.* New Delhi, India: Central Square Foundation (India).

Singh, M. (2003). Understanding life skills. Paper commissioned for the EFA Global Monitoring Report 2003/4, The Leap to Equality".

Slavin, R. L. (2002). Operative group dynamics in school settings: Structuring to enhance educational, social, and emotional progress. *Group, 26*(4), 297–308. doi:10.1023/A:1021021429606

Symonds, M. P. (1951). Introduction to the special issue on classroom dynamics. *The Journal of Educational Research, 45*(2), 81–87.

Talreja, V., Krishnamurthy, K., Sanchez, D. J. W., & Bhat, V. (2018). Mapping life skills in India: Research, policy and practice. *Dream a Dream.* Retrieved from www.dreama-dream.org/reports/mappinglifeskillsinindia.pdf

United Nations Children's Fund (UNICEF). (2019). Comprehensive life skills framework: Rights based and life cycle approach to building skills for empowerment.

Vranda, M. N., & Rao, M. C. (2011). Life skills education for young adolescents – Indian experience. *Journal of the Indian Academy of Applied Psychology, 37*(9), 9–15.

Wang, M. T., Degol, J. L., Amemiya, J., Parr, A., & Guo, J. (2020). Classroom climate and children's academic and psychological wellbeing: A systematic review and meta-analysis. *Developmental Review, 57,* 100912. doi:10.1016/j.dr.2020.100912

What are life skills and why teach them? (n.d.). Retrieved from www.britishcouncil.gr/en/life-skills/about/what-are-life-skills#:~:text=Life%20skills%20is%20a%20term,commonly%20encountered%20in%20daily%20life

What is skill development. (n.d.). Retrieved from www.igi-global.com/dictionary/gender-gap-in-skill-development/27090

INDEX

21st century 191, 232, 234–236, 242, 245

abstract 66, 68, 71–72, 76–77, 79, 83–85, 149
academic 26, 29, 38, 57, 87, 89, 114, 118, 129, 133–143, 147–148, 152–153, 157, 159, 161, 178–180, 185, 189, 191, 192–200, 204–205, 211–212, 220, 223–225, 227, 232, 235, 243
academic performance 29, 56, 89, 138, 143, 159, 197–198
acceptance 2, 29, 32, 108, 128, 134, 147, 158, 177, 184
access to education 33, 196
accomplishment 48, 83, 88, 180, 193
achievement 41, 50–51, 54–55, 58, 80, 84–85, 88, 114, 118, 128–129, 135, 138–139, 141, 143, 148, 153, 178, 180, 189, 200, 204, 222, 233–234
acquisition 49, 54, 57, 82, 147, 205, 224, 228–231, 238
adaptation 6, 59, 70, 81, 83, 161, 172, 178, 186, 188
adaption 40
adjusting 59
Adolescence Education Programme (AEP) 240, 245
adolescent development 3, 6–8, 10, 22, 24, 30–31, 34–35, 67, 80, 98, 104, 106, 111, 118–119, 127, 130, 132, 151, 158, 163, 229–230, 245
age-graded 104, 130
agency 8, 51, 83, 94–96, 98–100, 103–104, 111, 119–120, 137, 140, 144, 159, 164, 172, 174, 177, 183, 188, 209, 210, 212–217, 230, 233–234, 240, 244, 246–247; human 95–96, 98–99, 111, 177, 217; individual 8; personal 8, 99, 137, 144
agent-like perspective: self-organizing, proactive, self-regulating, self-reflecting 83
alternatives 12, 50, 71, 80, 135–136, 222
analytical 79, 103, 148, 233–237
anthropological 13
antisocial behaviour 88, 188, 196, 199
anxiety 116, 118, 123, 127, 159, 161, 178, 184–186, 194–195, 199, 222, 228
anxious 51
apprehensive 43
"apprenticeship in thinking": guided participation 82
approval 48, 87, 157, 204
arguments/counterarguments 67
aspirations 27, 49, 50, 95–96, 115, 134, 137, 140, 143, 159, 216, 244
assessment 90, 135, 156, 180, 194, 205, 225, 233, 241, 246
assumptions 64, 133, 145, 156
attachment 26–27, 84, 86, 118–119, 135, 143, 147, 150–151, 157, 188, 225
attainment 3, 23, 32, 67, 105, 193, 234
attention 11, 27, 49, 57, 72, 78, 81, 90, 99, 107, 119, 133, 140, 142, 154, 156, 158, 183–184, 187, 195, 199, 204, 212, 226, 245
attrition 87, 243
audience 69–70, 160

authoritarian 40–41, 114, 123, 128, 188
authority 11, 67, 76–77, 116, 120, 124, 128, 153, 159
autobiographical 84
autonomous 7, 26–27, 32, 45, 49, 55–56, 119, 127
autonomy 27, 40, 48, 54–56, 85–86, 113, 115, 118–121, 124, 134, 151, 156, 172, 174, 177, 185, 197, 224–225
autonomy – relatedness 119

Bandura, Albert 83
behavioural markers 13
beliefs 12, 27, 29–30, 32, 34, 41, 48–49, 56, 75, 77, 80–81, 83–85, 88–89, 95–96, 100, 107, 110–111, 121–122, 124, 127, 133–134, 137, 140–141, 143, 147, 149, 153, 158, 211, 212, 214–217, 222–223
belongingness 39, 57, 106, 136, 140, 148
bicultural identity 56
biography 47, 99
biological 8, 13, 22, 24–26, 35, 49, 57, 79, 83, 106, 124, 176, 199, 229–230
biopsychosocial transition 24
body image 28, 182, 185–187
bonding 57, 135, 140, 143
brain: prefrontal cortex 57, 74
Bronfenbrenner's bioecological systems 94, 100–102, 107, 177, 183, 188, 213–214, 225
Bruner, Jerome 82

capabilities 61, 65, 83, 89, 95, 147, 237
capacity 8, 26, 30, 71, 79, 84, 96, 98–99, 103, 119–120, 163, 181, 215, 228, 230, 232, 234, 240–241, 244, 246–247
career 12, 21, 23, 30, 50, 56, 83, 89, 99, 104–105, 114, 118, 134–135, 138, 162, 185, 232, 235–236, 242
caregivers 27, 86, 119, 156
caste 24, 32–34, 38, 100, 140, 152, 198, 214–215, 217, 223, 233
challenges 2, 27, 29–30, 32, 34, 47, 79, 81, 88, 90, 95, 105, 136, 140, 142, 144, 147, 182, 196, 200, 222, 224–225, 227–228, 231–233, 235, 243, 245
characteristics 2, 12, 27–30, 34, 44, 49, 74, 84–86, 101, 104–107, 113, 116, 125, 139, 140, 142, 151–152, 154, 157, 158, 172, 174, 181, 189, 193–195, 204, 212, 223–224
child-bearing 32–34
childhood 10–14, 21–23, 25–27, 31–32, 45, 48–49, 57, 78, 83, 85–88, 101, 106, 110, 113–114, 118, 132, 150, 154, 172, 176, 181, 185, 217, 222, 228–229, 235, 242
child rearing 10–12, 55, 118, 124, 130
citizenship skills 234
class based 32
classroom dynamics 211–214, 217, 222–223, 246–247
coexistence 101, 116
cognition 24, 57, 63, 66, 78, 81–82, 88, 90–91, 105–106, 184, 226
cognitive 24, 26, 30, 45, 49, 57–61, 63, 65–68, 71–75, 79, 80–85, 88–91, 94–96, 101, 107, 111, 116, 118, 133, 137, 142, 147, 163–164, 176, 184, 202, 204–205, 215, 224, 226, 228–229, 231–232, 235, 237, 239, 242–243, 247
cognitive development 45, 57, 59–61, 63, 67–68, 71, 74–75, 79–81, 83–84, 88, 101, 164, 224, 229; stages (sensorimotor stage, preoperational reasoning stage, concrete operational) 60
cognitive limitation (centration) 65
collective ethos 41
collective image 41
collectivist 32, 55–56, 85, 106, 114, 119, 124, 128, 153
community 5, 10, 22, 25, 33, 35, 39, 83, 101–103, 128, 136, 142, 158–159, 162, 172, 177, 183–184, 192–193, 196–197, 199–202, 224, 242–243, 244, 246
competencies 48, 86, 96, 107, 130, 164, 191, 224, 227–228, 231–233, 236, 238–239
competent 81, 229, 244
competitive 30, 90, 139, 196
complementary 59, 133, 223, 235
complex/complexity 5, 24, 37–38, 45, 72, 74, 79–80, 90, 96, 101, 106, 110, 133–134, 148, 153, 201, 205, 209, 211, 213, 228, 231, 244, 246
complicated 38, 49, 223
comprehensive 10, 12, 178, 201, 231–232, 241
conceptualization 12, 22, 46, 49, 105, 107, 177, 193, 213, 225
conditioned phenomenon 44
conductive 40, 154, 183, 228
conflict/conflicting 222
conformity 29
confrontation 45
confused 43, 68, 85, 87, 119
consciousness 10, 65, 90, 146, 184
consequences 21, 26, 68, 71, 74–76, 89, 121, 123, 139–140, 159, 186, 192, 194, 197, 200, 229–230, 238

conservation 62, 64, 65
"constantly lost and regained" 46
construction 24, 31, 38, 59, 84, 86, 105–106, 119, 137, 142, 159–160, 166, 185
constructivist 59, 71, 142, 224, 226, 229–230
contexts 24–27, 29, 34, 45, 49, 57, 74, 80, 82, 84, 86, 89–90, 99–101, 103, 105–106, 111, 115–116, 127–128, 132–135, 138–140, 142, 149–151, 154, 156–159, 181, 183, 188, 195, 201–202, 209–213, 215–217, 224, 234, 238–239, 247; cultural 49, 80, 156, 239; family 89, 99, 105, 154, 188, 239; peer 89, 99, 105, 151, 154, 183; school 29, 99, 132–135, 183, 201, 209; social 24, 27, 49, 80, 89, 99, 103, 111, 135, 157, 159, 181, 183, 188, 211–212, 239
contextual 7, 24–25, 79, 83, 94, 108–109, 118, 122, 158, 165, 200, 205, 214, 226, 231, 238–239, 243, 246–247
continuum 12, 31, 99–100, 181
continuity 12, 22, 38, 49, 106, 129
conventional 54, 63, 67
coping 6, 70, 100, 104, 130, 156, 174, 178, 183, 185, 188, 228, 229, 232, 238
creative 21, 67, 204, 228, 230, 232, 236, 242
critical bridge 25, 27
critical thinking 26, 222, 232, 234, 236–237, 242, 245
cross-cultural 56, 107, 236
crystallized 99
culture (of hope, of fear, of humiliation) 43
cultural construct 13
cultural structuring 22
cyclic 50

Darwinism 11
Datnow, Amanda 216–217
decision-making 26, 73, 74, 115, 134, 146–147, 153, 159, 228, 230, 232, 234, 237, 240
decontextualized 83
delinquency 11, 29, 116, 124, 178, 187–189, 197
Delor's Report 234
demographic 13, 142, 148, 152, 201, 245
depression 11, 159, 161, 179, 181, 185–189, 193–197, 199, 222, 228
deprived 55, 134, 197–198
determinant 12, 42, 55, 64, 94–95, 137, 200, 222, 226

developmental markers 22–24
deviating 12, 152, 154, 241
dialectically 83
dietary habits 34, 197
digital natives 161
dilemmas 70, 75, 79, 231
direction 26, 49–51, 80, 98, 109, 122, 132, 144, 155, 158, 210–211, 213, 228, 236; bidirectional 109, 122, 144, 155, 210–211; unidirectional 132, 155, 213
disagreement 45, 125
disapproving 88
disciplines 13, 25, 45, 90, 172; cognitive–developmental studies 90; humanistic psychology 90; life-span psychology 90; motivational psychology 90; narrative study of lives 90; social and personality psychology 90
discontinuity 12, 83
discourses 2, 5, 35, 37, 39–40, 45, 90, 104, 246
discrete stages 58
disparity 12, 34, 116, 242
dispositions 39, 41, 100, 156, 191, 209, 217, 235
disruptive 101, 225
distal 101
distinct 11, 14, 21–22, 31, 33, 66, 76, 100, 101, 114, 122, 127, 156, 189, 197, 222, 224, 242; yet transient 21–22
distinctive stage 53
diversity 8, 100, 155–156, 239
dramatic play 63; see also pretend play
dyadic relationships 29, 149
dynamic 2, 5, 13, 24, 31, 38, 89, 99, 103, 106, 114, 133–134, 149, 172, 205, 209, 211–215, 217, 222–223, 225, 229, 235, 246–247

ecological systems 9, 94, 101, 174, 177, 183, 188; microsystem, mesosystem, exosystem, and macrosystem, chronosystem 101
egocentricity 68, 70
egocentric speech 82
ego strengths 79
egotism/selfishness 11, 64
eight Stages of Psychosocial Development 47–48
Elkind, David 68, 70, 160
emancipating 41
embedded 2, 23, 99, 106, 119, 133–134, 181, 211, 214, 222
emotional reactivity 26, 108

emotional regulation 74, 88, 133, 188
emotions/emotional 11, 17, 24–27, 29–30, 34, 43, 45, 57, 69–70, 74–75, 87–89, 106–108, 115–119, 125, 129, 133, 135, 138–142, 146–147, 150–152, 156, 159, 164, 172, 174, 176, 180–181, 184–185, 188–190, 192–193, 205, 209–212, 222, 224–225, 227–232, 234, 238, 242–243, 247
employment 23, 33, 55, 116, 118, 162, 171, 204, 234, 242, 244–245
encouragement 54–55, 81–82, 89
encultured 34
Erikson, Erik 14, 46–50, 53–54, 79–80, 87, 105, 127, 135, 164
ethical-cultural 41
ever-changing 95
evolutionary 11, 24, 41, 110, 118
evolutionary passage 41
evolving 2, 22, 38, 41, 83, 100, 124, 205, 222, 235, 239
exclusion 44, 153, 213, 223, 233
"experience of engagement" 83
experiences 5, 11, 20, 22, 25–27, 30, 32, 42–43, 58–59, 61, 64, 66, 68–70, 72, 77–79, 82–84, 87–90, 114, 121, 124–125, 127, 134–135, 137, 140–142, 153–154, 156, 162, 176, 191–193, 195, 205, 210, 217, 223–224, 227, 229, 241, 247; educational 82, 191, 205; physical 64; sensory 64, 78; unpleasant and distressing 77
experiential cultures 68
experimentation 21–22, 30, 50
exploratory 27, 119, 134, 150
expressions 42, 43, 50, 117, 222
extracurricular 26, 136, 143, 191, 236, 241, 243

failures 74, 91, 120
fairness 72
family income 32
fatigue factor 89
favourable 77, 89, 118; unfavourable 137, 138, 217
feedback 85, 90, 130, 138–139, 154, 161, 226, 236, 238
feelings 29, 57, 65, 69, 71, 85–88, 137–138, 141, 149, 154, 174, 185, 188–189, 199, 229, 238
fertility 23, 28
flourishing 180, 194
formation of identity 49, 54, 56, 85, 90, 105; *see also* identity formation

fortuitous 96–97
framework 8, 67–68, 80, 89, 103, 108–109, 132–133, 144, 163, 177–178, 183, 188, 202, 203–204, 225–226, 231–236, 241
Freud, Sigmund 46
friendships 29, 87, 147–150, 152–153, 158, 161
future-directed 98

gender related 32
generations 12, 24, 32, 114, 129
genetic 5, 11, 24–25
Giddens, Anthony 38, 212, 217
Gilligan, Carol 77, 239
globalization 56, 152
goal-directed 41, 110
government initiatives 199
gradual progression 53
grounded 87, 89, 177, 183, 188
growth spurt 28
guidance 74, 81–82, 138, 158, 162, 192, 228

Hamre, B.K. and Pianta, R.C. 225; *see also* Teaching through Interactions (TTI) Framework
happiness 11, 56, 151, 157, 171, 176–177, 179, 193, 194
hierarchical 67–68, 79, 133, 184, 213, 223
hopelessness 43, 154
hormonal changes 34, 57, 199
hormones 28, 151; estrogen 28; testosterone 28
household chores 33, 55
Hubbard, Ryan 216–217
hyperactivity 11
hypocrites 71
hypothesis 66
hypothetico-deductive 67, 72; inverse, negation, reciprocation, correlation 78

idealistic 67, 70, 71
identical 2, 45
identity: "common-image" 37; identification, identity formation, identity development, identity consolidation, identity foreclosure, and identity resolution 46; "primordial identity" 38; "self-image" 37; "a symbolic construction" 38
identity construction 84
identity crises 14, 50
identity formation 45–46, 49–50, 54–57, 80, 83–84, 90, 103, 124, 127–128,

133–136, 140, 146, 152, 154, 159, 222, 235; *see also* formation of identity
"identity image" 39
identity phases: empirical ego to the self as a conscious subject 40; identification and individuation 39; "identification with the other" and "identification in the other" 40
identity statuses 50–51, 80; identity achievement 51, 54, 80, 128, 135; identity diffusion 51; identity foreclosure 46, 51, 80; identity moratorium 51
identity statuses, two components: commitment 50–51, 105, 127, 135–136, 142, 153, 159; exploration 50–51, 54–55, 105, 127–128, 134–136, 138, 142, 146, 153, 159
ideologically 38
ideologies 40, 84, 101, 212, 214–217, 223
illiteracy 33–34, 198
imaginary audience 69–70
imagination 61
imitating 83
immaturity 26
impulsive/impulsivity 30, 57, 74, 198
inadequacies 86
inanimate objects 65
incapability 49
inconsistency 50, 116
independent 23, 25–26, 32, 55, 75, 81, 124, 127–128, 162, 180
Indian 13, 22–24, 31–34, 55–56, 85, 88, 100, 106–107, 111, 113–119, 128–130, 141, 152–154, 156, 160–162, 183–184, 196–200, 217, 222, 232–233, 235–236, 240–246
indicators 89, 157, 164, 178, 194, 202, 204
individual differences 8, 29, 49, 74, 140, 149
infancy 3, 27, 48, 86, 110
influences, negative: aggressiveness, violence, unhealthy sexuality 29
information-processing 71–72
inherent reflexivity 41, 90
inherited 40, 45
initiation rites of passage: circumcision, arranged marriage 13
instructional 133, 138–139, 142, 211, 213, 223–227
integrate(d) 22, 24–25, 37, 72, 81, 85, 109, 177, 201, 235–236, 241–244
intellectual 4, 58, 65, 67–68, 81, 116, 140, 142, 188, 211, 229
intellectual development 4, 58, 67, 142, 211

intentionality 98, 163
interaction 13, 25, 32, 39, 49, 56–57, 61, 67, 79, 80–83, 99, 101, 103, 106–109, 111, 113, 119, 121–122, 125, 127, 129–130, 132, 134–136, 140, 144, 147, 153, 195, 202, 204–205, 209–217, 222–227, 229–230, 238, 244, 246
interdependence 83, 85, 106, 119, 211
interdisciplinary 24–25
interests 24–25, 96, 107, 130, 134, 139, 142, 148, 152, 157–159, 215, 225
intergenerational conflict 13–14, 129
internet 29, 155–156, 161–162, 197
interpersonal 72, 77, 80, 86, 88, 116, 119, 134, 136, 142, 145, 147, 149–150, 154, 161, 174, 184, 202, 211, 223, 228–230, 232–233, 235, 237–238, 240, 245; conflicts 88; relationships 72, 77, 86, 134, 174, 211, 223, 238
interplay 27, 56, 59, 89–90, 95, 134, 158, 177, 210, 213
interpretation 14, 40, 119, 124, 129, 137, 158–159
intervention 9, 29, 90, 129, 147, 162, 172, 174, 192–193, 199–201, 228, 231–232, 241–242, 246–247
intertwined 29
interwoven 80, 133, 216
intimate 29, 48, 54, 132, 149–150
intrapersonal 107, 202, 204, 229, 232
introspect 71
invulnerable 69
irreversibility 66
isolation 29, 48, 50, 81, 106, 147, 182, 195, 235, 241
issues associated with the adolescent life stage: initiation ceremonies, sexual practices, courtship, marital customs, intergenerational relations 13

journey 39, 50, 110–111, 144
judgments 26, 30, 75, 79, 127, 205

Kohlberg, Lawrence 75–77, 79

language 61, 63, 72, 81–82, 106–107, 215, 222, 226, 242
Lave, J. & Wenger, E. 83
learning as a social process 81; interpsychological 81; intrapsychological 81
legal 13–14
liberal comprehension 44
lifelong development 46–47, 80
life-shaping 27

life skills 193, 221–222, 227–233, 235–247; 21st century skills 232, 235, 242; employability skills 232; non-academic skills 232; non-cognitive skills 232; social and emotional learning (SEL) 232; social skills 232; soft skills 232, 242; vocational skills 232
life skills intervention models 242; curriculum-integrated model 243; formal in-school models 243; informal and school linked programmes 243; out-of-school programmes 242; stand-alone subject model 243
life span 3, 7, 22, 25, 47, 86, 90, 95, 106, 109–110, 119, 172, 231
lifestyle 12, 30, 32, 34, 56, 117, 161, 172, 181, 197–198; patterns 34, 56, 197
like-minded 57
livelihood 33, 55, 82, 242
longitudinal studies 6, 9
long-lasting 74, 229
long-term memory 59, 72

maladaptive conduct 88
malnutrition 25, 33–34, 197
manipulation 40, 57, 63
Marcia, James 49–51, 79–80, 127, 134
marginalized 33, 68, 100
marriage 2, 13, 23, 32–34, 54, 100, 117, 130, 152, 190, 196, 200, 222
mass identity 41
mastery 83, 89, 113, 139, 177, 224
maturation 5, 22, 28, 57, 58, 79, 110, 151, 187, 211
maturity 3, 11, 24, 26–27, 48, 116, 118–119, 149, 153, 181, 183
meaningful 22, 88, 136, 139, 142, 163, 179, 193, 204–205, 224–225, 246–247
media 27, 29, 34, 56–57, 69, 77, 90, 101, 103, 105, 109–110, 124, 129, 144, 152, 154–164, 186, 194–195, 197–198, 235–236
mediating 43, 55, 108, 183
memory 57, 59, 61, 72, 78, 81
menarche 22, 25, 28, 33; *see also* puberty
menstruation 28, 129
mental functions 81, 230; attention, sensation, perception, memory 81
mental representations 61, 68
methodical 73
Ministry of Human Resource Development (MHRD) 240, 245
"minority world" 56
mnemonic devices 72

mobility 14, 55, 153–154
modelling 77, 83, 90, 153, 189, 238, 240
models 3, 5, 25–26, 34, 83, 86, 89, 116, 122–123, 130, 138, 142, 189, 236–237, 240, 242–243
modern 10, 12, 14, 38, 44, 106, 116, 117, 204, 245
moral character 77
moral development, levels: preconventional, conventional, and postconventional 76
moral judgments 75, 79
more knowledgeable other (MKO) 81, 230
motherhood 13, 54, 116
motivating/motivational 87, 89–90, 98, 99, 110, 123–124, 138–140, 142–143, 150, 153, 157, 188–189, 202, 204, 216, 224–225, 238, 241
multidimensional 101, 171, 176–177, 180
multifaceted 27, 84, 123
multiple perspectives 24
multitasking 72
multitiered 46

NCERT 244, 245
negative identity 49
neighbourhood 25, 103, 152
nested 99, 101, 209, 213, 214
networking sites/platforms 56–57, 154–155, 159–162, 186
neurobiologically 27
neurological 72, 74
normative 22, 25, 27, 53, 83, 99, 106, 119, 121, 128, 130, 153, 181, 184, 215
nuptial knot 32
Nurmi, J. 103, 130
nutrition 25, 32–34, 182–183, 191, 197, 200, 238, 240

obesity 34, 181, 182, 185, 195, 198
object permanence 58, 61, 68
obstacles 39, 45, 99, 144
occupational choices 80
operationalization 80
operations 63, 67–68, 78–79, 142; concrete-'thought thinking about the environment' 67; formal-'thought thinking about itself' 67
opportunity 7, 12, 27, 32, 55, 104, 162
optimistic 9, 43, 174
Organization for Economic Co-operation and Development (OECD) 231, 233
orientations 43, 106, 139; life 43; motivational 139; psychological 106
other backward caste 33
"otherness" 44

overnutrition 34
overweight 29, 34

P21 framework 235; *see also* 21st century
parental attitudes 55, 128; control and overprotection 55
parental educational attainment 32
parental experiences/beliefs 124
parent-child 107, 118, 188; *see also* relationships, parent-adolescent
parenthood 2, 100, 117
parenting styles 77, 84, 114, 121–124, 127, 130, 157
participatory 83, 177–178, 183, 188, 240, 241
patriarchal 33, 55, 114, 117
pedagogical 132, 134, 140, 233
peer-rejected 29
peers 7, 9, 11–12, 22, 25–27, 29–30, 49, 56, 74, 77, 81, 83, 86, 88–90, 99, 100–101, 103–105, 107–110, 113–114, 118, 120–121, 124, 128–129, 134–140, 144–154, 157–159, 163–164, 174, 177, 183–184, 187, 188–189, 192, 194–195, 197–198, 200, 204, 209, 211, 213, 217, 222–223, 225–230, 238
perception 33, 61, 63–64, 68, 78–79, 81, 86, 99, 107, 113, 115, 117, 119, 129, 132, 138, 140, 143, 147, 158, 185, 187, 210–211, 214, 239
'period of transition' 13–14, 116
PERMA 179–180, 193–194; positive well-being 174, 179
personal fable 69–70, 163
personal identity 22, 29, 38, 40–41, 48, 134, 142, 185
personality development 41, 148, 162
perspectives 24, 45, 58, 64, 66, 71, 78–79, 90, 95, 99, 101, 107, 147, 151, 164, 176, 205, 214, 217, 222, 226, 229–230; cognitive 90; psychoanalytical 90; psychosocial 90; situated cognition 90; social cognitive 90
phases 4, 10, 31, 39, 199
phenomenon 11, 44, 78, 83, 148, 153, 176, 223
philosophy 72, 204, 224
phronesis 41
physiological 7, 11, 14, 69, 89, 177
Piaget, Jean 58–61, 63–68, 71, 75, 78–82, 229
plasticity 8, 9, 25, 181
pleasure-seeking 26
pluralistic 42, 114

policy vision 244–245
political 13, 23, 38, 40, 99–100, 140, 201, 205
positive development 9, 35, 88, 107, 143, 174, 181, 188, 213, 217
positive identity 43, 55–57, 147, 153
possibilities 50, 66–68, 71, 107, 154, 160, 245
postformal thought 70
potential 9, 29, 35, 50, 54, 56–57, 74, 100, 135, 143, 152, 156, 158–159, 162, 174, 177, 181, 182–183, 189–190, 192, 201, 205, 210, 216, 230, 240, 242
poverty 33–34, 183, 189, 196, 214, 217
power imbalances 33, 55
preadolescent 67, 88, 185
pretend play 63, 65; *see also* dramatic play
pre-thought 78
primary modes of identity: identity synthesis, identity confusion 50
principles 40, 66, 75–76, 78, 118, 159, 245
privileges 22, 55
proactive 83, 98, 231
problem-solving 57, 73, 152, 224, 232, 237
prosocial 26, 88, 135, 137, 138, 158
proximity 27
psychoanalytic 46, 90, 118
psychological 2, 13–14, 22, 24–26, 29, 47, 49–50, 59, 79, 81, 84–85, 87, 89–90, 98–99, 105–106, 117, 119, 122–123, 127–129, 138–141, 151, 172, 176–177, 180–181, 183–185, 188, 193–194, 205, 210–211, 222, 227, 230
psychological crisis 47
psychological moratorium: a period of delay 50 (*see also* 'Time out of Life')
psychosocial 26, 45–49, 53, 74, 79–80, 90, 95, 101, 114–115, 121, 128, 135, 158, 163, 188, 196, 227–228, 231, 233
puberty 2, 7, 11, 13, 22–25, 28, 32, 49, 57, 129, 151–152, 186, 199, 222; pubic, axillary, facial, breaking of the voice, spermatic formation for boys 28; pubic, axillary and menarche for girls 28
'push and pull' 34
positive youth development (PYD) 6, 181

questioning 45, 50, 123

realistic 30, 63, 70, 100, 154, 162, 163
reappearance 68
reasoning 21, 26, 57, 60, 64, 67, 71–72, 75, 77–79, 129, 224, 237, 246; deductive 64, 67; hypothetico-deductive 67,

72; inductive 64, 67; logical 64, 79; moral 75, 77–79, 129; scientific 67, 73; transductive 64
reciprocal 7, 82, 95, 113, 140, 153–154, 216
real-life 73
reappraisal 45
reflexive internalization 41
reinforcing 99, 214
relatedness 27, 119, 205
relationships 6, 14, 25–27, 29–30, 48, 51, 54–56, 72, 76–77, 86–88, 90, 100–101, 106–107, 113, 115–116, 118–121, 125, 127, 129–130, 132–138, 140, 142, 147–150, 152–154, 157–159, 161, 164, 177, 180, 183, 188–190, 192–194, 204–205, 211–217, 223–224, 229–230, 237–238, 246–247; parent-adolescent 54, 56, 107, 118, 120, 125, 130, 147, 183, 188 (*see also* parent-child); peer 138, 152–154, 158, 188, 194, 223, 227, 229; romantic 87, 115, 118, 129–130, 149, 150, 152–153, 183; student-student 223; teacher-student 90, 132, 134, 138, 212, 216–217, 223–225, 227–229
reorganisation of schemas: accommodation, assimilation 57
resources 89–90, 96, 99–101, 105, 110, 117–118, 132–133, 142–144, 158, 164, 174, 181–183, 189–192, 197–198, 200, 204, 210, 215, 224–225, 234, 244–245; capital, human, financial 89
response inhibition 72
responsibilities 22, 50, 83, 113, 117, 120, 124, 193, 234
responsive 35, 123, 142, 152, 212–213, 225, 229, 235, 247
reversible 78–79
risk takers 51
risk-taking 30, 73, 172, 192
Rogoff, Barbara 82
role confusion 48–50
role identity 27, 45, 159
role model 51, 83, 89, 116–117, 130, 138, 142, 189, 244
rudimentary models 86
rural 13, 24, 33–34, 55, 100, 113, 129, 140, 162, 197–198, 200, 222–223

satisfaction 56, 86, 98, 123, 164, 176, 179, 188, 192, 194–195
Scheduled Castes/Tribes 33
scientific thinking 67
scientific reasoning 67, 73

"secure base" 86, 136, 151
security 27, 40, 55, 128, 198
SEHER (whole-school health promotion intervention) 193
selective transmission 83
self: author 110, 111, 144, 163–164; conscious, preconscious, and unconscious 46; social actor 110, 132–133, 144, 164; social agent 110, 144, 164
self-awareness 84, 98, 163, 232, 234–235, 242
self-concept 30, 41, 66, 84–87, 89–90, 105–106, 138, 146, 184, 186
self-development 79, 86, 110, 151
self-direction 26, 51, 236
self-disclosure 57, 149, 150
self-efficacy 88–89, 239; sources (actual performances, vicarious experiences, forms of persuasion, physiological reactions) 89
self-esteem 30, 41, 51, 84, 86–90, 106–107, 110, 115–116, 123–124, 129, 136, 138, 140–141, 147, 151–152, 161, 178, 184–186, 188–189, 192, 194–195, 239–240, 244
selfhood 13, 41, 90
selfie 56; Facebook 56, 155, 186, 194; Instagram 56, 155, 194; Twitter 56, 155, 186; WhatsApp 155; YouTube 155
self-estimation 41
self-organizing 83, 98
self-reactiveness 98
self-recognition 84
self-regulation 26, 161, 197
self-reliant 55
self-representation 41
self-understanding 41
Seligman, Martin 179–180, 193
sensation seeking 74
sense of identity 29–30, 46, 107, 135, 146
sense of justice 79
sensitivity 11, 22, 26, 86, 124, 225
separation 11, 12, 22, 41, 54, 70, 86, 116, 127, 134, 151, 190
separation-individuation 86
sequence 3, 28, 58, 80, 95, 99–100, 163
sexual maturation 28
sexual orientation 140, 149–150, 153; heterosexual 153; homosexual 153; lesbian, gay, transgender 153
shortcomings 66
siblings 18, 19, 33, 55, 114

258 Index

social cognitive theory 83; agentic perspective 83, 98
social construct 13, 22, 24
social contexts 24, 27, 89, 94–95, 99, 103, 111, 135, 157, 159, 181, 183, 188, 211–212; *see also* contexts
social identity formation 56
social institutions 26–27, 40, 44, 99, 110, 144, 212
social isolation 29, 182, 195
socialization 41, 42, 44–45, 79, 90, 94, 103–105, 107–110, 113, 116, 134, 136, 145, 158–160, 197, 222, 235; four mechanisms (Channeling, Selection, Adjustment, and Reflection) 103
social milieu 95–96, 101, 111, 140, 144
social networking 32, 56–57, 154–156, 159–162, 186, 197
social perception 79
social phenomena 10
social process 81, 87, 103, 109, 144
societal order 76
societal relationships 76
society 7, 10–12, 14, 22–23, 28–30, 32–34, 39, 41, 45, 48, 54–55, 68, 77, 83, 91, 94, 96, 99–101, 103–104, 106, 108, 114, 117, 124, 128, 132, 140, 149, 152, 156, 158, 162, 197, 204, 209, 211, 214–215, 222, 231, 233–234, 247
socio-culturally 44–45
Sociocultural Theory of Cognitive Development 80
socio-economic status 25, 33, 55, 100, 113, 121, 128, 135, 137, 140–142, 149, 152, 183, 188, 215, 222–223, 233
sociological 25, 27, 38, 79, 98, 99, 214–215, 223
sociohistorical 13, 99
sources: of popularity, status, prestige, and acceptance during adolescence 29
Soutter, A.K. 176, 191, 202–203, 205; well-being framework (Assets; Appraisals; Actions) 202
special educational needs 90
stages 2, 3, 11, 13, 14, 25, 31, 47–49, 58, 60–61, 67–68, 75–79, 95, 110, 146, 149, 164, 183, 199, 229
stakeholders 10, 24, 90, 214, 229–230
Stanley, G. 10–12
state of equilibrium 58–59; formal operational thinking 58, 67
state of transition: "becoming" rather than "being 53
stereotypic 54, 140, 186, 197

storm and stress 11–12, 24, 222
strengths 79, 86, 142, 179, 244
stress 11–12, 14, 24, 56, 83, 87, 113–114, 118, 130, 153, 181, 182–184, 186, 192, 195, 198–200, 222, 231–233, 238, 242, 244, 247
structural model of the mind: id, the ego, and the superego 46
structural reintegration 78
substance abuse 88, 147, 152, 181, 186, 194, 197–200
successful 19, 26, 41, 47, 48, 50, 74, 87–89, 95, 137, 176–177, 193, 232, 241
supportive 87, 101, 123, 125, 136, 138, 157, 184, 190, 194, 198, 204, 213, 224, 228
susceptible 89
sustainable development 35, 229
symbolic 38, 61, 63, 68
synthesis 49, 50, 222

teacher agency 216–217
teaching-learning 191, 223
Teaching through Interactions (TTI) Framework 225; *see also* Hamre, B.K. and Pianta, R.C.
technological advances 32, 197
technical skills 228, 235
teen/teenager 2, 12, 16–18, 26, 29–30, 32, 56, 72–73, 75, 155–157, 159, 162, 195, 222
temporal 2, 23, 26, 87–88, 209
theory 10, 12, 25, 45–47, 49, 53, 58–60, 75, 78–80, 83, 86, 89, 95, 100–103, 107, 116, 118–119, 129, 139, 163, 177, 188, 195, 213, 216–217, 225, 230, 233, 238; Kohlberg's theory of moral development 45, 75, 76–77, 85, 101; situated learning theory 83
thinking 11, 26, 40, 42, 57, 58, 61, 63–64, 66–68, 70–73, 75, 78–79, 80–82, 104, 130, 132–133, 147, 156, 174, 202, 222, 226, 229–230, 232–234, 236–237, 242, 245, 247; egocentrism, animism and lack of conservation 64; intuitive 63, 64; sophisticated 63; transductive reasoning 64
"Time out of Life" 53
tolerance 12, 29, 149, 230
traditional 12, 14, 38–39, 41, 44, 55, 56, 85, 107, 114, 116, 123, 128–129, 154–155, 157, 193, 197–198
trajectories 8, 95–96, 98, 177–178, 225; self, agency, social milieu 95

transformations 14, 78, 121, 128, 230
transformative 216, 231, 247
transient 14, 21, 22, 32
transitional 31, 32, 68, 107, 172
transitions: childhood to adulthood 12, 14, 101, 113, 172, 222, 228
trial-and-error 73

undernourished 34
underprivileged 34, 68, 139
UNICEF 2, 33, 192, 231–234, 240–241, 244
unique 5, 12, 21–22, 26, 29–30, 37–39, 41, 44, 47, 49, 69, 91, 100, 105, 118, 127, 132–133, 140, 143, 147, 152, 154, 172, 181, 185, 223, 247
uniqueness 70, 116
'universal capacity' 99
upbringing 54
urbanization 56, 152
use of media 56, 156, 158–159

values 17, 19, 26–27, 40–41, 45, 48, 55–56, 75–77, 81, 84–85, 107–109, 114, 116, 122, 127–128, 130, 132, 134–135, 138–139, 149, 153, 159, 176, 198, 214–215, 223, 231, 241–242, 244, 246
variability 28, 106, 153
virtual world 56
vulnerable/vulnerability 11, 14, 33, 69–70, 79, 147–148, 184, 195, 201, 229, 233
Vygotsky, Lev 80–83, 107, 156, 229–230, 238; *see also* Zone of Proximal Development (ZPD)

well-being 27, 29, 35, 56, 83, 101, 105, 113, 117, 123, 128, 130, 138, 140, 150–151, 158–159, 161–162, 164, 171–185, 188–196, 198–206, 228, 244, 246; correlates 183, 201; hedonic/eudaimonic 176
WHO (World Health Organization) 2, 13, 28, 181, 199, 228, 231–232, 241
whole-school 193, 201, 244
window of opportunity 27

YUVA School Life Skills Program 245

Zone of Proximal Development (ZPD) 81, 230; *see also* Vygotsky, Lev

Printed in the United States
by Baker & Taylor Publisher Services